Praise for *The Post-Truth Business*

'At a time when there is so much disruption, trust is more important than ever. *The Post-Truth Business* provides invaluable insight into how brands can earn trust and play an authentic and meaningful role in consumers' lives. Sean Pillot de Chenecey has always had a knack for uncovering human truths and cultural insights, and he delivers again with *The Post-Truth Business*. It's a must-read and its publication couldn't be more timely.'
JOHN DUNLEAVY, GLOBAL PRESIDENT, M:UNITED//MCCANN

'A deep study into the culture of post-truth and what it means for brands. This book is a rigorous read for those who want to better understand the implications of our post-truth era.'
SARAH RABIA, GLOBAL DIRECTOR OF CULTURAL STRATEGY, TBWA\CHIAT\DAY

'Sean Pillot de Chenecey provides an incisive view of the troubled cultural and political landscape that modern brands need to navigate. But what makes this book "mission critical" is the rigorous research, laser insights and the intelligence briefings he has extracted from a broad range of experts. *The Post-Truth Business* is a field manual for marketers.' PAUL KEMP-ROBERTSON, CO-FOUNDER AND CHIEF BRAND OFFICER, CONTAGIOUS COMMUNICATIONS

'*The Post-Truth Business* shows how mistrust has been building in our lives over time. People are using social platforms to distort the truth and the more we are exposed to the lies around us, the more immune we become to the central idea of what is real – and right. This book goes beyond the standard text on fake news and digs much deeper, giving a more insightful and worldly view that demonstrates the interconnectedness of how consumers are now informed.' NICOLE FALL, CEO, ASIAN CONSUMER INTELLIGENCE

'Everything starts with trust – but how do brands reset their moral compass and gain trust in a post-truth era? Via brilliant storytelling and research, this hugely inspiring and insightful book shares compelling examples of leaders, brands and business models showing the way forward. I believe this is the ultimate handbook for anyone who wants to build reputation capital and future-proof their brand in a post-truth environment.'
ANNE-LISE KJAER, FOUNDER, KJAER GLOBAL FUTURES

'With such tangibles as trust, authenticity, reality and locality all in the air, now is the perfect timing for a book such as *The Post-Truth Business*. Deeply researched, it's an excellent atlas that will help all involved in brand strategy to navigate these very unclear and disruptive times.' DAVID SHAH, PUBLISHER AND CEO, VIEW PUBLICATIONS

'This book shows how and why we are now living in a post-truth world and how this is perhaps not as new a reality as we might think. Through a wonderfully wide set of interviews and examples from around the world, Sean Pillot de Chenecey shows a way forward for brands to rethink how they behave in order to regain meaning and trust. The rules have changed, perhaps for good, and *The Post-Truth Business* is a guidebook to help us navigate this new landscape.' GARETH KAY, CO-FOUNDER, CHAPTER

'*The Post-Truth Business* gets to the heart of why trust is vital in society and fundamental for businesses, now more than ever. Prioritizing and cultivating trust helps brands not only to stand out but to build a loyal following of dedicated advocates. The book explains clearly and intelligently how brands can benefit from being open, authentic and trustworthy and what they need to do to achieve this.' EMILY HARE, EDITOR, THE HONEY PARTNERSHIP

'*The Post-Truth Business* gives the reader an in-depth under-standing of why trust has been eroded in societies and markets, and why there is an increasing sense of frustration in the world. But that isn't the only reason why you should read this book. *The Post-Truth Business* shows a way forward, how reputation capital can be recreated and why positive brands can be trust-ed to show us true leadership. That is why you should read it. And when you've finished reading, please send your copy to a politician who will need to read it too! Enjoy the future.'
CARSTEN BECK, DIRECTOR OF RESEARCH, COPENHAGEN INSTITUTE FOR FUTURES STUDIES

'A constant search for trust, truth, commitment and action must set true north for every business and leader who intends to thrive in the uncertain and unsettling years ahead of us. Those who appreciate the value of authenticity, system-scale change, and of both small and beautiful will hold the keys to thrivability. *The Post-Truth Business* makes a clear and compelling case for change, with excellent examples of businesses and communities already making it happen. Read. Reflect. Act.' ANDY MIDDLETON, CHIEF EXPLORATION OFFICER, THE TYF GROUP, AND CO-FOUNDER, THE DO LECTURES

'With the explosion of social media has come a massive challenge for long-established and previously respected institutions. Trust in media and politics is being undermined in a way never seen before. Brands are not immune either, and yet no one has really set out to study the impact of our post-truth world until now with this timely, provocative and ultimately hopeful book.'
IAN MCGARRIGLE, CHAIRMAN, WORLD RETAIL CONGRESS

'As fake news continues to dominate our headlines, brands continue to misuse our data, and brand empathy and trustworthiness become ever more important issues, Sean Pillot de Chenecey has written an incisive, no-holds-barred account of how business is getting it woefully wrong, and what it now needs to change to rebuild trust with an increasingly sceptical and rightfully dismissive customer.' MARTIN RAYMOND, CO-FOUNDER, THE FUTURE LABORATORY

The Post-Truth Business

*How to Rebuild Brand Authenticity
in a Distrusting World*

Sean Pillot de Chenecey

Kogan Page
INSPIRE

First published in Great Britain and the United States in 2019 by Kogan Page Limited

Apart from any fair dealing for the purposes of research or private study, or criticism or review, as permitted under the Copyright, Designs and Patents Act 1988, this publication may only be reproduced, stored or transmitted, in any form or by any means, with the prior permission in writing of the publishers, or in the case of reprographic reproduction in accordance with the terms and licences issued by the CLA. Enquiries concerning reproduction outside these terms should be sent to the publishers at the undermentioned addresses:

2nd Floor, 45 Gee Street	c/o Martin P Hill Consulting	4737/23 Ansari Road
London EC1V 3RS	122 W 27th St, 10th Floor	Daryaganj
United Kingdom	New York NY 10001	New Delhi 110002
www.koganpage.com	USA	India

© Sean Pillot de Chenecey, 2019

The right of Sean Pillot de Chenecey to be identified as the author of this work has been asserted by him in accordance with the Copyright, Designs and Patents Act 1988.

ISBN   978 0 7494 8281 7
E-ISBN 978 0 7494 8282 4

British Library Cataloguing-in-Publication Data

A CIP record for this book is available from the British Library.

Library of Congress Cataloging-in-Publication Data

Names: Pillot de Chenecey, Sean, author.
Title: The post-truth business : how to rebuild brand authenticity in a
    distrusting world / Sean Pillot de Chenecey.
Description: 1 Edition. | New York, NY : Kogan Page Ltd, [2018] | Includes
    bibliographical references and index.
Identifiers: LCCN 2018027577 (print) | LCCN 2018029597 (ebook) | ISBN
    9780749482824 (ebook) | ISBN 9780749482817 (pbk.)
Subjects: LCSH: Brand name products. | Branding (Marketing) | Advertising.
Classification: LCC HD69.B7 (ebook) | LCC HD69.B7 P535 2018 (print) | DDC
    658.8/27--dc23

Typeset by Integra Software Services, Pondicherry
Print production managed by Jellyfish
Printed and bound by CPI Group (UK) Ltd, Croydon, CR0 4YY

Contents

Acknowledgements

Above all, I'd like to highlight the help given to me in developing the thinking behind this book by my amazingly talented and beautiful wife Helen, who, along with being a brilliant researcher, puts her empathy and creative skills at the service of the community. A massive hug goes out to my children Berry and Thomas, for putting up with my spending seemingly every waking moment in the office over the months that it took me to write *The Post-Truth Business*.

In writing it, I owe a huge debt of thanks to the superb team at Kogan Page; specifically to my brilliant editor Geraldine Collard and then, after she'd departed on maternity leave (congratulations on your son!), for the much appreciated help and advice of Chris Cudmore. I'd also like to thank Anna Moss, my initial editor, and Jenny Volich who helped clarify my original concept for the book, along with Annette Abel, Philippa Fiszzon, Amy Joyner, Helen Kogan, Christina Lindeholm, Matt De Bono, Courtney Dramis and Megan Mondi.

I'd like to thank the world's best-connected man, my marvellous agent Cosimo Turroturro, along with Julia Scott and Patrick Nelson at Speakers Associates.

I spoke with, and interviewed, many people while writing *The Post-Truth Business*, but in particular I would like to thank Chris Barron, Navaz Batliwalla, Carsten Beck, Adriaane and Graham Boynton, Michael Cohen, Stephen Colegrave, Jonathan Disegi, Katrina Dodd, John Dunleavy, Nicole Fall, Jane Foulner, Geoff Glendenning, Scott Goodson, Emily Hare, James Harkin, Stephen Hayward, Eithne Jones, Gareth Kay, Paul Kemp-Robertson, Anne Lise Kjaer, Steve Lacey, Andy Lee, Ian McGarrigle, Andy Middleton, Joakim Noren, Ole Petter Nyhaug, Sarah Rabia, Martin Raymond, Geoff Reynolds, David

Shah, John Shaw, Mark Shayler, Thomas Stoeckle, Jen Urich, Alex West, Marc Woodhouse and Nilgin Yusuf.

I should also point out that, while I believe that I've duly acknowledged every one of the hundreds of sources utilized in my research, if anyone has slipped through the net the fault is entirely mine and please accept my apologies.

Finally, I'd like to thank my mother, a remarkable woman who spent a lifetime helping those around her. If there's an antidote to our post-truth world, she embodies it.

Introduction

Brands are Built on Trust

I defy anyone to say that trust isn't a key issue of our time. In my view, it's the number one issue facing brands on a global basis.

Brands are built on trust, but in a post-truth world they're faced with a serious challenge when so much of modern life is now defined by mistrust.

A weakening of the vital trust connection between brands and consumers is causing enormous problems for businesses around the world. Linked to this, something has gone very wrong with a vital element of consumer engagement: authenticity often seems to be evaporating as a core brand pillar.

Trust is the number one issue facing brands on a global basis.

The ramifications for brands in all sectors are deeply serious, when 'reputation capital' is of such immense importance. The difference between Brand A and Brand B (and Brands C, D and E) so often pivots around those core questions of 'are they honest, competent and reliable?' If a brand isn't trustworthy, when choice is available it'll be rejected in favour of one that is.

This is why *The Post-Truth Business* goes into such detail explaining numerous interconnected issues, including the impact of fake news on the media and society, why the safeguarding of privacy is so vital, how creating communications with meaning is the way forward, why the issues of conscious capitalism and brand activism are increasingly important, how technology is revolutionizing transparency in areas from pricing to provenance, what we can learn about authenticity from artisans and innovators, points to note regarding national-branding initiatives, guidelines on cultural-marketing activity, and how one of the most successful advertising campaigns of all time was created – based on truth.

In the book, I've interviewed numerous industry experts, refer to a wide range of global research studies and reference leading media organizations and studies from think-tanks, along with quotes from fascinating authors.

I'm aware that there have been several excellent books about the post-truth issue that focus primarily on the political sphere. But I've yet to see a book taking a holistic look at numerous related areas from the point of view of business policy, brand strategy and communications development. This is why I decided to explore these issues, highlighting brands and organizations who are getting trust, transparency and authenticity 'right' as well as looking into how others undermine their own brands by doing the opposite.

Above all the other areas that I note of being of such importance in this book, truth and trust matter so deeply, on both a social and an individual level, that they're almost impossible to overstate.

Let's face it, the truth can be unwelcome, difficult and problematic for us all, as opposed to just 'going with the flow' and accepting what we're told, in a form of group-think. Of course, in an Orwellian environment, it can be safer to act in this way, whispering the truth only to ourselves. However, when no ideas are immune from criticism and when, based on reliable information, we're able to debate and choose what we believe to be the truth, then we have freedom of expression. That's why a free and independent press matters.

Of course, whenever the subject of 'truth' is debated, the first thing one does is to turn to philosophy, truth being one of its central preoccupations.

When writing about truth, you naturally have to reference Plato, who held truth to be the goal of philosophy. And you look to Nietzsche with his endlessly quoted 'there are no facts, only interpretations' perspectivism. That, of course, led to a long list of postmodern thinkers such as Derrida or Foucault, who saw truth as something to be attacked. Elsewhere, Wittgenstein explained that, while our understandings of the world are filtered through language and culture, this 'social construction' mustn't prevent us from trying to understand and make sense of it via enquiry, evidence and rationality.

I've therefore tried to explain the 'post-truth impact' on brands via detailed research, evidencing the information uncovered, before laying out a rational and progressive way forward. Obviously, I've done so while acknowledging that there's often more than a singular truth about most of the things that confront us, and we tend to choose truths that are either convenient or simply reflect our viewpoints. Of course, the twisting, or selective use of the truth can be done for constructive purposes, for instance to unite, inspire or transform; hence the ethical 'Noble Lie' as espoused by Plato. But when the phrase 'alternative facts' has become part of the fabric of political discussions on competing truths, we must heed the warnings given by Orwell, including the dystopian 'Ministry of Truth' in his fable of totalitarianism, *Nineteen Eighty-Four*.

Trust is also an intrinsic foundation of our lives, as without it society simply couldn't function. It is an indispensable element of nearly every relationship we have, every agreement we make and every endeavour we take; and an essential element of this is our sense of distrust. In the context of this book, a loss of trust can be devastating, as it has such an immense impact on the trustworthy brand choices we make as 'informed consumers'.

That trust is the number one issue for brands is evidenced by the detailed research you'll read in my book. It includes references to a wide range of national, international and global reports, from a variety of perspectives and via the viewpoints of consumers, agencies and brand owners. But when trust has fallen to historic lows across so many areas of life, including among business of all descriptions, brands face a critical problem.

Social psychologists tell us that, as individuals, we're social beings who must learn to trust 'wisely and well'. Humans are genetically compelled to make social connections from our first days, to rely on, cooperate with, and therefore trust others. We need these levels and types of trust and belief, as they go right to the core of who we are as individuals. When it comes to brands, they must behave in a manner deserving of our trust, in an era when they're under a media spotlight as never before, when technology is having a transformative impact on the way in which we trust, and while 'informed consumers' are ever more sceptical of brand claims. So, trust is the key factor in developing and maintaining the consumer–brand relationship. This means regular and consistent demonstrations of how the brand's trustworthy values are being actioned, reflecting their honesty, competence, reliability and empathy.

Before summarizing the various chapters in the book, I'd like to explain that the approach taken is to use a range of dynamic examples which illuminate best-practice. My aim is to provide an exploration of the social, cultural and business realities that are shaping international brand perceptions from a post-truth perspective; and to show how businesses can deal with the impact of these issues, for those interested in rebuilding brand authenticity in a distrusting world.

Here's an overview of some key areas in *The Post-Truth Business*.

Alternative facts and the war on truth

The overarching theme throughout the whole book is the enormously important issue that I outline in in Chapter 1. I explain that there's a problem that affects us all: we're living in a media landscape where the truth is deliberately manipulated, trust has been catastrophically devalued and organized misinformation is a growth business.

This is a fundamental problem, with transparency and truth being such key foundations for democracy. The situation has been leveraged by two issues, which combined to devastating effect: post-truth and fake news. These two issues affect consumers across all brand sectors, for the simple reasons that 'truth and trust' impact brands in every market.

This is underscored by a devastating lack of trust in media organizations. We'll look at issues such as what happens when the truth becomes devalued, what happens when social groups retreat into echo chambers that reinforce polarized thinking, and how the mainstream media became portrayed as the 'enemy within'.

I look into why tracking technology and System One and Two thinking are such important considerations, and finally how our social media platforms found themselves in the front line of the war on truth.

Privacy as a human right and a tradable asset

The privacy debate is a huge one, but in the context of this book, in Chapter 2 we'll concentrate on areas such as the key implications of the EU's General Data Protection Regulation (GDPR) statute, the consumer trust and privacy issues of in-home technology, and the impact of social media brands on consumer trust as it relates to data privacy.

Focusing on the ethical implications, I outline how the use and abuse of private data for consumer brand marketing purposes is causing enormous concern over civil liberties and personal privacy. An outcry has resulted in a tech backlash, and the chapter notes the problem for brands when consumers actively reject giving them access to their data, how 'personification' is key, and why GDPR in the EU is such a big deal.

We'll also look at the implications of several high-profile data breaches, including the issues around Cambridge Analytica and Facebook, and finally shine a spotlight on the issue of privacy increasingly becoming a tradable asset.

#SkipAd vs connections with meaning

The death of advertising has been foretold: Chapter 3 notes that there's no doubting that the communications industry in general, and the advertising world in particular, are in turmoil.

Technology has had a massive impact on the way adverts are created and the media used to publish, broadcast and promote them. So, naturally this chapter references creative technologies, including virtual reality, augmented reality and mixed reality, alongside the use of social technologies that include artificial intelligence, data analytics and machine learning. But I also note the unstoppable power that is 'word of mouth' and why influencer marketing is such a key area, albeit one that is challenged by declining consumer trust and advertiser confidence.

The realities of the marketing industry when brand trust is down and branded-comms rejection is up are explored, and we'll look at the growing disconnect between consumers and brands, agencies and brand owners, media owners and advertisers. But I'll highlight dynamic ways forward: from agencies creating fame-generating brand activity to those assisting brands to build 'cultural movements', along with others that help to create 'brands with soul'.

Conscious capitalism and brand activism

More and more people want to feel morally good about the things they consume. Added to this are the desires of an emerging generation who state the need for finding 'meaning and purpose' in their working lives – who are attracted to brands that reflect their viewpoints.

Chapter 4 explains how these themes clearly link to post-truth and authentic branding, and the types of action that brands are taking who demonstrate relevant best-practice. These actions include brand activism and joint value creation.

Aiming to play an active community role via linking with customers, partners and suppliers has become a bedrock of today's and tomorrow's brand. Rather than being a transient 'on-trend' piece of additional brand engagement, an increasing number of companies are realizing it's a core element of brand-building that's here to stay.

I look into macro issues that affect us all, sustainability and the circular economy. This directly connects brands, and brand communities, to an ethos where 'restore and regenerate' is an alternative to a traditional linear economy of 'make, use, dispose'.

A key foundation for a brand seeking to undertake community-linked activity is for the team running it to clarify the 'why' that sits at the heart of the brand. I therefore look into how brand teams can clarify that fundamental point. For companies that wish to future-proof their businesses, it is key that they think deeply about their social mission, and the implications of their activities from the perspective of the 'common good'. This issue of social purpose is of key importance for an emerging generation of young people, who are attracted by mission-based brands committed to being valued for their social commitment and enlightened business behaviour. This all goes towards building their 'social capital' in addition to the standard issues by which companies are valued.

Price, provenance and transparency

Brands that are seen to act with honesty, integrity and reliability demonstrate the way forward in our post-truth world. Leveraging transparency to gain and retain consumer trust is a fundamental element of this brand reality.

Chapter 5 looks into this as it relates to pricing and provenance, and how technological developments such as blockchain are providing a powerful way to strengthen the brand–consumer relationship. These are such catalytic areas, with incredible conceptual and product development activity happening across a wide range of categories on a seemingly non-stop basis.

I look at the dynamic pricing strategy activity undertaken by innovative brands in the fashion, beauty and music sectors, where an immense amount of price disruption is taking place.

There are few things more powerful, relevant and motivating than a 'good' brand strengthening their brand engagement by providing interested and informed consumers with a transparent view of the brand: this is the importance of provenance. And it's precisely here that technology is proving to be the 'means to an answer' that consumers and brands desire. Trend-forward areas that we will discover include omnichannel retailing and the future-focused health sector. These examples show how the vital issue of transparent information goes a long way in enabling consumers to make informed decisions. In turn, these informed decisions put them in far more control of the brand–consumer relationship. Technology, particularly in the form of blockchain, is helping to protect workers, manufacturers and others right along the supply chain. This is a huge step forward for consumer power, ethical and sustainable production, and thus for social good.

Makers, innovators and outsiders

Chapter 6 outlines a range of individuals, brands and organizations who define the truism that 'maker' brands are often cited as being the most authentic and, as a result, build strong emotional connections. When this bumps up against disruption, markets can get revolutionized.

The 'informed and interested, demanding and unpredictable' consumers of these brands, products, services and experiences are becoming a powerhouse of early-adopting and opinion-forming customers. They're eager to seek out the maker and/or innovator that directly links them to the 'Made By', thus reflecting their need for an ethos of intentional buying, where consumption is considered and deliberated.

We'll look at a range of creator-maker issues (and the personalities behind them), ranging from the street-food movement to singer-songwriters and independent craft-beer producers. Passion, purpose and identity tend to shine through these types of brands, where the common denominator seems to be the celebration, or enablement, of 'artisanal autonomy' and a 'be better' ethos.

While it's often the low-tech (or no-tech) brands and products that most readily lend themselves to association with authenticity, I'll explain that this isn't always the case, particularly when they're clearly linked to the 'aura of the originator'. In this way they have a direct and clear association with the brand image, and this includes some of the planet's most exciting hi-tech brands.

Reputation capital and national branding

Something that's guaranteed to crop up in the life of a marketer is linking consumer brands to national brands, by referencing the country within which their brand was created. Chapter 7 therefore considers national branding.

Endeavours to brand a nation are a hugely delicate task that requires deep knowledge of a place and genuine empathy with its people. Telling an impactful, engaging and motivating story is vital for those undertaking nation brand exercises, just as it is for consumer brands. But doing so in a way that has an authentic truth at the heart of that story is absolutely key.

Every country wishes to tell a good story about itself. This is of massive relevance to brand marketers, because of the ways in which brands can link to the 'positive narratives and myths' about their country of origin. It cuts across virtually every sector and, when done properly, it enables them to leverage incredibly powerful emotions.

When it comes to branding, 'nation of origin' affects us all whether we like it or not. Any cultural-marketing campaign in this environment must also be judged against geopolitical realities. At the moment, country brands are set in a context that is nationalistic and protectionist, with walls not bridges going up around the world, accompanied by huge demographic changes.

This chapter therefore highlights leading-edge and award-winning examples of national-branding campaigns, using these to illuminate a way forward for readers embarking on this type of activity, or who simply wish to remind themselves of the core principles.

The marketing of culture vs the search for authenticity

Chapter 8 looks at the way in which brands seek added authenticity by leveraging culture, and why there are clear lessons for businesses in a post-truth environment.

We live in a world where there is more and more branding of culture, but less and less genuine cultural connection. We think that most cultural marketing produces connections between people and brands, but actually the opposite occurs.

This chapter uses, as an example, the worst campaign fail of all time, which is a fairly staggering achievement, given the strong competition. On a more positive note, we see examples of brands that are getting it right, illustrating how they utilize authentic cultural looks and icons that endure, and what the key lessons are that brands can note from an 'ultimate' example of cultural branding.

What these examples show is that the search for authenticity, at the heart of culturally based brand activity, is an 'always on' endeavour that requires the brand to get as close as possible to the core of that cultural issue. And they must do so in a respectful manner that entails the brand adding to the culture, instead of purely taking from it, which is what so many brands do in this context.

Truth, lies and advertising

In corporate terms, can you think of anything more 'Post-Truth' than the tobacco industry? That's the question at the start of Chapter 9, referencing an industry whose promotional activity is steeped in deceit and deception to an astonishing degree.

It doesn't matter what sector a brand is in; if young people make up a significant portion of the target market, then the fundamental law of youth marketing applies. This is that every brand attempting to engage with young consumers is obsessed with chasing two things: authenticity and cool. When it comes to attempting to engage with young people, the tobacco industry effectively wrote the youth marketing handbook. So, it was in this context that a leading-edge agency was briefed to create a hard-hitting public health campaign. The task they'd been set was to change social norms and reduce youth smoking – which is about as inspiring a challenge as an agency is likely to get.

I discuss how the 'Truth' campaign, which is one of the most successful marketing campaigns of all time and has saved many thousands of lives along the way, came into being. It also illustrates why truth beats lies – a core theme of this book. That the campaign was enabled by having a clear 'moral compass' will hopefully be noted and considered by those seeking inspiration.

The Post-Truth Brand Manifesto

My aim is that this book clearly illustrates a range of crucial issues that cannot be ignored by marketers as they aim to rebuild levels of reputation capital.

I firmly believe that more and more consumers are attracted to brands in which they can genuinely trust and that reflect some of their relevant personal values. When we find a brand that matches our beliefs and expectations, or fails to match them, we increasingly tell others about it, with word of mouth being the most trusted of endorsements, or indeed warnings. As I highlight throughout this book, when choice is available, if a brand isn't trustworthy it'll be rejected in favour of one that is.

Finally, in Chapter 10, I draw the strands of the book together, giving an overall viewpoint of what I see as being the key lessons for business, which I set out in a 'Post-Truth Brand Manifesto'.

Welcome to the post-truth business.

Alternative Facts
and the War on Truth

As highlighted in the introduction, there's a problem that affects us all. We're living in a media landscape where the truth is deliberately manipulated, trust has been catastrophically devalued and organized misinformation is a growth business.

This is a fundamental problem for democracy, with transparency and truth being such key foundations. The situation is based on two issues that combined to devastating effect: post-truth and fake news.

A debate at the World Economic Forum meeting in Davos noted that due to 'hacking, leaking and disputing the facts, it's never been easier to distort the truth. Fake news and digitization present a major threat to global democracy. Social media in particular has changed the way we consume and share news and information and accelerated the spread of inaccurate and misleading content' (World Economic Forum, 2018).

This is underlined by a lack of trust in mainstream media organizations. A poll from Gallup noted that Americans' trust in mass media peaked at 72 per cent in 1976 (Swift, 2016). By 2016 that figure had plunged to 32 per cent overall, but just 14 per cent among Republicans, a 'polarization' point that illuminates the increasingly toxic nature of partisan politics around the world regarding the inflammatory use of social media by politicians and voters from both ends of the political spectrum. The United States is hardly unique in having a population that mistrusts the media, but according to the *Financial Times* 'in few countries are views of journalists more defined by party allegiance and in no other has a president so weaponized that mistrust' (Edgecliffe-Johnson, 2017).

While this book focuses on rebuilding brand authenticity in a distrusting world, as the political sphere plays such a major part in undermining people's trust in the world around them, it's vital to illuminate that overall context. In terms of political bias (let's face it, we all have one), I'll aim to take an even-handed approach to the subject; but as certain key personalities and countries are so prominent in this debate, those players will naturally figure strongly throughout this chapter.

Of course, truth is the crucial foundation here. A report from the Rand Corporation titled 'Truth Decay' explored the diminishing role of facts and analysis in, for instance, US public life. Their report identified four trends that characterized the issue: 'increasing disagreement about facts and analytical interpretation of facts and data, a blurring of the line between opinion and fact, the increasing relative volume and resulting influence of opinion and personal experience over fact, and declining trust in formerly respected sources of facts' (Rand Corporation, 2018).

From a business point of view, the issues that I'll cover relate to brands of all varieties, as post-truth and fake news impact the people who consume brands in every sector, for the simple reasons that 'truth and trust' impact brands of every type. I'll discuss issues including what happens when the truth becomes devalued, the polarizing impact of social groups retreating into niche-interest echo chambers, how the mainstream media became portrayed as the 'enemy within', why tracking technology and System One and Two thinking are such important considerations, and finally how our social media platforms have found themselves in the front line in the war against terror – which, once again, affects us all.

A government of lies

It's generally accepted that the playwright Steve Tesich coined the phrase 'Post-Truth' back in the 1990s, in an article titled 'A government of lies' which he wrote for *The Nation* magazine in reaction to the Iran/Contra scandal.

A quick recap on that infamous episode goes like this: President Reagan shocked the world when he went on US TV to inform the public that, despite repeated denials, his administration had covertly organized and funded US support for the Contra anti-Sandinista Government rebels in Nicaragua – support which had been specifically banned by Congress. To give this an additional twist, the funding was linked to an illegal deal swapping weapons with Iran, a country that was the subject of an arms embargo. The reason for that deal was to gain Iranian influence in assisting the release of US hostages who'd been kidnapped by Hezbollah in Lebanon.

As political intrigue goes, that one takes some beating. To quote an old saying, what could possibly go wrong? When the inevitable happened and this politically explosive story broke, the phrase 'Iran-Contra' became a talking point around the world, summing up incompetent government, political arrogance and dishonest public officials.

But it was the words that President Reagan used in his TV address, and the thinking behind them, that so intrigued Steve Tesich. The president said: 'A few months ago I told the American people I did not trade arms for hostages. My heart and my best intentions still tell me that's true, but the facts and the evidence tell me it is not' (Reagan, 1987).

Americans were unfortunately familiar with being lied to by a president, with memories of Watergate still fresh in the mind. That scandal had shone a spotlight on President Nixon and his advisers, and their actions had horrified a public who at that point still generally viewed the United States as being a beacon, the shining 'City on a Hill' – a place where politicians, and presidents in particular, simply did not lie to the US public.

An impeachment process against Nixon 'for high crimes and misdemeanours' was started, although he resigned before matters were taken further. That meant Americans could feel good about themselves again, because, following the uncovering of his actions by a strong and independent press, governmental processes clicked into action and the democratic system had been seen to work.

However, what seemed to happen as a result of this 'public image catastrophe' for Brand America, linked in the public mind with the seemingly never-ending misery of the Vietnam war, was that hard truth became ever more intrinsically linked with bad news. And, without wanting to sound trite, US citizens wanted good news.

When Steve Tesich saw the result of President Reagan's admitting that he'd lied 'for emotional reasons' eventually leading to renewed popularity with the US populace, after a short dip, he wrote how the president 'perceived correctly that the public didn't want the truth. So, he lied, but didn't have to work hard at it. He sensed that we would gladly accept his loss of memory as an alibi. It had simply "slipped his mind" what form of government we had in our country' (Tesich, 1992).

The implications for the US republic were shocking and far-reaching, and Tesich's words resonated. Years later, at the International Populism Conference in Prague, Attila Antal referenced him as stating: 'We are rapidly becoming prototypes of a people that totalitarian monsters could only drool about in their dreams. In a very fundamental way we, as a free people, have freely decided that we want to live in some post-truth world' (Attila, 2017).

President Reagan sensed that his supporters liked what he was doing and simply didn't care if what he said didn't actually correspond with the truth. Which, when you're in charge of the most powerful country on the planet, doesn't bode well.

So that's where the post-truth story 'officially' began, with the *Oxford Dictionary* defining it as 'relating to or denoting circumstances in which objective facts are less influential in shaping public opinion than appeals to emotion and personal belief'. They also stated that it had gone from being 'a peripheral term to being a mainstay in political commentary, often used by major publications without the need for clarification or definition in their headlines' (Midgley, 2016).

However, as noted by the *Financial Times*, a vital difference in contemporary meaning is that 'Tesich used it to mean "after the truth was known" rather than our modern definition of a situation where the truth is irrelevant' (Noble and Lockett, 2016).

The president sensed his supporters liked what he was doing and didn't care if what he said didn't correspond with the truth.

Reagan was also the first president to be in charge when 24-hour news reporting became the new normal, which was to have enormous implications for both post-truth and fake news with the ability to feed unverified stories, at speed, into the news cycle.

The origins of fake news go back through history, but there are clear links with the 'Proclamation for the Suppression of Coffee Houses' made in 1672 by Charles II 'to restrain the speaking of false news, and licentious talking of matters of state and government' along with the salacious rumours spread by the political pamphleteers of the French Revolution, which was itself 'a revolution of the media'.

It's generally accepted that it was the blogger David Roberts who came up with the term 'Post-truth politics' in a piece he wrote for the US environmental magazine *Grist* in 2010 with that title. In the post, he said that 'voters don't generally know much about politics or policy' and that they 'used crude heuristics to assess legislative proposals which ran counter to the idealized Enlightenment view'. He went on to say that we now existed in a time of 'post-truth politics: a political culture in which politics (public opinion and media narratives) have become almost entirely disconnected from policy (the substance of legislation)' (Roberts, 2010).

For reasons of brevity (and to keep within the parameters of this book), I'm going to take a massive jump forward a couple of decades to begin to bring things up to date, and consider a world in which public discourse appears to be increasingly anti-fact. The manipulation of emotion clearly seems to work for politicians who've taken a lead from the classic consumer-brand handbook where any advertising agency will tell you that 'feelings beat facts'. This issue was outlined by the journalist Michael Deacon, who wrote: 'It's why modern political campaigners love using the words "positive, negative, optimism, pessimism": as they enable easy dismissal of criticism. Thus a politician who lies is "running a positive campaign", while opponents are "engaged in personal attacks". It's simple but effective. Facts are negative. Facts are pessimistic. Facts are unpatriotic' (Deacon, 2016).

Meanwhile, something that didn't exist in the initial Reagan 'Post-Truth' years came along and turned everything upside down for us all, journalists, voters and politicians alike. That was, of course, the internet and its intrinsic element, social media. So, let's look at how this impacted politics in particular.

Social media, where 'everyone has a voice'

It was during the presidency of Barack Obama that we saw the internet transform mass communication between government and citizens. The first president to be in office in the 'social media age', Barack Obama, took what was then seen as the radical step of broadcasting his weekly national address via YouTube. He was the first president to put up photos on Instagram, use a Snapchat filter, make a podcast, post on Myspace or go live on the newly ubiquitous Facebook. Back in 2010, he'd also sent the first ever 'presidential tweet'.

When this ultra-democratic medium first began to gain mainstream international usage in the mid-2000s, the links between social media and political debate seemed wholly positive. Everyone could have their say – from bloggers to web activists to citizen journalists to just 'anyone with a view' – and so everyone could be heard. What could be healthier for politics than an open media where everyone could freely join the conversation, and all voices and viewpoints would be given equal access to the debate?

That sounds unbelievably naïve now, yet it really did seem to be that way, back in the dim and distant past of 2006. This was the year that Twitter was founded, two years after Facebook, a year after YouTube and four years before Instagram. But then reality kicked in.

How social media was intended to be used, and how it is used, are two very different things.

Or should I say kicked back. And kicked back hard. How social media was intended to be used, and how it turned out to be used, proved to be two very different things.

Because, along with all the positivity that social media brought, a dark side that really hadn't been considered soon began to show itself via extraordinarily divisive shows of strength across the political spectrum. This parasitic link is what the VR pioneer Jaron Lanier refers to as 'toxoplasmosis'.

A pivotal thing to note relating to the lack of connection between voter and politician is the incredibly low levels of trust in media coverage given to politics – a lack of trust also being a key fault-line between consumer and brand, as portrayed throughout this book. According to the Pew Research Center, when it comes to Americans having trust in religious leaders versus the news media, more than twice as many do so 'a great deal' (Kennedy, 2016). In the United Kingdom an Ipsos MORI veracity index indicating trust in professions also showed that more than twice as many people trusted priests to tell the truth as trusted the media (Ipsos MORI, 2017).

With reference to populist politicians leveraging this issue, the *Financial Times* pointed out that while Trump 'didn't invent the idea of mainstream reporters being left-wing, elite bogeymen who hate America, he's rebranded it masterfully for the #FakeNews age' (Edgecliffe-Johnson, 2017). On people with this attitude, in his book *Alt-America* the author David Neiwert states that 'they cannot believe any kind of official explanation for events, actions, or policies, but instead seek an alternative one. This alters – or rather distorts – their relationship to authority' (Neiwert, 2017).

This is a key point to consider, because to quote the journalist Evan Davis: 'In 2016, the great political schism to divide Western societies switched from being a left–right one to being about liberalism and populism, each with different priorities, values and tribal allegiances. It's not hard to see why the term post-truth emerged; there were genuine changes in the way public discourse was conducted' (Davis, 2017). This polarization can also be seen as dividing between polarized stances such as 'openness and change' vs 'authority and order'.

In terms of 'genuine changes in public discourse', what we were then to see from President Trump was a use of social media in particular that confused US and international politicians, the mainstream media (or 'MSM') and the general public alike. For example, in a now famous tweet he declared: 'Fox News is much more important in the US than CNN, but outside of the US, CNN Int'l is still a major source of (fake) news, and they represent our nation to the world very poorly. The outside world does not see the truth from them!' (Trump, 2017).

This attack on one of the key foundations of democracy, a free and independent press, became a hallmark of Trump's behaviour from the time he began campaigning. But when it came to accusations of fake news, as *Foreign Policy* magazine said: 'President Donald Trump is right. There is an epidemic of fake news in America. Only it's being perpetuated not by his political opponents but by him and his supporters' (Boot, 2017).

Alternative facts and fake news

A key issue going to the heart of fake news is quite simply one of clarification. While everyone's using the term, the problem is that its common use has grown to mean everything from actual lies to just something a politician doesn't agree with. Alongside this are increasing accusations of a 'deep state' made up of shadowy, autonomous power-brokers, using behind-the-scenes actions to undermine democracy to their own ends.

But a fundamental problem is that there isn't a globally defined illustration of 'fake news'. While each main media outlet may have its own working definition, I defer to the one used by the Atlantic Council's DFR Lab. Their definition of fake news is 'deliberately presenting false information as news'. They differentiate this from disinformation, which they consider to be 'deliberately spreading false information', and misinformation, which they take to mean the 'unintentional spreading of false information' (DFR, 2017).

According to Joseph Khan, Managing Editor of *The New York Times*, 'there's a spectrum between propaganda and spin and totally false maliciously created fake news. So, you can dispute where on the spectrum stories (like those relating to politicians) fall' (Khan, 2018). To illuminate just how widespread this issue is seen to be from a global perspective, where a lack of confidence in the media undermines trust and truth, in the annual Edelman Trust Barometer (probably the biggest study into trust) they found that on average 'nearly 70% of us worry about false information or fake news being used as a weapon, with the media now the least trusted institution'. By the way, it should be noted that Edelman reported 'people use the term "media" as both content and platforms in their findings, but while trust in platforms declined, trust in journalism has rebounded' (Edelman, 2018).

This 'issue with the facts' was shown to starkly visible effect as soon as President Trump took office, with his notorious claim that one and a half million people attended his inauguration and with Sean Spicer, the White House Press Secretary, famously backing up the claim (Ford, 2017). Those comments in turn were then supported by Senior White House aide Kellyanne Conway, who went on to NBC's 'Meet the Press' show to say that Sean Spicer hadn't been lying but had given 'alternative facts' (Jaffe, 2017).

That inauguration took place shortly after post-truth had been named 'Word of the Year' by the *Oxford English Dictionary*. The *Financial Times*, referencing the dictionary definition, commented that 'a less verbose way to describe the same phenomenon would be to say that it was the year in which emotion trumped fact. Or cruder still, it was the year of the lie' (Thornhill, 2016).

The mainstream media vs political partisanship

Taking this to a level of partisanship unseen in the mainstream media in recent elections has been radically biased, hyper-partisan news that tells niche audiences gathered in so-called 'filter bubbles' or 'echo chambers' what they want to hear. This classic case of confirmation bias is brought to them c/o media falling either side of the political spectrum. These include right-wing ones like Breitbart, Infowars and the Drudge Report, while on the left there are Slate, NPR and Mother Jones. I'll let you decide just how politically far 'right or left' these are....

This is noted by Yale historian David W Blight, who says: 'Millions of Americans on the right get their information from selective websites, radio shows and news networks, possessing all sorts of conspiratorial conceptions about liberals. Many on the left also know precious little about the people who voted for Trump; coastal elites sometimes hold contemptuous views about people they "fly-over"' (Blight, 2017).

Just because these audiences are niche doesn't mean they are small; quite the opposite. These are the days of 'massive niche' groupings, so beloved of marketers who find them ideal targets for branded messaging. And even more so for political parties, who love preaching to the converted, when it's often niche voter groups that win elections owing to generally falling mainstream voter turnouts in elections. For instance, the winning margins in the 2016 US Presidential Election in states such as Wisconsin, Michigan and Pennsylvania were wafer-thin, being less than 1 per cent of voter turnout in each case – and only about 55 per cent of the US voting-age population cast their vote in the election, according to CNN (Wallace, 2016).

This is a serious problem if you consider that, according to a Pew Research Survey, '67% of American adults rely on social media platforms such as Facebook, Twitter and Snapchat for news' (Shearer, 2017). Many of them are accessing information via niche groups that have wildly skewed world views, views which are duly passed on and spread on a viral basis.

Vice Media had an interesting take on this in 2018 with their #LikeWhatYouHate campaign, which encouraged people to consider other points of view via bursting the filter bubble of their Facebook news feed. To do this, the creative agency Virtue Scandinavia and the digital studio Koalition created a tool to disrupt the Facebook algorithm by proposing people, organizations and parties that you disagree with, or hate, in order to balance out those fed to you by Facebook. According to Frederik Andersen of Vice Media Scandinavia: 'We made the tool to remind everyone about a world beyond our social filter bubbles and to show how easy it is to create a greater perspective and respect each other's views and opinions. I hope that we can help open that mindset and spark debate' (Kiefer, 2018).

That approach links with the one taken by the renowned *AllSides.Org* which, according to their site, 'provides balanced news, perspectives and issues across the political spectrum. There is no such thing as unbiased news or truly non-partisan coverage – we use technology and the crowd to provide balance.' This is vital when so much electioneering takes place 'in the dark', ie via data-driven micro-targeted ads.

Martin Raymond, co-founder of The Future Laboratory, told me:

> When a problem is that the truth might be inconvenient or diffi-cult, social media allows us to develop 'truths' which aren't just fake and convenient but also allow people to create a different filter bubble and ecosystem, and I think that happened across the market. The Millennial Hipsters saw social media as a legitimate way to communicate but are now realizing that in fact within 'the lake' there are parts of the lake which are poisonous and parts of the lake that are good for them; whereas previously they were just interested in being part of the lake because they thought that was all that was important. The traditional media side has had a rude awakening in that it now needs to make really brilliant and carefully calculated statements and underwrite them in an honest way. Hence when I look at *The New York Times*, *The Guardian*, *The Wall Street Journal* or *The Washington Post*, their big push is towards verification. While it used to be about breaking news, now it's about verification journalism. There's a desire now to verify and to authenticate. What is interesting is that the same thing is happening online, and if the current generation of media publishers or even a new generation of media publishers get it right, they will become the new voices of truth and honesty and of authenticity.

I discussed that point with Emily Hare, who'd just left the strate-gic and creative intelligence experts Contagious to become Edi-tor at The Honey Partnership. Her view was that:

> the public have it as a consideration now more than they had in the past, when they began to realize how they were being misled.

It's tied into how people access information, which is what has led to Facebook changing its algorithms because so many people get their news through that. And it's led to people questioning sources that they would previously have seen as reliable. In some ways it's good for established sources. There's less investigative journalism going on with a lot of media companies; and it doesn't really help them build up their trust. So there are going to be a lot of people questioning sources and where their information comes from.

On 'questioning of information' and the way that fake news is passed on, it's also important to note that it isn't always the case that this is done in an unthinking manner. An article on Medium referencing the 'Ironic Truths of Meme Culture' pointed out that 'even people who share fake news are trying to tell a kind of truth too'. That piece went on to reference the annual SXSW Edu event, where it was argued that 'the assumption people really believe the claims they share, and therefore are stupid, is actually not so simple. They post it because they're making a statement and are offended if you say they've been duped' (Owens, 2018).

But it's the rage-filled and insulting nature of contemporary political debate that concerns so many. According to the journalist Janice Turner: 'There is an arms race of rage in politics, escalated by social media. Each side clings to a childish stance: the others do it too, their trolls are worse, their threats more vicious. In truth, they have a common language. The aim is to vaporize those with whom you disagree' (Turner, 2017).

As for the viewpoints of those in charge of the platforms, as Jack Dorsey, CEO of Twitter, put it: 'We have witnessed abuse, harassment, troll armies, manipulation through bots and human-coordination, misinformation campaigns, and increasingly divisive echo chambers. We aren't proud of how people have taken advantage of our service, or our inability to address it fast enough' (Dorsey, 2018).

Identity politics

In terms of this social divide and 'who we all are', at this point I need to say something about personal identity and the way in which voters appear to make their political choices in the modern age. This political division, by the way, also seems to have implications for consumer-brand choice: in the United Kingdom, research conducted into Brexit voters and their brand affinity by the polling organization YouGov showed that while Leave voters preferred brands like HP Sauce, Bisto and Birds Eye, Remain voters opted for Instagram, Airbnb and Spotify (Mohan, 2016).

Tim Marshall is a leading authority on foreign affairs with more than 30 years of reporting experience in 40 countries. According to him, 'Walls are going up. Nationalism and identity politics are on the rise once more. Thousands of miles of fences and barriers have been erected in the past decade, and they are redefining our political landscape' (Marshall, 2018). This defining of the political landscape is something that really interests Sarah Rabia, Global Director of Cultural Strategy at TBWA\Chiat\Day in Los Angeles. She refers to the documentary filmmaker Adam Curtis, whose work concentrates on psychology, sociology, philosophy and political history. He's made some absolutely stunning documentaries, including *Paranoia and Moral Panics, Bitter Lake* and *HyperNormalisation*. As she points out, 'we are living in a world of extremes. Adam Curtis talks about how governments and institutions create this good v evil narrative and they try to make it really simplistic, so they can control people and create a kind of fear and a sense of instability.'

Occasionally, a book comes along that makes policy-makers sit up and take notice, an example being *The Road to Somewhere* by former editor of *Prospect* magazine David Goodhart. In it, he shows how political affiliations and voting patterns are now formed by identity rather than class and that people are divided into voter tribes he named as 'Anywheres or Somewheres'. According to the *New Statesman* magazine: 'Anywheres dominate our culture and society, having portable "achieved" identities, based on educational and career success. Somewheres are more rooted in geographical identity who find the rapid changes of the modern world unsettling. They have lost economically; their working-class culture has disappeared, and their views are marginalised in the public conversation' (Marr, 2017).

Back in the United States, voting for a man who said he would 'drain the Washington swamp' clearly felt like a highly positive step for his supporters, which demonstrates the levels of emotion – as opposed to rationality – involved when people consider which party or candidate for whom to vote. In the book *Democracy for Realists*, the authors describe how most voters 'simply decide which candidate they like and then ascribe policies they approve of to him or her, which are often completely incorrect. Most people have an incredibly weak understanding of what their chosen political party's policies actually are, not really knowing what it is that each party actually stands for' (Achan and Bartels, 2016).

It's the effect of the highly emotional information that voters get that led *The Economist* to state, in a special report on social media vs democracy, 'not long ago social media held out the promise of a more enlightened politics, as accurate information and effortless communication helped good people drive out corruption, bigotry and lies. Yet... far from bringing enlightenment, social media have been spreading poison' (*The Economist*, 2017). When 'spreading poison' is being done by social media, it's worth swiftly noting how and why the issue of speed is such an important factor, reflecting how the brain processes information.

System One and System Two

As any advertising agency will tell you, a key issue about how we use social media (in fact how we absorb any messaging) links directly to so-called System One and Two thinking. In summary, the brain works on a dual-process model: System One is fast, driven by instinct and prior learning. Why this is important for ad agencies is because we don't concentrate on the vast majority of advertising, it just takes place while we're chatting to someone else or simultaneously looking at another screen, and so on. So, it's a big deal for people making TV commercials, as you might expect.

System Two, however, is slow, driven by deliberation, effort and logic. Even when we believe we are making decisions based on rational considerations, our System One beliefs, biases and intuition are what drive many of our choices. It's the 'secret author of many of the judgments you make', according to psychologist Daniel Kahneman in his book *Thinking, Fast and Slow* (2012).

So... System One thinking drives which ads consumers unconsciously pay attention to, as well as what brands they buy as they rush around a grocery store while dealing with constant distractions. It has big implications for social media and politics, and thus all those creating political messaging.

In social media terms, political commentary (heard as part of the daily background buzz which surrounds us all) that sounds vaguely agreeable to our point of view is noted while in System One 'automatic browsing mode' and is therefore the mode by which most of us unthinkingly pass on information. You've done this and so have I, many times. And that 'pass it on' messaging – essentially digital word of mouth, ie tweet to retweet – is precisely the form of communication that is most believed by others we know ie those we're linked with on social media.

So, we pass on important messages without thought, they're received by friends and acquaintances as having added credibility as they arrive from a known source, ie us, and they're often then retweeted without hesitation. Thus the pattern goes on and the message is spread.

Now, the implications of users utilizing System One behaviour are a great thing if you're a consumer-brand advertiser with an impactful, likeable and motivating message to communicate, ie if you're a Huawei, Kotak, Visa, Itau or Sky. But for a healthy democracy, this approach to social media is a terrible thing when it comes to political word of mouth.

The antidote to this is clear: if we just thought about what we were doing – literally just actively thought about it for even a few extra seconds – our System Two 'dual process' would kick in and perhaps make us question what we were reading, consider the ramifications of the contents of that post, and stop our potential 'automatic' retweet.

This is why a quick method of verifying factual vs fake news is to simply check to see if other major news organizations are reporting on the same story – if they are, then the chances are that the story stands up to an 'instant fake check'.

Why is this so important for politicians and elections? This worrying situation was given a sinister twist when social media platforms found themselves weaponized.

Disinformation warfare

In print-media terms, fake news can actually be traced back to the days of Stalin, as in the doctoring, defacing or deletion of 'actual news imagery' which was discovered by the journalist David King in the early 1970s when he was researching the Russian Revolution and communist propaganda.

Francis Fukuyama spoke of 'Fear, Uncertainty and Doubt' being key macro issues impacting society, and the deliberate blurring effect of fake news in a post-truth world is what I'll highlight now, as it builds on a post-truth environment to create an 'infosmog' of falsehood, twisted truth, 'whataboutism', confusion, false-flag operations, deepfakes, so-called 'crisis actors' and blatant lies. This results in a situation where having a crystal-clear picture of 'The Truth' to which we can all refer becomes an ever more difficult, and sometimes impossible, goal.

It gets worse. The ability to create fake news is easy and fast – unlike real journalism – as its creators can create a false story (of the outrageous click-bait or 'intended to confuse' type), put it up online and move on to the next story at high speed.

A report for CNN titled 'The Fake News Machine' highlighted Veles in Macedonia, where numerous website creators are based and who manufacture false stories. According to CNN, 'the scale is industrial, with profits coming primarily from ad services such as Google's AdSense, which places targeted advertisements around the web. Each click sends cash back to the content creator. But, and this is crucial, what the fake news producers are doing isn't illegal in their country' (Soares, 2017).

Leaving aside the 'location-legality' issue, taking on a fake news story and proving that it is fake also takes (or wastes) endless amounts of time. Many false stories that we 'know' are false are virtually impossible to disprove and so are left to float around in cyberspace or the public consciousness.

Causing even more of a problem is that this situation is also misused and cynically reframed by politicians who began, and continue, to simply deride as 'fake' any story that casts them in a bad light. Which, as Joseph Heller might have said, is about as classic an example of Catch-22 as you're likely to get.

But while fake news may be terrible for ethics, it's correspondingly great for business, because people don't bother watching or reading 'boring' news, and if there's one thing that's actually reliable about fake news, it's that it is never boring. Fake news is loud, outrageous and shocking. Which means the mainstream media finds itself currently kind of… stuck. To put it politely.

And the effect is, of course, global. The impact on Baidu's Tieba, Tencent's WeChat and Alibaba/Sina's Weibo in China, despite their very strict state rules to tackle false news, is immense, and has led to ever tighter regulation.

Social media go to war

The core aim of those state actors behind much of the fake news destabilization that we've seen over recent times has been to reduce everything reported by the mainstream media to the same 'maybe/maybe not' level of believability as that published by extreme sites and via word-of-mouth rumour. That is an issue of staggering importance. In what has now become a hugely reported official enquiry, Russian social media manipulation of the US 2016 Election was officially organized, meticulously planned and ruthlessly conducted. According to an Atlantic Council case study: 'The Russian government's propaganda and influence operations use a "full spectrum" model spanning social and traditional media. Some channels are overt and official; others are covert and claim to be independent. All work together to create the appearance of multiple voices and points of view, masking a coordinated approach' (Nimmo, 2018).

Once it began its domination of the social media universe, it didn't take too long for Facebook, and the implications for utilizing it in destabilizing society, to catch the eye of the intelligence networks. Fake news strategists aim to blur reality and reposition facts as just 'potential answers' from differing partisan perspectives. Manipulating trust, or rather the lack of it, and causing confusion, and particularly a lot of it, can cause utter chaos among enemies. Therefore, Facebook and other key platforms found themselves swiftly involved in a new digital version of espionage.

It didn't take long for Facebook, and the implications for utilizing it in destabilizing society, to catch the eye of the intelligence networks.

According to the British MP Damian Collins, chairman of Parliament's Culture, Media and Sport Selection Committee, who has shown immense leadership in challenging the people, organizations and governments involved in fake news and media manipulation: 'In the US election (of Donald Trump) the top twenty fake news stories were far more widely shared than the top twenty real stories. That's fake as in really fake; fake quotes, fake facts' (Rifkind, 2017).

The type of fake news that we've unfortunately become used to has been taken to a whole new level by the latest innovation, augmented reality, and by advances in artificial intelligence, video editing and computer graphics, which includes voice-morphing and face-morphing technology. The implications of this were noted by Damian Collins at a debate into 'Restoring Trust' at the London School of Economics, where he talked about this delivering:

> a worrying level of sophistication and fakery that's becoming so good, that for people who want the truth, they may have no option but to fall back on trusted news brands. Augmented Reality makes it easy to create fake films, of people giving fake speeches, being at events they never attended; with the quality being so good, you can't tell the difference between that and the real thing. Who do you trust in that environment? That doesn't mean to say that there aren't very good young news companies that use social media really well, like 'Now This' in New York. But in short, greater transparency on where information is coming from is one of the best things that we could achieve; because that at least allows the consumer to weigh up the evidence of what they're viewing and use their own judgements on whether they think it's true or not. (Collins, 2018)

The statistic that really highlighted the scale of the problem was when Facebook admitted that Russian-purchased adverts had reached nearly 130 million Americans during the Trump/Clinton 2016 election battle (White, 2017), supplemented by staggering amounts of online posts on social media platforms. Let's not forget that Facebook owns Messenger, Instagram and WhatsApp, with the majority of 'active users' reposting their social media messages on a cross-platform basis. It should also be noted that WhatsApp is causing ever-growing concern in countries from India to Brazil to Kenya.

The Guardian noted how US lawmakers 'released a selection of Facebook ads bought by Russian operatives and listings of imposter Twitter accounts, revealing how foreign actors sought to sow division among Americans. The ads and profiles targeted liberals and conservatives on a range of hot-button topics, including police brutality, immigration, race relations, Islamophobia and LGBT rights' (Solon, 2017).

Elsewhere, the journalist Ben Macintyre wrote that 'President Putin manages a steady flow of disinformation and fake news through the Kremlin's troll farms, to sow division and confusion, and in the Russian phrase "powder the brains" not only of his own people but a worldwide audience' (Macintyre, 2017).

As investigations into attempts to influence the 2016 US Presidential Election got under way, the Digital and Cyberspace Policy Program run by the Council on Foreign Relations reported that 'more aspects of Russia's approach to information warfare are coming to light. A steady stream of new disclosures reveals a complex blend of hacking, public disclosures of private emails, and use of bots, trolls, and targeted advertising on social media designed to interfere in political processes and heighten societal tensions' (Giles, 2017).

Meanwhile, in the summer of 2018 special counsel Robert Mueller's investigation (re: Russian interference in the 2016 presidential election and possible collusion with members of Donald Trump's campaign team) dropped a geopolitical bombshell. The US Department of Justice indicted a dozen Russian GRU military intelligence officers for, as *The Times* reported, 'hacking into servers belonging to Donald Trump's rivals and local election boards. The suspects had covertly monitored the computers, implanted hundreds of files containing malicious computer code and had stolen emails and other documents' (Philp, 2018). A few days later, Donald Trump stunned the world while at a summit with President Vladimir Putin in Helsinki. In response to media questions about Russian interference with the 2016 US presidential election, he described the Mueller investigation as a 'disaster for America' and sided with Russia against the FBI. Huge attention was then focused on the bipartisan DETER Act (the acronym standing for Defending Elections from Threats by Establishing Red Lines) regarding the automatic imposing of severe sanctions on those engaged in any future election interference, or 'information warfare' as it is increasingly being termed.

Regarding fake news, the World Economic Forum debated this issue in Davos, where a panel including Jimmy Wales (founder of Wikipedia) and Joseph Khan (Managing Editor of *The New York Times*) witnessed Zeinab Badawi from BBC News highlight a range of accusations that Russia 'weaponizes information'. As she said, 'there are many accusations from various sources including NATO, the French President, the British Prime Minister, the German Government, and the American Government. They all say that Russia as a state actor is a perpetrator of fake news, and it uses stations such as RT' (Badawi, 2018). She also quoted President Macron of France, who said 'Russia Today and Sputnik were agents of influence and propaganda that spread falsehoods about me and my campaign' (Serhan, 2017).

RT, the Russian media company, were represented at the debate by Anna Belkina, their deputy editor in chief, who said those accusations 'were false, in fact demonstrably false, and that RT had been a target of false information spread about it' (Belkina, 2018).

Noting the Russian side of the story, it was interesting to hear that Russian President Vladimir Putin's government warned the United States not to meddle in their 2018 election. The Russian Foreign Ministry spokeswoman Maria Zakharova accused the United States of 'direct interference into the electoral process' after the State Department criticized Russia's decision to ban anti-corruption activist Alexei Navalny from running for president (Mosbergen, 2017).

Facebook, Google and Twitter have testified in front of congressional committees to discuss Russia's alleged attempt to influence the presidential election by spreading misinformation online. The three companies had already admitted that, unknown to them, Russian-backed accounts used their respective sites to share and promote content aimed at stirring political unrest. At those official hearings, Facebook's General Counsel Colin Stretch said: 'The foreign interference we saw is reprehensible. That foreign actors, hiding behind safe accounts, abused our platform and other Internet services to try to sow division and discord to undermine the election, is an assault on democracy that is directly contrary to our values and violates everything Facebook stands for' (Shaban, 2017).

When Mark Zuckerberg testified in front of Congress, he said that 'the highly sophisticated Russian approach to spreading its influence online had left Facebook at a distinct disadvantage. We're in an arms race with Russia but Artificial Intelligence will save us. Our idealistic and optimistic company failed to understand that Facebook could be used for harm as well as good' (Groll, 2018).

So, fake news, which started out as a jokey catch-all term for something fun, has also become deadly serious. Social media giants have morphed from being set up as high-tech cash machines that enable advertisers to sell us more stuff that we very probably don't need, to now being repositioned as AI-driven election-winning behemoths.

Facebook or Fakebook? Twitter or Twister?

It's clearly the responsibility of the massively powerful social media platforms to stand up against fake news, as with their epic financial power comes a huge social responsibility to fight against this onslaught, just as they've been forced to do against issues ranging from cyber bullying to trolling and online hate speech. It was depressing to note that Mark Zuckerberg told Congress that the 'best solution' to misinformation (AI technology) wouldn't be ready for up to another decade.

In order to enact legislation to force them to do so, Damian Collins, the chair of the UK Government's DCMS committee looking into the matter, suggested that, as far as their obligations and responsibilities were concerned, 'the government should introduce an offence of "Failing to Act" when material has been reported to a company either because it was illegal or against that company's own community guidelines' (Collins, 2017). But as he also said, 'the evidence handed over by Twitter to investigators so far is only the tip of a very large iceberg' (Mascarenhas, 2017), noting that 'Twitter has identified 2,752 accounts linked to the St Petersburg-based Internet Research Agency, a Russian "troll factory", which sent out 1.4 million messages in just over two months. The same accounts also posted content relating to UK politics' (Whale, 2017).

In the UK, ground-breaking research by *The Sunday Times* found evidence of attempts by Russia to influence the result of the UK General Election in 2017. As their report stated, '16,000 Russian bots tweeted on British politics. 80 per cent of the automated accounts had been created in the weeks before the vote'. On fake accounts identified by *The Sunday Times*, it wrote that 'academics said these were just the tip of the iceberg and called on Twitter to investigate fully the true scale of Russian meddling in British politics' (Insight Team, 2018).

The New York Times reported how senior Facebook executives faced much tougher questioning by the UK's DCMS parliamentary committee than Mark Zuckerberg had during his testimony before Congress, and that one member noted dryly: 'I'm delighted to hear that Facebook has a head of integrity.' That piece also quoted Damian Collins of the DCMS committee as saying: 'many people would look at what's happened recently and say the case for greater regulatory scrutiny of the way the tech companies work is appropriate. I don't think you can put that genie back in the bottle' (Satariano, 2018).

There is, however, some good news about activity that has taken place and that continues to do so. Facebook told millions of users who liked or followed any of the hundreds of Facebook and Instagram pages created by Russian actors that they were ensnared in an alleged misinformation campaign (Nicas, 2017). (Users have access to a tool to check if they followed any of the pages, which were designed to look as if they were run by Americans but were actually created by the pro-Kremlin Internet Research Agency.)

Google announced back in 2017 that it had made major changes (called 'Project Owl') as part of its efforts to fight against fake news that was 'polluting' its search results. This enhanced the public's ability to analyse results and report content, enabling users to inform Google if they came across something wrong or objectionable. Another major change to the search engine was that they started to give more weight to what they termed 'more authoritative' information.

But, as reported by the *Los Angeles Times*, when Mark Zuckerberg appeared in front of Congress in early 2018, 'it highlighted how unprepared Congress is to impose game-changing rules on the social network. The proceedings brought into stark relief how San Francisco innovation can be more nimble than Washington bureaucracy' (Halper, 2018).

Which brings us to the killer point impacting media brands that seek to be authentic in a post-truth world inundated with fake news. These organizations have a clear and present danger around them (including attempted sting operations aimed at undermining the credibility of the media) and a horrendous task ahead of them. An example of a sting happened to *The Washington Post* with the Roy Moore scandal, where the BBC reported that 'a source told the newspaper she had been impregnated as a teenager by US politician Roy Moore. The Post said its research debunked her story, and that she worked for a group called Project Veritas, which "targets the mainstream news media"' (BBC, 2017).

The 'horrendous task ahead of them' includes the basic business-model issues, where the need to get effective subscription models set up and to wean them away from advertising is, currently, seemingly the most obvious way to destroy the click-through model which is itself so destructive, and so tied into the world of fake news.

That key problem was summed up by Gillian Tett in the *FT* who suggested that the next time you complain about the media, ask yourself how you expect 'fair' mass-market journalism to be funded and run – and if you are willing to pay for it. But she also noted a core human issue that also drives the situation: 'the trouble is that partisan social media is free – and readers seem to be hungry for this. So how can we support real news when most voters keep flocking to entertaining stories that are (at best) partisan and (at worst) deliberately fake?' (Tett, 2017).

As we've seen, some media organizations have already fought back and others are joining the fight to earn our trust. This is truly vital. According to *The Economist*, 'The stakes for liberal democracy could hardly be higher' (*The Economist*, 2017).

Fighting back re: the war on truth

The implications for international press freedom could not be more serious. To quote Brian Klaas of the LSE and author of *The Despot's Apprentice*, 'American efforts to promote press freedom in authoritarian regimes abroad have been destroyed by Trump's tweets. Imagine trying to press Myanmar to release its jailed journalists from the State Department while the Myanmar government screams "fake news!" and cites his tweets' (Klaas, 2017).

In response to all this media abuse and fake news, there have been some great instances of the mainstream media fighting back. *The New York Times* campaigned to 'unite the nation against alternative facts'. *The Drum* magazine, noting how media brands have used marketing to turn accusations of fake news into page views, reported on numerous advertising campaigns. Those included *The Wall Street Journal* 'attempting to forge trust with the public by positioning itself as the antithesis of fake news'. The *FT* took a stance against fake news with their 'Thinking Beyond Black and White' campaign, and *The Atlantic* magazine encouraged more cynicism from readers by urging them to question its answers (McCarthy, 2017).

Sarah Rabia from TBWA/Chiat/Day Los Angeles referred to this when I spoke with her, where she started the conversation by talking about polarization:

> We see two main approaches when it comes to this: either think smaller – identify your tribe (Seth Godin wrote a great book on this called *We Are All Weird*) where it's about getting more radical about a shared issue alongside those people who you really connect to. Or you try and break the filter bubbles, which are connected to trust and fake news. *The Guardian* and *The New York Times* both have slogans about the whole picture and that the truth has never been more important.

She went on:

> There are lots of media organizations popping up now: a company called All Sides.org was created by a Republican that worked in Silicon Valley and he said 'we thought that the internet would make everything fairer and give us a broader world view but actually it has narrowed our view and put us in these bubbles'. His site reveals media bias, it shows you the same story but how it can have different angles. What we saw in our Pan-Activism study is there is a desire to see different sides of the story. So people are really making an effort to engage in a conversation with someone with different beliefs or they are reading a different newspaper with a different agenda, because people want a balanced view.

I think that's interesting as a new form of activism. Things often aren't simply black and white. I think the middle ground will re-emerge because there used to be a moderate majority and now maybe we've all become too tribal and subcultural. Why is this important to us? Because brands in particular are trying to find commonalities and connection points.

Talking about the other side of the story, in this instance the media advertising messages focusing on fake news, Russia Today ran a #QuestionMore campaign which took aim at those who might accuse it of being part of the problem. For instance, following the US Elections, RT ads poked fun at Hillary Clinton with roadside posters that said 'Stuck in traffic? Lost an election? Blame it on us!'

There's been a lot of discussion about antidotes to all this, one idea being those on either side of the political spectrum acting as whistle-blowers on fake news coming from their own side, ie the left wing denounce fake left-wing-generated stories, with the same action taken by those on the right.

Most politicians on either side are, of course, 'good people' who just disagree on the most effective means of implanting positive change in society. Both sets of them see fake news and the world of post-truth damaging the world around them, and thus their voters' lives. This isn't to deny everyday reality in some sort of utopian fantasy. Politics will always be a tough, and less than entirely clean, environment. To quote the *Financial Times*: 'Lies, seduction, persuasion, hypocrisy and flattery have always attended public life; alternative facts and fake news have been part of the feedstock of politics and journalism for centuries' (Barber, 2017).

A way forward that may appear from the world of entrepreneurs is (as pointed out by Mark Zuckerberg) artificial intelligence. According to Dhruv Gulati in a *Wired* magazine piece about his 'Factmata' start-up, 'the idea is a system that uses AI to detect stuff that is potentially misleading, including fake news, rumours, hoaxes. Everything, in short, that isn't entirely true. If a statement deviates in any way from the strict truth, his system will be able to spot it' (Manthorpe, 2017). The FT also reports on companies looking for ways to help clients willing to pay for taking on fake news. 'Some such as Crisp or New Knowledge started out fighting terrorism. Others such as Cisco and Digital Shadows are seeing the parallels with cyber security, using tactics developed to defend against hackers to battle against fake news' (Kuchler, 2017).

Dealing with next-generation entrepreneurs is obviously key for the dominant media platforms in a world driven by likes, clicks and attention; but do they have what it takes and are they genuinely willing to take action? Moves from those like Facebook suggest that action is indeed (or 'finally' some might say) being taken. They will, for instance, expose users to more 'Related Articles' that show a wider range of perspectives about particular issues. According to Samidh Chakrabarti from Facebook's civic engagement team, talking about how it thinks its technologies have impacted global democracy: 'I wish I could guarantee that the positives are destined to outweigh the negatives, but I can't. Facebook has a moral duty to understand how tech is being used and what can be done to make our community representative, civil and trustworthy (Ingram, 2018).

That statement, according to Axion, shows 'a continued effort on Facebook's part to be more transparent about the way its platform has steered away from its original mission of promoting openness and democracy' (Fischer, 2018).

The key issue of 'platform responsibility' remains the absolute killer question, together with safe-harbour liability provisions concerning whether the likes of Facebook are 'conduits of information' or publishers, with the legal status that follows. It has long been argued that Facebook is a tech company, not a media company, and that it acts as a conduit for information and discussion rather than as a publisher (Brown, 2018). The social media expert Mari Smith, following Zuckerberg's appearance before Congress, said, 'When over 45 per cent of Americans get most of their news from Facebook, it's a publishing platform' (BBC Newsnight, 2018). It was therefore fascinating to see Facebook launching its own quarterly magazine, *Grow*, which they describe as a 'thought leadership platform' aimed at business leaders. Soon after, their lawyers told a US court that Facebook was indeed a publisher. *The Times* said, 'Their statements represent a U-turn and could have implications on how it is viewed by lawmakers' (Bridge, 2018).

But along with all the positive elements of social media that we mustn't forget, the psychological effects that it has across society are also, finally, causing Silicon Valley to pause and reflect. The anti-tech backlash is pushing back against 'tech-utopianism'. Now 'tech-humanists', whose nucleus is the Center for Humane Technology in San Francisco, argue that social media products 'are designed to be maximally addictive, in order to harvest as much of our attention as they can'. The unintended, or perhaps intended, consequences of this business strategy 'where everyone is distracted, all the time, is that their products threaten our health and our humanity'. The way out of this mess is improved design 'intended to be less addictive and less manipulative... building products that don't hijack our minds' (Tarnoff and Weigel, 2018). Good intentions to be sure, but to work they'll need a genuinely catalytic form of disruption.

The anti-tech backlash is pushing back against 'tech-utopianism'.

Looking away from the corporate perspective to a governmental level, Britain and various other European countries have historically taken a far tougher line than the US Government in relation to regulating the major tech brands that distribute fake news. The UK Government announced that it had taken action to combat numerous methods of information warfare used by states such as Russia and had set up a 'National Security Communications Unit' to combat fake news. According to *The Times*, 'A national security capability review identified a gap in Britain's ability to tackle state-sponsored disinformation operations designed to influence and disrupt daily life, as is alleged to have happened during the US presidential elections'. The prime minister's spokesman said: 'We are living in an era of fake news and competing narratives' (Haynes, 2018).

To begin to draw this chapter to a close, following Donald Trump's infamous 'Fake News Awards', a clarification of what actually constitutes 'fake news' vs truthful information is an ever more vital issue. According to Reporters Without Borders, 'Predators of press freedom have seized on the notion of "fake news" to muzzle the media on the pretext of fighting false information' (Reporters Without Borders, 2017). Referencing the US presidential campaign, PolitiFact, the fact-checking website, found that '51% of Donald Trump's statements were mostly or completely false' (Thornhill, 2016).

On the 2020 US Elections, and many other forthcoming elections in other parts of the world, something we now know is that recognizing fake news is only going to get harder, with new technology (as demonstrated at places such as the Consumer Electronics Show) meaning that we now need to question not just what we read in the papers, but things that we see and hear in the online and broadcast media. Owing to facial and speech copying technology delivering 'more real than real' images and sounds, to quote The Tyrell Corporation, this is going to become a 'Fake News Mk2' issue, with the weaponizing of information moving on from the basic type of fake news and misinformation that we've unfortunately grown used to in recent years.

According to a piece about what journalists can do about machine reality and deepfakes, the *Columbia Journalism Review* stated that 'nothing online is quite as it appears, now less than ever. Thanks to a new breed of neural network machine-learning algorithms, video, images, voice, and text can be synthesized. Imaginary faces can be realistically fabricated by computer. Videos of politicians produced as you might control a puppet' (Diakopoulos, 2018).

In social media terms, and with reference to the fallout from the role played by Facebook in the 2016 US Presidential Election,

Facebook has taken up the battle against fake news by utilizing third-party fact-checkers, starting by fact-checking images and videos as just one of numerous updates to protect civic engagement. As part of these actions, 'Facebook will focus on combating foreign interference, removing fake accounts, increasing ad transparency, and reducing the spread of fake news. In addition to monitoring for the spread of misinformation, Facebook is proactively readying itself for upcoming campaigns that seek to sway political and cultural events in different countries' (Perry, 2018).

It was also highly encouraging to note the announcement from the Atlantic Council that their Digital Forensic Research Lab was launching a partnership with Facebook, 'aiming to ensure that the tools designed to bring us closer together aren't used to instead drive us further apart'. The report went on to say that they were 'building a digital solidarity movement, a community driven by a shared commitment to protect democracy and advance truth across the globe. This partnership's a crucial step towards forging digital resilience' (Kempe, 2018).

Facebook announced what they called 'major new initiatives' on fake news, which included 'launching an updated "news literacy campaign" to teach users how to identify false news and prevent it from spreading, ... [they] called upon academics to help measure the volume and effects of misinformation on its platform, and released a short film, *Facing Facts*' (Jefferson, 2018).

The scale of the problem with which Facebook are confronted was summed up by an announcement that, in three months alone, they'd uncovered and disabled nearly 540 million fake accounts, which were in addition to the millions of fake accounts that they prevented daily. But as *The Guardian* responded when also noting the increasing movement of 'bad actors' to WhatsApp owing to its encryption software, 'this is interesting as it seems to suggest either a dramatic change in external circumstances or that the company, wilfully or unknowingly, underestimated the problems of fake accounts in the past'. To deal with this, 'Facebook is betting the ranch on artificial intelligence as the solution to the problem' (Naughton, 2018).

But the problem that Facebook itself poses to society was summed up during the questioning of Mark Zuckerberg by MEPs at the European Parliament. One of them, Guy Verhofstadt, who called on Facebook to cooperate with the EU's anti-trust authorities and said that they 'enjoyed a monopoly', asked Zuckerberg, 'are you in fact a genius who has created a digital monster that is destroying our societies?' (Rankin, 2018).

As *Wired* magazine stated in an exclusive about fake news and future elections, 'what'll happen as the problem gets more complex? False news is only going to get more complicated, as it moves from text to images to video to VR to, maybe, computer–brain interfaces. Facebook knows this and says "Two billion people around the world are counting on us to fix this"' (Thompson, 2018).

'Fixing things', or perhaps 'fixing things badly', was done in fake news terms when the Russian journalist Arkady Babchenko, aided by the Ukrainian authorities, faked his own assassination. This was then widely reported by the world's media, who were outraged when the trick was revealed a day later. 'Journalists warned that Mr Babchenko had effectively given Russia free rein to write off its alleged involvement in any other extra-judicial killings as fake news. RT mocked publications and broadcasters who had reported on the apparent murder, saying huge apologies had to be made by Western media organisations' (Bennetts, 2018a). *Wired* magazine reported that 'the faked murder plot has raised concerns from Moscow-based journalists who say the plot may further erode trust in the media. Establishing the truth in Russia is incredibly difficult, in part because so few independent outlets exist' (Matsakis, 2018). *The Times* reported that 'the staged death could only lead to more accusations of fake news at a time when the distinction between credible and non-credible sources was becoming more crucial'. Reporters Without Borders described it as a 'pathetic stunt' while the president of the International Federation of Journalists said that 'by spreading false evidence the Ukrainian authorities have seriously eroded the credibility of information (Bennetts, 2018b). As also reported by *The Times*, 'A free society depends on public trust in official truthfulness. Ruses corrode that confidence, at home and abroad. Russia is rightly criticised for using news as a political weapon. To critics, Ukraine just did something similar. Defending our societies against Putinism will be fruitless if we resort to Putinising ourselves' (Lucas, 2018).

Orwell lives on

To be clear about just how vitally important this all is, in her excellent book *Who Can You Trust?* Rachel Botsman states that 'without trust, and without an understanding of how it is built, managed, lost and repaired, a society cannot thrive. Trust is fundamental to almost every action, relationship and transaction' (Botsman, 2017).

With reference to this issue, Kantar conducted a 'trust in news' global survey in 2017 (via 8,000 people) which found that 'social media and digital-only news platforms have sustained major reputation damage as a result of the "fake news" narrative during recent election cycles. People retain a strong belief that quality journalism is a fundamental cornerstone of a democratic society. However, news organizations are under more scrutiny than ever before' (Cooke, 2017).

The concept of fake news demonstrates that the battle to defend objective truth is as important as ever.

The impact on those news organizations regarding their advertisers is, of course, a critical issue when, according to CNN, 'many brands have been startled by the rise of fake news'. The editor in chief of CNN Digital Worldwide stated that 'the concept of brand safety should be expanded in a way that more clearly demarcates trustworthy content sources from purveyors of fake and misleading material. Marketers want an environment that stands for truth, facts and integrity' (WARC, 2018).

So, we *all* have to face facts, and to do that, the lying has to stop. Because, and to quote the journalist David Aaronovitch, 'democracies partly rely on journalists whose aim is both to arm citizens with the knowledge they need to make decisions and also to connect them with each other as a civil society. If you debase this, then nothing is sacred, least of all the facts' (Aaronovitch, 2017).

It was well reported that, with remarkable serendipity, the election of Donald Trump coincided with George Orwell's dystopian novel *Nineteen Eighty-Four* becoming a bestseller once again.

The preface to the recent *Orwell on Truth*, referencing a description by President Trump's spokeswoman of a comment by him 'as an "alternative fact" rather than a lie', noted 'the concept of fake news could have come from the Ingsoc regime in the superstate of Oceania. These developments demonstrate that the battle to defend objective truth is as important as ever, and that George Orwell lives on' (Johnson, 2017).

The problem, of course, is who gets to decide what is the truth and what is a lie. The *Financial Times* points out that President Donald Trump 'has blurred the boundaries, apparently giving licence to would-be demagogues across the world. For Mr Trump, fake news is what is propagated by his critics. For his critics, it is the dissemination by Mr Trump and his supporters of "alternative facts" to explain persistent anomalies in their account of reality' (Financial Times, 2018).

'But don't despair,' stated Timothy Garton Ash, 'if Orwell and Solzhenitsyn did not surrender in the face of Goebbels and Stalin, it would be pathetic for us to give up now.' He referenced the great poet John Milton, 'who wrote of Truth with a capital T', quoting 'Let her and Falsehood grapple; who ever knew Truth put to the worse in a fair and open encounter', but as Garton Ash noted, 'there is much we can do to make the grappling fair and open' (Timothy Garton Ash, 2016).

The media is at the forefront of the war on truth, but society, and thus the people acting as citizens or consumers within it, needs to be able to trust the media (of all descriptions) and rely on the information they're given.

It's encouraging to note that some individual journalists and a small number of newspapers, sites and broadcasters are so rightly admired for the extraordinary efforts they go to in order to gain such trust and respect from the public. But a large percentage of the media, of all descriptions, needs to urgently rebuild their levels of public trust and thus regain their brand authenticity, in a distrusting world.

I'll begin to finish by quoting an advert and an article, both of which appeared on World Press Freedom Day. The advert was part of a series for UNESCO which ran across top media titles, with the intention of encouraging media plurality and for us to engage with different perspectives. (Reporters Without Borders also marked the day with a strong campaign that attacked fake news and disinformation.) And for anyone who thinks that facts are subject to debate, I would simply recommend they read the superb book *Factfulness* by Hans Rosling.

The ad ran in *The New York Times*. Created by Droga5, it proposed that we 'Don't just read The New York Times, read the Wall Street Journal, Atlantic, National Review, Guardian, Economist, Financial Times, Los Angeles Times, Repubblica, Helsingin Sanomat, Chicago Tribune; watch the BBC, CNN, NBC, MSNBC, and listen to NPR. Read more. Listen more. Understand more. It all starts with a free press.'

As for the article, it was published by the 'ideas and perspectives' platform *Medium* and, explaining the context of journalism in the current era, highlighted 'Local news under siege. Reporters targeted for doing their jobs. Facts subject to debate. Lies spreading faster than truth. Quality journalism in peril. And the stakes – for our personal wellbeing, for the health of our democracy and the world – are just beginning to be understood. What can help? Quality journalism' (Levien, 2018).

And as for quality journalism, a series of print ads created by TBWA\Chiat\Day for CJR illustrated how everyday Americans actually access their news, by showing them reading newspapers whilst on the daily commute. What stands out in these ads is that the titles of the newspapers have been switched for 'dubious' sources as opposed to real ones; ie they now feature names like 'Retweets from strangers' or 'Some guy's blog'.

For the final industry quote in this chapter, I'll turn to Sir Martin Sorrell. Commenting on the Silicon Valley tech giants at the 2018 Cannes Lions festival, he said, 'the only serious challenge to Google and Facebook is government regulation. Cambridge Analytica, fake news, and possible intervention in elections have changed everything' (Waterson, 2018).

So it was reassuring to hear shortly afterwards that Facebook had been fined by the UK's Information Commissioner's Office with its first financial penalty over the vast Cambridge Analytica data breach. The Information Commissioner said it was 'the most important investigation that the ICO has ever undertaken. But while fines and prosecutions punish the bad actors, the real goal is to effect change and restore trust in our democratic system' (Hern and Pegg, 2018).

CHAPTER TWO

Privacy as a Human Right – and a Tradable Asset

Go to any marketing industry conference, and you're guaranteed to find that a key topic is consumer privacy.

However, it's important to note that the privacy battle, or debate, sees very different attitudes being taken by citizens and legislators around the world. Cultural sensitivities towards privacy, and expectations of it, vary widely. While many of us perceive privacy as a fundamental human right to be protected at all costs, others seem far more relaxed about the subject. It's far from a clear-cut issue where all attitudes and behaviour are the same. Hence a common view in boardrooms is that, while many consumers are increasingly concerned about how much of their personal data is being tracked, some are increasingly willing to trade privacy for things that clearly benefit them.

To quantify this point, a high-profile international study into online privacy, involving over ten thousand interviews, was conducted by ComRes (before the latest scandals involving social media companies) in the United Kingdom, Germany, France, Spain, India, Japan, South Korea, Brazil and Australia. Their research found that of the global respondents interviewed, '79% were concerned about their privacy online, while 41% felt consumers are harmed by big companies gathering large amounts of personal data for internal use. Consumers in South Korea, UK, Australia and France were the most critical, while consumers in Brazil, India and Spain were the most sympathetic' (Big Brother Watch, 2013).

The UN has passed its latest 'Right to Privacy in the Digital Age' resolution. This recognizes that 'more and more personal data is being collected, processed, and shared; and expresses concern about the sale or multiple re-sale of personal data, which often happens without the individual's free, explicit and informed consent' (Brown, 2016). Since the first resolution, the UN has evolved its approach from being a mainly political response to mass surveillance to looking into more complex issues around data collection and the role of the private sector. When private sector companies are facilitating digital surveillance, this means that those businesses may be complicit in human rights abuses.

> *The most consequential war being waged today is over data protection.*

The privacy debate is a huge one, but in this chapter I focus mainly on areas such as how the leverage of psychographic data by the likes of Cambridge Analytica has led to enormous public outrage, the impact of social media brands on consumer trust as it relates to our data privacy, the consumer trust and privacy issues relating to in-home technology, and the key implications of the EU's GDPR regulations.

It comes at a time when, as *Wired* magazine put it, 'the most consequential war being waged today is over data protection. ... One ideology puts the control of personal data in the hands of the individual, the other cedes control to the corporation [or state]. Will ... 2018 be remembered as when the right to privacy was enshrined as a fundamental human right?' (Pendergast, 2018).

Privacy + data = democracy

As illustrated by the questioning in April 2018 of Mark Zuckerberg by the US Congress, which we saw in Chapter 1, the debates over privacy and use of our data go much further than companies simply collecting that data to recommend a new product to buy. Just as brands such as SBI, Baidu, AT&T, HSBC and Coca-Cola aim to understand consumers by tracking their behaviour (when allowed), political pollsters aim to reboot their voter knowledge by utilizing an extraordinary range of analytical and machine-learning software.

On the personal data issue, I'd discussed the analysis and use of this with David Plouffe, Campaign Manager for Barack Obama, when we were both on the same speaker-panel at a conference in the Middle East a couple of years ago. At that event, he gave a fascinating talk about the leverage of data by the Barack Obama campaign team.

That activity was reported by the *New York Review of Books*: 'They did so by gathering millions of data points on the electorate from public sources, commercial information brokers, and their own surveys, then polling voters with great frequency and looking for response patterns. All this was used to create predictive models of who was likely to vote for Obama' (Halpern, 2017). The use of analytics by the Obama campaign enabled them to group voters into specific potential voting sub-sections based on predicted psychographic profiles, and therefore tailor fine-tuned campaign communications targeting these voters in their filter-bubble groupings.

Looking to target individuals or small groups of voters is nothing new, just like knocking on doors or holding hustings to speak with voters face to face. Knocking on doors is still a great way to connect with existing, lapsed or potential voters. But it's in the digital realm that elections are clearly now won or lost, and elections can be decided by niche groups of voters who just need exactly the right 'nudge'. This can now be done on either a genuinely individual or 'mass-niche' basis.

The Washington Post revealed that 'political consultants from Obama's earlier presidential campaign also siphoned huge amounts of data about users and their friends, developing deep understandings of people's relationships and preferences'. That article noted how the director of data analytics for the 'Obama for America' campaign had 'built a database of every American voter using the same Facebook tool used by CA'. That developer said they had 'ingested the entire U.S. social graph. We scraped it all' (Dwoskin, 2018).

So it seems that the protection of personal data was given low priority, and the implications for the US Presidential Election that followed were extraordinary. Unless you've taken an extremely long break from access to any media, you'll be well aware that the use of data was sent into hyperdrive by Donald Trump's 2016 campaign consultants, Cambridge Analytica (Kranish and Romm, 2018).

Facebook, Cambridge Analytica and the US presidential election

That media organizations need to re-earn our trust was underlined in the most explosive of ways via the results of some incredible investigative journalism in the United Kingdom. The journalist Carole Cadwalladr of *The Observer* was at the centre of the superb investigation which took more than a year to bring together in order to expose, in early 2018, 'Cambridge Analytica's alleged harvesting of the data of over 50 million Facebook users to influence the US presidential elections'. *The Observer* took the decision to share the scoop with Channel 4 News and *The New York Times* prior to publishing (Tobitt, 2018).

In their scoop, the investigation showed how '50 million Americans had their data harvested and shared improperly by

Global Science Research, which shared it with Cambridge Analytica' (Lewis and Hilder, 2018). Just to illustrate the complex story that was later to be unravelled by investigative reporters, Cambridge Analytica had previously worked for Republican presidential candidates Ted Cruz and Ben Carson, along with conducting data research for the 'Leave.EU' campaign. The billionaire Robert Mercer co-owned their parent company, SCL, which had also played a key role in the Brexit campaign. Steve Bannon, who was Donald Trump's former chief strategist, also used to be Vice President of Cambridge Analytica. As widely reported, Cambridge Analytica then 'used the data to build a system that could profile individual US voters, in order to target them with personalized political advertisements' (Osborne and Sabbagh, 2018). That figure was later revealed to have climbed to 87 million people, including over a million UK users.

To complete the tangled company web that I mentioned just now, SCL was set up by Aleksandr Kogan and Joseph Chancellor as an equal partnership. But when the data breach scandal was exposed, while Facebook was to focus on Kogan, laying the blame on him for the misuse of the data used by Cambridge Analytica, Chancellor escaped the public eye – until it was later revealed that he was working as a quantitative social psychologist at, yes, you've guessed it, Facebook. (When this was also later exposed, the company then, according to BuzzFeed, placed him on administration leave and launched an 'employment investigation' into him (Mac, 2018).)

Noting the Brexit angle, the whistle-blower Christopher Wylie told a committee of MPs in the United Kingdom that 'the EU referendum was won through fraud', saying it was striking that Vote Leave and three key pro-Brexit groups all used the services of the little-known technology firm AggregateIQ to help target voters online; and that AggregateIQ was effectively the Canadian arm of Cambridge Analytica and its parent SCL (Hern and Sabbagh, 2018).

Cambridge Analytica then became the subject of US special prosecutor Robert Mueller's probing of the company's role in Donald Trump's presidential election campaign, along with being investigated by the UK authorities. As for Facebook, as reported by virtually every news source in the world, Mark Zuckerberg finally apologized after the allegations about the harvesting and exploiting of data from all those many millions of Facebook users, calling the incident 'a major breach of trust' and saying that Facebook would audit thousands of apps as part of a major crackdown, restrict developers' data access and introduce a tool for every user to assess the apps they've used and offer an easy way to revoke their permission. He posted on Facebook that 'We have a responsibility to protect your data and if we can't then we don't deserve to serve you' (Zuckerberg, 2018). The Chief Operating Operator of Facebook, Cheryl Sandberg, also posted a message saying exactly the same thing.

Facebook has a responsibility to protect your data and if they can't then they don't deserve to serve you.

This followed on from the 'Privacy Principles' that Facebook had already announced, regarding the company's approach to how individual users could control their privacy on the platform. Facebook's Elliot Schrage told the DLD conference in Germany: 'We have over-invested in building new experiences and under-invested in preventing abuses' (O'Brien, 2018).

In response, just before Zuckerberg was called before Congress it was announced that lawyers in the United States and Britain had started a class action lawsuit against Facebook, Cambridge Analytica, SCL Group and Global Science Research, for the alleged misuse of the personal data of more than 71 million people. In terms of mind-boggling numbers, it was announced that Facebook provided Aleksandr Kogan (the researcher involved in the Cambridge Analytica data-harvesting scandal) with a dataset of 57 billion Facebook friendships. This dataset was of 'every friendship formed in 2011 in every country in the world at the national aggregate level' (Wong and Lewis, 2018).

With respect to the technicalities of that, it was reported that Facebook 'failed to compel Cambridge Analytica to delete "derivatives" of personal data it had obtained without users' consent, enabling the consultancy to retain predictive models derived from users' profiles'. Facebook had asked Cambridge Analytica to delete data it had obtained without consent, and all its derivatives. But in response, Cambridge Analytica merely stated that 'it had deleted the data, making no reference to derivatives' (Bridge, 2018c).

At that Senate hearing, and in a dramatic moment which *The Times* described as 'one of the most revealing of the two-day inquisition', Zuckerberg casually revealed that Facebook had been 'quietly constructing a vast database of "shadow profiles" of people who had never consented to use the social media platform'. He also said that 'in general, we collect data on people who are not signed up for Facebook for security purposes' (Fortson, 2018).

Soon after that hearing, *AdAge* reported that Zuckerberg, 'appearing somewhat defiant', said 'we will keep building.' He also announced that Facebook was 'working on a dating service to compete with Tinder, Bumble, Match and all the rest. He claimed that it would match people based on shared interests and would encourage deep connection. How exactly it would do that was unclear' (Sloane, 2018a). Unfortunately, following that statement, *The Times* reported that 'Facebook has introduced thousands of Islamic State supporters to one another as "suggested friends". Facebook, in its desire to connect as many people as possible, has inadvertently created a system which helps connect extremists and terrorists.' The article also referenced research from the Counter Extremism Project, which said 'its research laid bare Facebook's inability or unwillingness to address extremist content' (Bridge, 2018b).

On the impact that can result from a 'brand minus trust' equation, an article about the 'Anti-Social Network' stated that the company 'claims motivation by a noble calling. But if it has benefited society, it's done so as a by-product of harvesting personal data and using it for profit. Facebook must face up to its responsibilities towards the law, society and democracy. If that hits their vast profits, that is their problem' (*The Times*, 2018).

This point was mirrored by Tim Cook, the Chief Executive of Apple, who as noted by *The Times*, 'accused some of his rivals of turning people into products' and had previously accused Facebook 'of building a business based on an invasion of privacy'. Apple 'regarded privacy as a basic human right and has built the company around that belief'. The Apple CEO also thinks that 'the sprawling, intimate personal data profiles that companies like Facebook and Google compile shouldn't exist' (Hoyle, 2018).

Perhaps as a reaction to this overall situation, both Facebook and Twitter announced that they would be taking action that they hoped would alter the way people used their services, with Facebook aiming for a 'time well spent' strategy, meaning fewer unwanted interactions with brands, while Twitter would aim for improved 'conversational health' by users of its platform.

As a postscript to this issue, and from a strictly political-advertising perspective, I should mention that in the United Kingdom, following months of heated public debate, questions in Parliament and an immense amount of media attention, it was good to read a report in *Campaign* magazine that the IPA (Institute of Practitioners in Advertising, the world's most influential professional association relating to marketing communications) challenged the Electoral Commission and political parties to suspend all micro-targeted ads following the data scandal involving Facebook and Cambridge Analytica. The IPA has also called for all political-advertising creative work to be listed for public display in a bid to increase transparency (Oakes, 2018b).

IPA president Sarah Golding explained: 'There's nothing wrong with using data to micro target advertising for holiday destinations or sports cars .... However, in an age where consumer trust has been heavily eroded and the quest for truth and transparency is paramount, we feel it incumbent upon us to call for this moratorium' (Oakes, 2018a).

Cambridge Analytica, the company at the centre of the Facebook data breach scandal, closed down in mid-2018. It was a long fall for Andrew Nix, the CEO, who had so memorably claimed credit for getting Donald Trump to the White House, telling an undercover reporter from Channel 4 News that 'we did all the research, all the data, all the analytics, all the targeting. We ran all the digital campaign, the television campaign and our data informed all the strategy'. That media report went on to say that 'he also revealed the firm used a self-destruct email server to erase its digital history' (Solon, 2018a).

Soon after their closure, the BBC reported that the UK's data watchdog, the Information Commissioners Office, 'had ordered the parent company of Cambridge Analytica (SCL Elections, which continues to trade) to hand over all data it held

If Cambridge Analytica can be shown to have misused data, it could open itself up to class action from the entire US electorate.

on a US citizen, the academic David Carroll. The move could open the floodgates for millions of other claims against the company which was involved in the Facebook data harvesting scandal. The ICO said that if SCL continued to refuse to engage with it, it could become a criminal matter' (BBC News, 2018).

The Guardian also reported on the story, noting that 'this would have been unimaginable a year ago. It's a real landmark.... Cambridge Analytica has claimed to have up to 7,000 data points on 240 million Americans.... If it ... can be shown to have misused data, it could open itself up to class action from the entire US electorate' (Cadwalladr, 2018a).

As also reported by *The Guardian*, 'Facebook used its apps to gather information about users and their friends, including some who had not signed up to the social network, reading their text messages, tracking their locations and accessing photos on their phones, a court case in California alleges. The claims would amount to mass surveillance' (Cadwalladr and Graham-Harrison, 2018a). Noting that Mark Zuckerberg is facing allegations 'that he developed a "malicious and fraudulent scheme" to exploit vast amounts of private data to earn Facebook billions', the same journalists also reported that Facebook is being sued by a company which 'claims the social network's chief executive "weaponised" the ability to access data from any user's network of friends – the feature at the heart of the Cambridge Analytica scandal' (Cadwalladr and Graham-Harrison, 2018b).

Personalization and customer predictive modelling

We're now going to look at a very different aspect of privacy. One of the leading consumer trends of our time is hyper-personalization. We're told that customers are ever more de-manding, with a strong desire that brands perfectly fulfil or even predict their needs, this being a vital brand connector for consumers who want everything to be accessible, but also to be customized and unique.

Linked to this, we see a continued rise in extreme convenience where brands increasingly shape and personalize their offerings to fit in with consumers' ever-busier lives. To do this, business teams need accurate data on which to base their operational and marketing plans, hence they are using things such as customer predictive modelling software that doesn't wait for 'actual' de-mand. This sees brands activate future consumption by intelli-gently applying data gained from everything from store cards to in-home connected devices.

We now have the brave new world of omnipresent digital services, illustrated, for instance, by the continued rise of Ama-zon's next-generation product portfolio.

Trend speakers at 'Future of Retail' conferences often talk of ever-increasing numbers of people using in-home voice assistants, conducting their shopping without using a screen, and voice technology being utilized in more and more public spaces and consumer devices.

This also sees the home as an ever more commercial space where the 'Internet of Everything' is shown by Google's Assistant built into cookers, fridges and washing machines. Amazon and Microsoft have set aside (some) competitive differences to allow Alexa and Cortana to collaborate with each other. The latest move in mass-market robotics from Amazon is the new 'home-droid' embodiment of Alexa, which is camera and microphone equipped. Amazon's robot also has an in-body phone recharging station, possibly useful as it follows you around and tries to sell you things. *The Times* noted the concerns of critics that these 'creepy data-gatherers could be hacked by third-parties to spy on their masters'. Facebook 'has filed a patent for a Segway-style "self-balancing robot" that would follow users, monitor their surroundings using cameras and microphones and give access to Facebook on a screen' (Bridge, 2018a).

Contagious magazine recently noted that '55% of US homes will have a smart speaker by 2022, whilst 30% of web browsing will be done by voice by 2020. As smart-speaker technology improves, brands will have to think about developing a voice of their own, too (Swift, 2018). The implications for product purchases increasingly made via voice-activated AI devices that are 'always listening to get to know you better' are immense. A very real voice-search concern for brands though, is a 'brand bypass' situation where, if we don't demand a specific brand, this will be 'chosen' for us via third-party promotional deals.

Elsewhere, smartphone health monitoring means that we'll effectively see our doctors daily and is transforming the way health companies serve us. In terms of personalized digital health services, the text-based Lysa chatbot app (developed by an ex-member of the digital health team at Google) uses AI to mimic the benefits of talking directly with a nutritionist, but at a far more affordable rate, therefore being accessible to a much wider audience.

Hyper-targeted advertising

However, all this 'getting personal' technology clearly has its critics. In the context of marketing, a recent UK report by You-Gov into hyper-targeted advertising, ie those 'personalized for the right audience', found that 'over half of British adults say personalized adverts creep them out. But, targeting the one-third that are more likely to engage with adverts which are tailored to them can yield strong return on investment. Understanding consumers' appetite for personalization and finding that balance is critical' (Sevak, 2018).

For all those individuals who are concerned, this is a very big deal, and one that marketers simply have to take on board. A superb article in *Marketing Week* by Mark Ritson noted that most British adults detest the idea of hyper-personalized advertising: 'Just because we can do a more advanced job of targeting, doesn't mean that consumers want any part of it. In fact, we can be certain they do not.' His report went on to say: 'How marketers respond to all of this is, quite literally, the biggest question our discipline has faced in decades' (Ritson, 2018).

At the SXSW festival this year, Hector Ouilhet and Laura Granka from Google Search suggested that media are transitioning to a fourth human experience, following the third stage of 'mobile multi-modality' (device centricity) to one of 'fluidity' (device un-centricity), meaning 'ambient media and devices everywhere around you'. A report on their presentation suggested that 'in a 2025 world in which media is everywhere around you, and content turns on just for you as you walk past screens and audio ports and scores of different glass panel tools, data about *you* will be the only thing that matters' (Kunz, 2018).

This is a perfect time to reference industry guru Faris Yakob, who said 'the only people who think Minority Report was a positive vision of the future, work in marketing' (Yakob, 2016).

Privacy as collateral damage

Do you read the endless 'terms and conditions' documents or unintelligible privacy policies that come with our shiny new tech products? Seemingly none of us do, but this must change as we need to be far more critically aware. An example of this relates to issues such as the 'listening in' of voice-activated hardware. Here a red line seems to be forming for an increasing number of people as the 'privacy intrusion' of these products becomes more apparent.

A UK 2017 survey stated that '76% of us are fearful of smart home gear, with unauthorised data collection the most-cited issue' (ICO, 2017). For an example of why there's growing concern, recent reports noted that Google's Home Mini smart speaker left their devices recording everything, almost constantly, and transmitted the recordings to Google (Sulleyman, 2017). The BBC also reported that those devices, described by some as 'Trojan horses', put tech companies right at the heart of people's lives. They noted that, while Amazon's in-home voice-activated AI technology currently activates when someone uses a wake-phrase such as 'hello Alexa', they had patented 'voice-sniffing' technology 'to be deployed via its Echo speakers; enabling it to listen-in to entire conversations, using trigger-words such as like and love, indicating a level of user-interest, to build a profile of customers. The system could then offer targeted advertising and product recommendations' (BBC Technology, 2018) While the product will have its fans, others clearly feel that this is the stuff of smart-home nightmares, where consumers see that their cool new piece of technology has actually turned into an Orwellian surveillance machine.

Concerning the 'privacy legalities' of all this, the law fortunately appears to be on the side of the individual. In the United States,

Albert Gidari, director of privacy at the Stanford Center, said in a recent article that 'If they do not disclose the functionality, they have liability. If the device collects data without user knowledge, then the FTC and State Attorneys, as well as class action plaintiff lawyers will respond.' He noted that 'Privacy violations usually mean big fines and we have strong criminal laws against unauthorised recording of communications' (Williams, 2018).

Despite this, numerous reports highlight that transcriptions of voice recordings, as opposed to the actual audio recordings themselves, are being used by the tech giants to get around the voice-data issue. Other uses of our recordings identify us by anonymous 'random identifiers', as opposed to our own personal details, to avoid potential privacy-breach issues. Elsewhere, voice recognition software is being used more often to enable, for instance, access to government services. When it comes to governmental policy, several high-profile cases have already taken place in the United States and Europe. These include access to personal data and voice recordings made by the likes of Google and Apple, usually over issues such as terrorism. Regarding the privacy of private citizens, this is taken far more seriously in some countries than others, of course, an obvious example being the United States where this is dealt with under the protection of the First Amendment.

I won't delve deeply into the matter of state use of facial recognition and citizen surveillance hardware and software, as it's outside the brand-based subject of this book. However, it is worth highlighting issues such as the Data Retention Directive, which requires the various EU member states to store and grant the security and police services access to information on every phone call, text message and e-mail sent or received for up to the past two years.

In a country such as Germany where memories of communism ensured that state snooping was a taboo subject, the threat of terrorism has now made public video surveillance a commonplace sight. Elsewhere, the use of the Social Credit System in China, which is intended to be fully operational by 2020, aims to reinforce the idea that 'keeping trust is glorious and breaking trust is disgraceful'. It focuses on four areas: honesty in public affairs, social integrity, commercial integrity and judicial integrity. 'Trust-breaking' citizens with a low score relating to their 'social credit' face restrictions, such as on travelling or being banned from senior-level jobs (Chinese Govt State Council Notice, 2015). According to Business Insider, 'The system is run by city councils and private tech platforms which hold personal data. Like private credit scores, a person's social score can move up and down depending on their behaviour' (Ma, 2018). Good behaviour will get you access to better hotels or even improve your profile on Chinese dating sites, such as Baihe, while bad behaviour can also relate to things such as posting fake news online, in addition to criminality.

The overall privacy issue, and a forward-looking scenario, was summed up well by the futurist Richard Watson in his excellent book *Digital vs Human*. Writing about the things that should concern us in relation to privacy, he said that these are 'individual freedom, mental privacy, and self-determination, especially what happens to the private self if it is constantly spied upon. It's possible that we'll trade the idea of governments gathering information about us in return for the promise of security, in which case privacy will become collateral damage' (Watson, 2016).

On that last point, *China Daily* noted, 'though concerns about privacy exist and big efforts are needed to protect personal data, companies are eagerly embracing the new technology. The images captured by cameras won't be stored on computers. They are encrypted and just used for real-time image matching with the public security bureau's database' (Si, 2018).

But there's a problem: consumers are actively rejecting giving access to their data in favour of privacy. According to Jeremy Waite, Global Leader of CMO Programs at IBM, '55% of UK consumers say they no longer wish to share any data – at all – with marketers, and 90% of consumer conversations are now invisible due to their conversations happening on "dark social"' (Waite, 2017). (See more on how marketers are acting around 'dark social' in Chapter 3.) The implications seem to be that we trust technology in terms of product performance, but we increasingly distrust the usage of our data.

What will be next for marketers in this context if they can't access accurate 'personalized data' at will? If they are unable to offer hyper-personalization due to data being withheld by such things as GDPR rules, how will they provide a service?

Brands don't actually need to know everything about you; they just need to know a few things about a lot of people.

Talk to a data scientist, and they'll tell you that brands don't actually need to know everything about you, they just need to know a few things about a lot of people. This is known as 'personalization'.

IBM offer predictive analytics through 'Mood Graphs'. These interpret personality traits via the digital behaviour of someone's social media activity. The ability of their 'Personality Insights' app and the resulting 'Mood Graphs' gives a view into an individual's agreeableness, conscientiousness, extraversion, emotional range, and openness. It also gives a 'deep dive' into their needs and values. One obvious implication of this could be for human resources departments to judge whether you might be suitable to join their staff. This may lead to ever more people reconsidering their social media posts, and tone of voice.

The tech counter-reaction and General Data Protection Regulation (GDPR)

The issue of trust in relation to privacy and the use of our personal data is where GDPR will have a radical impact on both business and society at large.

The aim, and hopefully the result of the GDPR legislation in the EU, has been to increase society's trust and confidence in how a wide variety of companies, organizations and institutions gain and use our personal data and information. It gives the individual much more power over what information these groups can hold on them, and also gives individuals access to that information and the right to have it erased in certain circumstances.

GDPR has received spectacular media attention, with responses from governments around the world. International legal regulation is being taken at a UN level, providing hard-hitting and clear-cut action protecting the digital rights and privacy of citizens.

In Europe, GDPR is delivering stronger privacy protection for individual citizens by putting a legal firewall around personal privacy, via the protection of personal data. In an article about privacy law, Jeffrey Chester, founder of the Center for Digital Democracy, said: 'GDPR is changing the balance of power from the giant digital marketing companies to focus on the needs of individuals and democratic society. That's an incredible breakthrough'. According to David Carroll, Associate Professor at the Parsons School in New York, 'Consumers have been abused. Marketers have succeeded in making people feel powerless. GDPR gives consumers the chance to renegotiate that very unfair deal' (Solon, 2018b).

This issue of the EU protecting individuals and society and the growing 'tech backlash' was explained in a *Financial Times* article, stating that the EU has 'led the way in enforcing antitrust law against Google, privacy law against Facebook, and tax law against Apple. Plenty of people are threatening to follow suit, on the left and right. The new technology tools are destroying both trust and truth, creating a hunger for community and authenticity' (Slaughter, 2018).

The ramifications for brands are huge. As noted by *Marketing Week*, 'Only 20% of the public has trust and confidence in how organizations store their personal information. If marketers can embed the ethos of GDPR into how they talk to consumers, that combined with education will build trust' (Vizard, 2018).

The very fact that consumers have a lack of 'trust and confidence' about their private data is hardly surprising given the number of data breaches in the past few years. Yahoo still tops a sorry list of brands who have seen this happen to their users, with *The Wall Street Journal* memorably reporting that 'a massive data breach at Yahoo affected all of its three billion user accounts. Compromised customer information included usernames, passwords, and in some cases telephone numbers and dates of birth'. This breach was further complicated owing to many of those affected having had numerous accounts across various Yahoo-owned sites, such as Tumblr and Flickr. This followed other cyberattacks that showed the vulnerability of technology companies, which as *The Wall Street Journal* also reported, included a data breach at Equifax 'that affected more than 140 million consumers' (McMillan and Knutson, 2017).

In 2018, Facebook announced an overhaul of their data collection rules, and admitted that the public profiles of most users could have been 'scraped'. According to Abbas Razaghpanah, a specialist in mobile privacy and security, 'once that data is scraped, there is little Facebook can do to regain control of that information. There's a number of ways public information can be abused. Somebody could use this to impersonate you in a number of ways, none of which is good for the person being impersonated' (Sloane, 2018b).

In response, there's been a myopic reaction to these data breaches from advertisers. *AdAge* reported: 'Advertisers are more concerned Facebook will cut off access to data than they are about privacy, it seems. Far from boycotting the social network over highly publicized data lapses, most brands appear worried about their ability to reach their desired consumers if stricter privacy policies take root' (Sloane, 2018c). The reaction of Bob Hoffman, a leading commentator, was swift, as he posted on Twitter that the 'Ad industry's irresponsibility continues unabated' (Hoffman, 2018).

Surveillance capitalism

A huge amount of attention has been paid to GDPR, which was designed to protect and empower EU citizens' data privacy, an essential element of it being the legality of personal 'opt in' rather than 'opt out' protection.

After the Zuckerberg 2018 Senate hearing, *The Guardian* noted that with 'regulation very much on the table, the EU's GDPR is everyone's favourite' and that 'European regulators are suddenly the heroes of the day'. However, they also stated that 'Multiple congressional representatives asked Zuckerberg whether or not he would enforce GDPR for Americans, a question he repeatedly dodged by promising GDPR "controls" rather than "protections"' (Hern, 2018).

According to Reuters, Facebook confirmed to them that 'the social network is keen to reduce its exposure to GDPR, which allows European regulators to fine companies for collecting or using personal data without users' consent. They're planning to make their 1.5 billion members in Africa, Asia, Australia and Latin America not fall under the EU's GDPR rules' (Ingram, 2018).

Jonathan Taplin, author of *Move Fast and Break Things*, talked about Facebook being in the 'Surveillance Capitalism business' following Mark Zuckerberg's appearance before Congress. He feels that 'GDPR, if it's adhered to, will change Facebook radically in Europe, as it means users have the choice of opting in or opting out of sharing their data. That will make a huge difference' (Taplin, 2018).

Back in the US, the impact on corporate business models from American regulators with their historically more lenient privacy laws, looks set to be extensive, following the Consumer Privacy Act passed in California that comes into effect in 2020.

It was interesting to read an article by Sandy Parakilas (who led Facebook's efforts to fix its privacy problems) in *The New York Times* where she commented: 'What I saw was a company that prioritized data collection from its users over protecting them from abuse. As the world contemplates what to do about Facebook in the wake of its role in Russia's election meddling, it must consider this history. Lawmakers shouldn't allow Facebook to regulate itself. Because it won't' (Parakilas, 2017).

The likes of Facebook and other social media platforms may squeal about the law of unintended consequences but, at the same time, certain organizations have clearly set out with sinister intentions over the leverage and abuse of individual privacy, and the result of this weaponization of data is the vital need for protective legal regulations. While we see the EU GDPR rules (and possibly the Consumer Privacy Act throughout the US) being implemented, it will be fascinating to see which other governments use similar regulations to protect citizen and consumer rights.

Privacy as a tradable asset aka 'anonymous data monetization'

In some areas, a lack of privacy can clearly be seen as being beneficial, for example elderly people being able to hold on to their independence by living at home, albeit while under the 'watchful eye' of home robots and other IoT-enabled devices, which record things such as heart rates and whether they have an accident or fail to take medicine on time. The healthcare industry is obviously a big player in this huge global market, which shows enormous future growth.

At the same time, genetics-testing services are growing in popularity, and this is an area where, once again, the issues of privacy cannot be overstated, when it comes to trusting companies such as 23andme to hold and use our data securely. Elsewhere, what was once essentially the preserve of the so-called 'quantified self' movement has since exploded into a myriad of sectors where brands offer personal tracking technology. This includes a vast number of wearables, to enable us, and employers or others in authority, to track the individual. Health or insurance companies that reward us for leading active lives, or employers who do the same in recognition of our activity at work, reflect a world that sees us being rewarded for the exchange of our personal data.

This is where 'privacy as a tradable asset' also comes into the picture. An interesting debate that's frequently discussed at trend conferences is whether, increasingly, we shall see privacy (specifically our personal data) being used as a tradable asset, rather than something to be guarded, simply given away, or taken from us without our consent.

When it comes to consumer brands, people are realizing that their data has worth. Part of the problem with all the data scandals that hit the headlines in 2017/2018 was that, essentially, most people appeared not to have given much thought as to the value of their data. This issue has now truly been put under the spotlight.

These are early days for monetized privacy, but if we do so by trading our data, then trust will naturally be a key pillar of any brand with which we choose to share that data, whether we sell it on an individual basis or by aggregating it anonymously with others'. Another route could be to share it piecemeal, bit by bit, specifically relating to the usage required by the recipient involved.

Even before the recent Facebook scandal, and I mentioned a series of other data breaches earlier in this chapter, the privacy issue was of prime importance. As a *Harvard Business Review* podcast put it: '97% of people are vaguely nervous about the fact that companies are gathering data and are vaguely aware that something is being gathered. But they're not quite sure what. That's a dangerous combination; nervousness and ignorance. Those two feed off each other, uncertainty feeds the fear of the unknown' (Green, 2015).

A *Harvard Business Review* article linked to that podcast stated that 'companies are sweeping up vast quantities of data about consumer activities, both online and off. Numerous studies have found that transparency about the use and protection of consumer data reinforces trust.' The article surveyed a wide range of companies and ranked them as being 'completely trustworthy, trustworthy, untrustworthy or completely untrustworthy'. As their report noted, 'Finance firms such as PayPal and China's Alipay received the highest rankings. Social networks like Facebook came in last' (Morey, Forbath and Schoop, 2015).

What does this all tell us? That for those consumers who see their privacy as something to be taken seriously, indeed who view it as a fundamental human right, brands must be seen to be acting on the side of the consumer, respecting them and guaranteeing the safety of that privacy, and rewarding the individual for the use of their personal data. The use, or abuse, of our personal data being one of the key ethical issues in the world of today and of the future.

Brands must be seen to be acting on the side of the consumer, respecting them and guaranteeing the safety of their privacy.

This issue has huge implications in the global 'FAANGS vs BATS' commercial battle, regarding their different approaches to the subject. (Those acronyms meaning Facebook, Amazon, Apple, Netflix and Google/Alphabet vs Baidu, Alibaba and Tencent). We need to view our data as being genuinely 'ours', ie the same way we view 'our money' or 'our bodies' or 'our homes'. This needs managing in a transparent manner, and the security, usage and management of that data is of the upmost importance.

Brands have a fundamental role to play here, when, even leaving aside social media brands, the data that will be transmitted about us by over 20 billion connected devices in the world by 2020 will be truly incredible. Unless the safeguarding of that data is up to the task, an equally incredible, and tragic, thing will be the disappearance of our privacy.

Following the EU's GDPR ruling, which included strict rules about data portability, the 'DTP' (Data Transfer Project) collaboration was then announced by Facebook, Google, Microsoft and Twitter. This enabled platform users to back up their personal data (and in that respect therefore wasn't dissimilar to the 'Download Your Data' offering from Google), delete a network or join a different one; but crucially, by taking their data with them, users wouldn't have to begin completely afresh. The end result for consumers being those key buzzwords: flexibility and control.

I shall draw this chapter to a close with two final quotes relating to the demise of Cambridge Analytica not actually being the end of that particular story. Ongoing enquiries by the Information Commissioner's Office are still in action. In addition, special counsel Robert Mueller's investigations into connections between Donald Trump's presidential campaign and the data-mining firm are specifically looking into whether they'd used data improperly obtained from Facebook to try to influence elections.

An excellent article in *The Observer* stated that unfortunately it wasn't 'the end of the use of personal data in ways in which we may not even be aware, but it's a triumph. News has won over fake news. Facts over lies. A mainstream news organisation over false narratives crafted by expert manipulators and seeded across the internet by untraceable websites' (Cadwalladr, 2018b). (And at this point I should also mention that Carole Cadwalladr won the Orwell prize for journalism, in recognition of her superb investigative work into Cambridge Analytica.)

The vice chairman of the Senate Intelligence Committee, referring to the growing scandal over Cambridge Analytica's involvement with the US 2016 Presidential Election campaign, said that it was 'more evidence that the online political advertising market is essentially the Wild West. Whether it's allowing Russians to purchase political ads, or extensive micro-targeting based on ill-gotten user data, it's clear that, left unregulated, this market will continue to be prone to deception and lacking in transparency' (Lemire, 2018).

So, whether it's in this most macro of political contexts, or that of the day-to-day impact on our individual privacy from mainstream consumer brands, they have clear questions to answer about the trust-based consumer relationship that is so vital: whose side are they on, and why should we trust them?

CHAPTER THREE

#SkipAd vs Connections with Meaning

The death of advertising has been long foretold, but there's no doubting that the communications world in general, and the advertising one in particular, is in turmoil. How this connects to the topics highlighted in the previous chapters can immediately be shown by comments from the Advertising Standards Authority in the United Kingdom. In reaction to media reports that record numbers of advertisements were amended or withdrawn in 2017, their chief executive said that 'an increase in complaints to the ASA is a function of our wider awareness of ... seemingly unrelated or only peripherally-related issues or events like Cambridge Analytica, concerns about privacy and so on' (Hammett, 2018).

If you take a look back at the 'golden age' of advertising, and yes, I am talking Mad Men-esque territory here, things used to be enviably simple. Basically put, the real-life Don Drapers were faced with a very narrow set of media with which to connect with consumers, and a very different set of consumer attitudes towards brands and advertising, ie both were broadly positive.

In this chapter I'll look at the causes of a growing disconnection among consumers and brands, agencies and brand owners; but also at how senior industry figures are illuminating a way forward to rebuild those connections.

To begin, I'll drop in a famous industry statistic that most brand owners and agencies wish had never been uncovered. The Havas Group 'Meaningful Brands' survey (which questioned more than 300,000 people in over 20 countries) found that the majority of consumers 'wouldn't care if 74% of brands they use vanished, and also that 60% of the content produced by companies is poor, irrelevant or failing to deliver'. The report, covered by CNBC among many others, also went on to say that 'We have an overload of brands, opportunities, and too much communication: so you need to be meaningful' (Handley, 2017a).

That 'meaningful' word needs clarifying. Rather than just delivering the standard combination of 'faster/bigger/newer' that so many brands aim to bring to market, the Havas report suggests that what people actually want are brands that, as their Global MD Dominique Delport puts it, 'functionally work, are value for money and make life easier, as well as considering the impact they have on communities' (Handley, 2017b).

Trust in brands has been falling for decades

Of course, there's also the huge issue of trust. As the Havas report puts it, it is about the way that the relationship between people and brands is broken: 'Much of the trust, respect and loyalty people had for many brands has disintegrated. You see it in the level of cynicism, scepticism and indifference that people have towards many brands. The reality is, trust in brands worldwide has been falling for three decades' (Havas, 2018).

This lack of trust also points an accusing finger at the advertising industry. In the annual Ipsos MORI Veracity Index, nurses and doctors are at the top of the 'public trust in professions' list, while trust in journalists is also at a record high, gaining its highest score since the survey began (Ipsos MORI, 2017). Trust in the advertising industry is generally held to be so low that it doesn't even make the report. So whom do we trust? The report notes that whom we actually trust most is ourselves, the ordinary man/woman in the street; hence the agency world's obsession with 'word of mouth'. This is, without doubt, the most valuable form of marketing ever invented – quite simply because we believe each other far more than we believe branded messages.

'Word of mouth' is the most valuable form of marketing ever invented – we believe each other far more than we believe branded messages.

A fairly obvious key to this is that friends and family don't tend to have a vested interest in selling us something. There are also the inbuilt issues of relevance, trust and reputation along with the basic point that the recommendations we give to each other are hopefully done for the 'right' reasons. Nor do we always exaggerate the potential impact on our lives of every single product out there. Which, essentially, is the strategy behind most advertising.

This basic but staggeringly important point was taken up by McKinsey, who state that 'Marketers may spend millions on advertising, yet often what really makes up a consumer's mind is not only simple but free: a word-of-mouth recommendation from a trusted source. As consumers overwhelmed by choices tune out the barrage of traditional marketing, word of mouth cuts through the noise quickly and effectively' (Bughin, 2010).

Their report also suggests that word of mouth is the primary decision-making factor in up to 50 per cent of all purchasing decisions, and also notes that word of mouth is incredibly disruptive. We can all relate to being in a store or looking at a website, about to make a purchase, when someone close to us suggests an alternative and we've taken their advice. Up until that point, those branded messages and the brand connections that we'd taken note of or had remembered were working – and then word of mouth completely changed our minds. That goes to explain why eMarketer goes further than McKinsey, and reports that word-of-mouth marketing is the number one purchase decision influencer in countries as diverse as the United States, Brazil, the United Kingdom and China.

I spoke about this with one of Asia's most renowned consumer experts, Nicole Fall. The last time I'd seen her was when I was conducting focus groups in Japan, but on this occasion she was in Singapore. Nicole told me that:

> In Singapore there's a huge culture of influencer marketing and I've never seen a market quite like it. What this translates into is campaigns, from Dyson to the Singaporean Government, turning to influencers to spread the message. In China there's also a huge influencer culture. Consumers feel that even though they know these influencers are being paid to spread these messages and stories, it's more genuine when they market in this way. That's not to say people believe everything influencers say, consumers aren't that gullible. But there is a sense, particularly in Asia, where reputation counts, that if you are endorsing a product then you should believe in it.

It's not just consumers making these types of claims: '64% of marketing executives indicated that they believe word of mouth is the most effective form of marketing,' stated the American Marketing Association, 'but only 6% say they have mastered it' (WOMMA and AMA 2013).

Marketers used to concentrate obsessively on the four Ps, ie Product, Promotion, Place, Price. However, according to a *Forbes* magazine interview with the president of the Word of Mouth Marketing Association, 'Now marketers need to focus on the 3 Es: Engage (Listen to what they tell you. Be part of the conversation. Be a presence in your fans' lives), Equip (Give them reasons to talk about your products and service), Empower (Give consumers different ways to talk and share)' (Whitler, 2014).

Continuing this deliberate blizzard of facts to underline just how much of a big deal this is, the results of a study conducted by Nielsen in 60 countries, which took in Asia-Pacific, Europe, Latin America, the Middle East, Africa and North America, showed that '83% of consumers believe recommendations from friends and family over all forms of advertising' (Nielsen, 2015).

In an article referencing the veracity report that I mentioned earlier, Charles Vallance of VCCP noted that 'the deference/reference pyramid has been fully inverted. People no longer even vaguely trust upwards, they trust sideways. This correlates directly with the rising importance of word of mouth, customer advocacy and brand talkability' (Vallance, 2017). So, it's clear that adland has a problem. Chris Hirst, Chief Executive of Havas Europe, puts this bluntly: 'Skip-Ad is a metaphor for the public's relationship with ads. Creating more meaningful connections is the answer' (Hirst, 2018).

Word of mouth can essentially be divided into three broad categories, the first being those that are product or service experience based, the second those that arise as a result of exposure to a marketing campaign, and finally those that are impacted by paid influencers, for instance celebrity vloggers. The second category, termed 'consequential' by McKinsey, has a direct link to the type of behaviour related to fake news (which I dealt with in the previous chapter), while the final one, 'intentional', as also termed by McKinsey, is the focus of adland's laser-like concentration on influencer marketing, very much including 'dark social'.

That issue of 'dark social' will be discussed later in this chapter in more detail. This 'earned or paid' influence revolves around the core routes of influencers creating their own content and having an impact via the extent of their social reach (as in the number of people who follow them on Instagram, for example).

Noting the connection that people have with their celebrity blogger of choice, The Fashion Law site says: 'word of mouth has always been a trustworthy tool for marketing but now it's even bigger as people look to Instagram, Twitter, and Snapchat for recommendations' (The Fashion Law, 2018). The vital part in that statement was trust. The influencer–follower relationship is incredibly reliant on it. Because if we believe that the influencer isn't being straight with us, the value we associate with their brand-relevant messages declines massively.

Referencing this at Cannes Lions 2018, Keith Weed of Unilever said, 'Brands need to take urgent action to rebuild trust. The one thing influencer marketing requires is confidence in the influencers' (Moore, 2018). Meanwhile, the basic problem of 'influencer overload' was neatly summed up by David Kershaw, co-founder of M&C Saatchi, who says that 'the competitive nature of influencer marketing is so high that I can't see how all these people are going to be able to sustain it long term' (Frean, 2018).

Meanwhile, one could also argue that the reason word of mouth has historically worked so well amongst women is that most advertising targeting them is either incredibly annoying, ignores the differences between them, lacks inspiration or simply misunderstands the realities of their lives.

#Infosmog and Adtech

For more context about the overall problem, let's not forget that we exist in a time of so-called #Infosmog owing to the sheer amount of advertising, social media, general background information, real and fake news, and entertainment, all of which are vying for people's attention 24/7.

Add to this the staggering amount of ongoing disruption throughout these areas (and more), and the manner in which we consume media and entertainment of every conceivable type means that we're living in what marketers love to call the 'Attention Economy', where the battle to win our attention generally involves every person, brand and company involved essentially trying to shout louder than each other. The result is chaos. Hence the rise and rise of adblockers and every conceivable method that most of us can think of to avoid being interrupted and intruded upon by these unwelcome outsiders.

Technology has had a massive impact on the way ads are created and the media used to publish, broadcast and promote them. Consequently, things aren't so simple anymore. Note the trend, for example, of using creative technologies, including virtual reality, augmented reality and mixed reality, alongside the use of social technologies that also include artificial intelligence, data analytics and machine learning.

The above list normally leads one to the type of 'Future Adland' described by *The Economist* in which they paint a nightmarish world where 'you're manipulated by intelligent advertisements from dusk till dawn. Your various screens flash constantly with commercials that know your desires. Driverless cars bombard you with personalized ads once their doors lock, and if you try to escape by putting on your VR headset, all you see are synthetic billboards' (Schumpeter, 2018).

So, what to do? Before we move on to some ways forward, it's also worth looking at another side of the trust issue when it comes to advertising, in all its forms: the relationship between the advertisers and media owners, particularly when it comes to the world of digital communication. It's a relationship that is fraught, because it seems that fewer and fewer marketers believe in what they're being told or sold by the 'medium or media' suppliers.

Marc Pritchard, Chief Brand Officer of Procter & Gamble (the world's biggest advertiser), has a fundamental problem: people really don't want to watch ads, particularly on social media. Pritchard pointed to the average digital-ad viewing time of 1.7 seconds, with only 20 per cent of ads viewed for more than 2 seconds. That's one reason he believes the marketing world collectively is only delivering low-single-digit sales growth, despite $200 billion in digital and $600 billion in broader marketing spending. 'Obviously we stopped wasting money on 30-second ads. We're designing ads to work in 2 seconds where the next generation of ads is likely to revolve around utility and the concept of "mass one-to-one marketing"' (B&T, 2017).

He says that P&G is working with Amazon and Alibaba among others to serve ads based on consumer shopping and purchase patterns because 'you can understand more about the behaviour, and thus deliver the ad in context, when it's more useful at the right time, when it's relevant and not annoying' (Neff, 2017).

In an exposé that shocked the industry, it was announced that Facebook had 'vastly overstated average viewing time for video ads for years, by up to 80%'. The miscounting also fuelled concerns about so-called 'walled gardens' that Facebook and Google are often described as operating: keeping a tight grip on data, and only allowing limited third-party tracking firms to plug into their systems (Vranica, 2016).

Procter & Gamble's move to cut digital marketing spend had little impact on its business, proving those digital ads were largely ineffective.

P&G, Unilever and others who have outside firms measuring viewership weren't surprised by Facebook's recent revelation that it had been overstating video view times. Marc Pritchard said: 'our patience has run out. It's time to insist that all media partners adopt common, transparent measurement standards and accept third-party verification' (Neff, 2016).

According to Keith Weed, Unilever's Chief Marketing Officer, 'the industry is making progress on ad fraud and viewability, but there is still a long way to go. It's equally important that verification is independent, and we are not in a position where big players are "Marking their own homework"' (Weed, 2017).

But even if the advertiser and digital media owner relationship is rebuilt, there's still another faulty link: between advertiser and agency. Ken Auletta summed this up memorably in his book *Frenemies* when he said 'you can't immerse yourself in this industry and not be punched in the nose constantly by the growing level of mistrust between client and agency'.

On the effectiveness (or otherwise) of digital advertising, a fairly breath-taking announcement was made by Procter & Gamble back in 2017, when, as quoted by *The Wall Street Journal*, 'its move to cut more than $100 million in digital marketing spend in the June quarter had little impact on its business, proving that those digital ads were largely ineffective' (Bruell, 2017).

Many consider the industry 'voice of reason' to be the infamous #Adcontrarian Bob Hoffman. In his book *Badmen* he discusses how we're being held hostage by the likes of Amazon, Google, Facebook *et al*. On his advice to brand owners: 'Ad tech is stealing your money, threatening your security, alienating your customers', P&G say that 'precision targeting' – the great value proposition of ad tech – actually harms their marketing. After giving a list of other issues, ranging from middlemen taking their cut, to the fact that advertisers may be inadvertently funding terrorists and political extremists, to fraudulent activity and so on, he goes on to state that '70% of marketers are dissatisfied with online advertising. Ad tech, tracking and surveillance marketing are the mortal enemy of transparency' (Hoffman, 2017).

Just to show how important and serious this issue of ad fraud is, let me just quote a fairly stunning statement from the World Federation of Advertisers: 'Ad fraud is likely to exceed $50bn globally by 2025. On current trends that's second only to the drugs trade as a source of income for organized crime. Brands should apply caution to their digital investment until the advertising technology industry takes decisive action to deal effectively with the problem' (WFA, 2016).

So, if brand trust is down and branded-comms rejection is up, what are brands to do in this context?

If no one notices your advertising, everything else is academic

As a quick aside, I'm deliberately going to leave out detailed discussion on the use of humour in advertising, because we can hopefully all agree that the power of it as a tactic is such a proven way of connecting with consumers that it's not worth reiterating in depth. But if you really want a couple of examples, let me just point you towards two very different brands using humour in a great way: the Swedish oat milk brand Oatly and the skate brand Palace, whose tone of voice and approach to communication are incredibly engaging, motivating and relevant.

Let me also just state for the record that some things have stayed the same, of course. The most basic point, 'being noticed', is still the primary task of any communication. As the great adland sage Bill Bernbach said, 'If no one notices your advertising, everything else is academic' (Roberts, 2014).

Talking of great adland figures, Dave Trott of GGT fame is endlessly quoted at industry events. One of his conversation-stopping stats about advertising from his book *Predatory Thinking* states: 'We know that 4% is remembered positively, 7% is remembered negatively, and a massive 89% isn't noticed or remembered. But if the audience doesn't notice the advertising, what's the point in doing it?' (Trott, 2013).

Assuming you've got past the stage of actually having whatever it is that you've created being ... noticed, then a primary issue for today's marketer is 'does the consumer trust the brand and believe what we say?' Because without trust, any brand–consumer relationship isn't going to get very far. So, what are brands up to in order to achieve this?

The Future Laboratory works with many leading communication agencies, so I asked co-founder Martin Raymond for his take on the subject. His view was that:

A lot of brands are being caught out. This is where there's a big problem, because a lot of advertisers can't cope with the truth that is required; and a lot of them have forgotten about the creativity that used to be needed to get you over that problem. A good creative ad would allow you to skip the truth for the sake of a good story. The whole notion now is that advertisers have to become cleverer on the creative side or embrace truth in a different way. I think creativity is back in a major way because I think it had gone missing both from advertising and general ways of engagement and debate. I think we are no longer believing that the consumer is always right, ie the safe space issue in universities. So I think we will begin to go back into awkward spaces of debates again which is good, because the simplicity that we created over the past decade, based either on political correctness or social media filter bubbles – we're now understanding that that's actually not good for us. Without any kind of controversy, there is no creativity. That's what I think with truth: we have to reassess what we mean by it, to communicate it and how we ultimately want to broker it. All those debates are making us just rethink advertising and marketing and publishing generally.

For a completely outsider view from the world of agencies, I talked with renowned brand expert, David Shah, Publisher and CEO of View Publications. I asked him what he thought about the issue of trust and transparency. He told me:

Public trust in all things has gone down by about 80% and that, of course, includes corporate, includes branded products. Originally the whole raison d'être of brand was 'trust': it was a pact between you and the company you chose that if you were buying into their product you were getting the best value, quality, design equation available.

Now, the values that lie behind a brand have completely changed: the internet, inquisitor culture and public opinion tell you everything you could ever possibly need to know about a company and its brands. Today, quality is a given, just as in the future sustainability and recycling will also become givens; that means brands now have to sell by their moral values. It's all about relevance in the complex, confusing world of today and the personal relationship they have with their customers – EQ and connoisseurship. That's a major shift in our understanding of brands.

It doesn't stop there. The pressure to be transparent in a post-truth world is one thing. They have to deal with the consumer move from an experiential culture to a transformational one, where consumers are looking for products that help them lead 'better', more 'fulfilled' lives. Research has shown that people are prepared to pay more for a brand that delivers wellbeing, mindfulness, quality of life and so on, but it has to be sincere, not reek of marketing, green washing, cashing-in. Remember the consumer is not a fool anymore.

Building 'connections with meaning'

To deal with that major shift, and to provide some clarity, I'm going to concentrate on a few key areas that seem to illuminate some alternative ways forward in order for brands and their agencies to create 'connections with meaning'.

When trying to understand trends in the world of brand communications, an obvious place to note is the annual Cannes Lions Festival. This event, while it's come under increasing fire over recent years for being both too expensive and dated in its approach, is where key players from global agencies and (some) brands gather each year to discuss the state of play and where things are going next.

The issue of cost was one of the things that WPP highlighted, and that the Publicis Groupe cited when deciding to skip the 2018 event and invest the money saved on developing 'Marcel', their own artificial intelligence platform which will enable roughly 80,000 staff in 130 countries to anticipate client requirements.

Over the past few years, some big themes that have come out of Cannes, alongside a range of other international advertising events, include 'High Ground' brand purpose, which basically illuminates the core organizing principle and aim of the brand, along with 'Heritage Storytelling', which relates to the geographical and historical background of the brand's provenance.

Bringing the consumer–brand relationship to life is where researchers are briefed to find powerful insights via uncovering and clarifying the true contemporary connection between brand and consumer. So, the basis of the ongoing development of communication has tended to revolve around the core areas of either 'brand storytelling' or 'brand purpose' or 'trust and transparency'. Agency planners often talk of combining all of these together, in the hope of creating campaigns than really 'connect with meaning'. Sy Lau, Chairman of Group Marketing and Global Branding at Tencent, put another twist on this when he told the assembled masses at the 'China Day' run at Cannes that 'CMOs must evolve from the Big Idea to Big Data, from Precision Marketing to Predictive Marketing' (Tencent, 2017).

The challenge, that agencies must move on from the 'Big Idea' mantra of David Ogilvy (the founder of the industry giant Ogilvy & Mather), is a really big deal, coming as it does from Tencent who are themselves a very big deal. The premise that David Ogilvy suggested about the big idea was that 'you will never win fame and fortune unless you invent big ideas. It takes a big idea to attract the attention of consumers and get them to buy your product. Unless your advertising contains a big idea, it will pass like a ship in the night' (Ogilvy, 2014).

However, the problem with that point (which was made many years ago) is that in today's context, the whole environment in which advertising works has undergone fundamental change. The days of a limited number of TV channels being regularly watched at the same time by giant chunks of society have essentially gone (unless it's a genuinely major viewing occasion being broadcast), when the name of the game was effectively to hammer home a distinctive message enough times to embed it in the minds of the population. Today, that reality really is generally a dream for agency planners and creatives who have an infinitely more difficult task, and usually far less time and a lot less budget at their disposal.

Something that's supposed to help them, particularly when it comes to understanding and indeed predicting our consumer behaviour, is Big Data. The number of articles, books and reports written about the combining of data and algorithms is quite phenomenal. The key issue they note remains that crunching vast amounts of data on customer behaviour, ie genuine consumption or search activity, means that businesses are able to fine-tune their targeting efforts in a far more precise manner. This also leads straight into the area of programmatic advertising, where the real-time and automated bartering of advertising, leveraged by algorithms, means that advertisers can lower costs dramatically while hopefully increasing the accuracy of their consumer targeting.

This is all how it's supposed to be, of course, but as pointed out earlier, things usually don't work out so neatly. Still, to use a phrase that's used at every advertising conference on the planet, 'the technological revolution is all around us'. As the independent news source *The Conversation* says, 'Chatbots are replacing humans, data threatens our privacy, and blockchain links it all together'. Advertising is now 'a world of software, ultra-high-speed networks and processing power, statistics, optimisation, operations research, heuristics, data science and a range of related disciplines coming together in dealing with large volumes of rapidly changing data' (Livingstone, 2017).

In overall marketing terms, it's obviously not just adland that's being impacted. According to Bain & Company, 'Big Data and advanced analytics present opportunities for all companies to increase performance and are creating profound new opportunities for businesses; yet we found that only 4% of companies are able to combine the right people, tools, data and organizational focus to take advantage' (Bain & Company, 2018).

I talked about that with Emily Hare, just after she'd left Contagious to join the Honey Partnership, and she told me that:

> Marc Pritchard has been talking a lot about the drop in trust in social platforms that came about with fake news, but advertisers

are also starting to question things: 'Are the metrics we're getting accurate, where is our advertising appearing, what content is it running next to?' I think there is an impetus to change and it's good to see that advertising and media are trying to drive that on social media. But they also have to think about how their company is or isn't transparent and how they can build trust through other ways, not just through social platforms.

However, to structure an agency in order for them to be best set up to deal with all these myriad required changes, it's worth quoting The Network One, who are generally viewed as having the inside track on the industry. As one of their post-Cannes reports said: 'Agencies don't need to reinvent but do need to redefine themselves, according to what they really are, or want to be. There's plenty of space for creativity, and all the more if you're willing to experiment and learn – and if your approach is inclusive, collaborative and non-hierarchical' (The Network One, 2016).

They then have to work out a way of taking their offering to market in a distinctive, credible and meaningful way. This most basic of positioning issues is something that the agency world has struggled with, seemingly since time began. They make fortunes from advising clients on creating or fine-tuning brand positioning (and communicating the results), but most are notoriously dreadful at doing it themselves, for their own agency brand.

An agency always cited as being superb is R/GA, so I'll quote them as actually having a superbly succinct way of describing themselves. That snappy one-liner is: 'we help brands capitalise on disruptive technologies and emerging behaviours' (R/GA, 2017).

Culture vs collateral

Agencies are endlessly trying to redefine themselves to ensure they're always on-point regarding emerging marketing trends.

To implement that, the talk in industry circles is of adland essentially being divided into two distinct types of agency. According to David Golding of Adam & Eve, 'The first will work to create culture through campaigns that generate fame, talkability and memetic power. The second will create collateral driven by data and the ongoing ability to precisely target and reach audiences in new ways. So "culture versus collateral". That's the big divide' (Golding, 2017).

On the first of those types, the dust is still settling on a campaign that really shook up adland and which put a small statue of a very brave girl centre stage, facing down the charging bull on Wall Street. (The banks may have moved on, but the point remains the same.) The #FearlessGirl campaign, created to promote State Street Global Advisors (SSGA)'s fund that only invests in companies that have a female presence at the CEO, board or senior leadership levels, was set up on Wall Street the day before International Women's Day.

The #FearlessGirl campaign has gripped the world's attention. Its simplicity in the use of symbolism transcends geography, language and culture.

As reported by Contagious, Wendy Clark, CEO of DDB Worldwide and a Cannes Lions jury president, said: 'This gripped the world's attention, and it will do for years to come. Its simplicity in the use of symbolism transcends geography, transcends language and transcends culture. For us, it elegantly captures women's journeys … and it also encapsulates our hopes and ambitions for every little girl in the world' (Jeffrey, 2017).

The campaign won best outdoor, best PR, best in gender equality (the Glass Lion) and the Titanium award. The Network One's Cannes Report for that year put it thus: 'A simple but brilliant image of the gender equality which Wall Street lacks and State Street has committed to improving, a "big idea" proving that such a thing still exists – a commercial objective achieved through an expression of corporate purpose and social responsibility'(The Network One, 2017).

The stats about the campaign are fairly mind-blowing. After the statue was set up, *The Wall Street Journal* stated that the 'the social media exposure the brand generated with Fearless Girl was valued at up to $38 million' (Vranica, 2017). In terms of just one platform, Twitter, it received nearly five billion impressions overall, with a billion of them happening in the first 12 hours (Nudd, 2017).

The international press noted that Fearless Girl made an incredible impact for SSGA's SHE Fund. *Adweek* noted that 'Fearless Girl was created on a shoestring budget with no paid media, which made it even more of a marketing marvel. It generated $7.4 million in free marketing across TV, social media and radio. Daily trading volume for the fund shot up 384 per cent following the debut of the statue (Richards, 2017). Alongside its 2017 Cannes Lions awards, it also went on to win the coveted 'black Pencil' award in 2018 from D&AD (the global association for creative advertising and design), where the crown of 'most awarded brand' also went to SSGA.

Going back to the 'most meaningful' brands that I mentioned earlier, that report highlighted some major brands, including Microsoft. I asked John Dunleavy, Global President at m:united McCann in New York, about their approach to developing or reinforcing brand trust and authenticity. He told me: 'A lot of it depends on the brands and the category, the relationship with the consumer, how long they've had it; and how authentic and deep is the relationship. There are brands like Microsoft for example that people have had a relationship with pretty much all of their lives. That relationship may have had some bumps in the road but it's a relationship that's built on products that work and has therefore gained our trust.'

On their advertising, he went on to tell me that:

Microsoft have a campaign that we loosely call 'Real People' for a range of products and services. We go to great pains to find real, interesting people (to appear in the ads) and we don't pay them for an endorsement, we just pay them for an opinion and that's a big difference. What we tend to do is, if someone is a designer, and they've been using a Mac for the past 10–15 years, we'll give them the product, give them some training on the product and then we'll go back and interview them with a director and a film crew and ask them about their experience. So, it's not made up or scripted, it's this person telling you about their experience of the product. We get great lines like 'I couldn't do that with my Mac' and that's a genuine line, something that this real person has said versus a line that an actor or a paid endorser would say. The net effect is it comes across as authentic because it is, and even though it's within the confines of a 30-second commercial, it comes across to the consumer as very authentic, believable and honest. It's worked really, really well for us.

This approach is a great example of the 'bringing the consumer–brand relationship to life' that I mentioned earlier, where researchers unearth the true connection between brand and consumer and, in this type of case, help the agency planners to liaise with the creatives in order to develop motivating, entertaining, impactful and relevant communications. This approach is one that I've taken many times over the years, and it's always incredibly satisfying.

As the Fearless Girl campaign had been created by McCann Erickson New York, I also asked John Dunleavy about this. He told me:

The timing was everything. It was the right idea at the right moment. It was also just so symbolic and a different way to communicate an idea through one of the oldest forms of art in the world – sculpture. What's amazing about it is, if you go down to the site any day there are just as many people now, maybe even more people having their photograph taken with the Fearless Girl than the Wall Street Bull. It's taken on a life of its own!

As a final note about that truly amazing creation, and noting that Fearless Girl had just been awarded the Grand Effie at the 2018 Awards Gala in NYC, *AdAge* commented that she had become 'the industry's darling, winning big for SSGA and McCann NY at the Cannes Lions, The One Show, the ANDY Awards, D&AD, the Clios, the Webby Awards and *AdAge*'s own Creativity Awards'. By also gaining the Grand Effie award, 'with that, it's over. There are no more major industry awards left for her to win. A creative coup' (Sherwood, 2018).

Weaponizing audiences

An interesting take on this was offered by Paul Kemp Robertson, the founder and chief brand officer of Contagious Communications. In an article in *Forbes* magazine about a talk he gave for the Berlin School of Creative Leadership, he talked about the principle of 'Weaponizing Consumers' where 'if brands get their content and platforms right, they turn people into media, willing to spread their brand's gospel. Adidas refer to a new kind of "eye-to-eye relationship" – meaning they build a marketing concept based on audience insights, and then hand the spreading of the product over to their audience' (Gallen, 2017).

Now, linking with your consumers as a means of 'encouraging' them to do your marketing for you is nothing new, of course. I've already mentioned the increasing trend for brands to utilize overt influencers, but what is a more recent addition to the marketers' arsenal of tricks is so-called 'dark social'.

In this instance, Adidas are an example of a brand who utilize 'dark social' tactics, ie social sharing that can't be tracked by web analytics platforms owing to those shares and referrals being made via private messaging apps. This has become an ever more popular method of leveraging the power of word of mouth care of opinion-forming consumers. As reported by Digital Sport, 'the WhatsApp "dark social" campaign sought to bring together a community of influencers who formed a sort of a club that others wanted to be a part of – and it's that Fear of Missing Out, that desire to be a part of something cool, that drove the engagement' (McMullan, 2016).

What Adidas did was to build what they term 'squads'. The idea, according to *The Drum*, was 'to track the untrackable, by building hyper-local communities in cities across the world. These "squads" initially launched in Berlin, London, Paris, Milan and Stockholm, before going global. Dark Social isn't the hard sale but about building a relationship making sure there's something there for both parties' (Goodfellow, 2016).

Another great example of a brand leveraging the power of the consumer as a 'weaponized audience' is the French fashion-brand Sézane, who essentially rely on their almost fanatically loyal consumer base to post images of the items they've bought (delivered c/o their superb e-commerce offering and attractive packaging) alongside reposting the imagery they put up on Instagram. This effectively means that, apart from commissioning a photographer and a model, their marketing budget is incredibly low compared to the fashion, beauty and other lifestyle brands in their competitive set.

Sézane are also renowned for their innovative use of physical retail – in this instance a handful of 'apartment-style showroom stores' in which, to quote *Vogue* magazine, 'a lifestyle shop is disguised as an actual home (albeit your coolest friend's well-decorated and perfectly edited home), which offers an intimate, highly curated experience that's very much in the physical realm. Shoppers can peruse goods integrated into a living environment, then buy on the spot or shop online later' (Dash, 2015).

Brand experiences and brand movements

Elsewhere, in the brutally competitive world of retail brands, what's very clear is that the future of modern brand-building in this context lies in creating meaningful and memorable experiences. Now that anyone can buy anything from anywhere with an internet connection, stores are staying relevant by also offering highly curated and immersive physical and social experiences, which increasingly link both the physical and virtual worlds, ie those involving augmented, mixed and virtual reality. The fact that 'experience' is so important for retailers was shown by a *Marketing Week* survey which found that '83% of marketers believe customer experience is more central to their role than just five years ago' (Chahal, 2016).

Of course, the incalculable impact of social media drives the importance of word of mouth which links right back to things like … brand experience.

We'll see stores become 'less about being a place to consummate a transaction than a place to immerse yourself in a lifestyle. So, retail is no longer merely about buying stuff, the overall tone of what we do in traditional retail spaces has changed', according to *Forbes* (Finkelstein, 2017).

Shops have basically become a location for gathering information and to look, feel and experience brands before committing to purchase: the outside world is becoming more about discovering and testing brands before we then decide to bring them into our busy, cluttered and increasingly chaotic lives. To sum that point up, I'll quote a much-used McKinsey phrase referenced by my fellow speakers at the World Retail Congress over the past couple of years: 'Shops are reinventing themselves as "fun tech places to help you buy", essentially becoming leisure destinations' (Herring, 2014). Develop this issue of experience elsewhere, in a compelling way, and people may genuinely interact with brands that are themselves providing genuinely useful services, and in doing so are creating 'meaningful connections'.

Scott Goodson, founder of the 'Movement Making' firm Strawberry Frog, has a fascinating take on this. As he told me:

I've been banging on about movements for a long time. We are focused on creating these cultural movements and I think in today's world they are relevant more than ever before. You have to create a movement – starting with what people care about and from there tie it back to the brand benefit or brand purpose in some way, that's how you create meaningful connections. Then it's about a brand experience that is truly inspiring and every time you connect to that brand, you feel better for it. So that to me is the magic of it all.

The financial sector is a typical example of one where brand differentiation seems almost non-existent, and many people struggle to tell any discernible difference (in terms of product range and service approach) between the various banking brands in the market.

I asked Scott about how brand movements can be utilized in this area:

We've been working with a top ten bank in the United States called Suntrust. We created a movement for them which was to tackle the biggest challenge that Americans in this generation were facing, which is financial security. Financial security is something that drives a lot of the pain and fear that leads to people making political decisions like Trump. If you feel you have no financial security, you make decisions that otherwise you wouldn't make if you had a little better security.

As for the results of that activity, he told me:

the Suntrust movement has been incredible in driving internal passion and conviction and creativity, and has really brought that organization together in a way that they've never had in the past. The other side of the coin is the consumer, particularly the younger consumers who are just really passionate about engaging with this brand, and we're talking about a bank! If you go to their website 'onup.com', you'll see that there are over 2.6 million people that have joined the movement. Who'd have thought that a bank could engage 2.6 million people to participate in a movement? It is pretty mind-blowing!

In contrast, too many banks appear satisfied to just churn out the same old bland advertising approach, which sees entirely unconvincing claims and narratives essentially trying to reframe the sector's image away from its links with the latest financial crisis. As reported by *Marketing Week*: 'Most of the time banks are on the front pages because of a fine for some sort of dodgy behaviour. Ever since the financial crash in 2008, most bank brands have not been in the public's good books and have had to battle a strong sense of distrust among consumers' (Roderick, 2017). That's why I find the 'movement' strategy taken by Scott and the Strawberry Frog team to be a really inspiring example of an agency approaching the marketing issues facing brands in a catalytic way that really adds value to both the consumer and the business.

Brand soul

I'll finish this chapter by highlighting some of the deeply insightful points given to me by one of the leading brand strategists on the planet, Gareth Kay. He was the Chief Strategy Officer of Goodby Silverstein in San Francisco, before later co-founding Chapter where he's a real evangelist for brands that play a positive role in society.

As he told me:

Undoubtedly there has been a dramatic crash in trust of brands. I think this fall in trust might be a result of the oversupply of brands. Brands and their agency partners have to essentially lie to create some sense of distinctiveness and differentiation. Brands are trying to separate themselves by literally a hair's breadth of difference. I think the reality is there has to be a change in the marketing and communications model, from a world where brands are essentially created on fantasy, to brands that are going to be built much more on substance and around proving their value in people's lives.

I asked him to tell me about some examples of brands who are getting it right:

> I'm excited by brands who are trying to genuinely do stuff and then communicate it. For example, a brand like Everlane who've taken a fresh point of view in the fashion world by being radically transparent. They clarify how much an item costs, including the cost of the supply chain and what their mark-up is going to be.
>
> Or a brand such as Google who have always been very much a case of 'let's make something that's valuable to people and then document it'. They put things into the world that make you feel that they're genuinely trying to do stuff that is useful and valuable for people. You compare that with some of the other tech brands where essentially you're left with a question of 'what is the value I'm really getting for all this data I'm giving?' They are not really creating any sense of new value creation.
>
> It just feels like there is definitely a move to people respecting brands with soul, and that changes the marketing model. But this isn't new, it's back to the future. It takes the marketing model back to where it was originally, back in the 1950s and 1960s. I believe brands should be better social citizens and have a role in the world to try and create a better environment and a better place for people to live.
>
> Firstly, understand what people need, work out what you are good at doing and build a bridge between the two things. I think brands should think about what people want, and then deliver against that. I think our tendency to practise the opposite, where we say 'we could do this, let's try and make people want it', is what causes the sense of a lack of value that brands are feeling nowadays. There is a need for brands to get back to having a real sense of soul.

That idea, that brands need 'a sense of soul', is something that really fascinates me, and I think Gareth is absolutely correct in the way he believes marketers need to be increasingly focusing their attention. When it comes to communicating a brand message, the oldest saying in adland is that 'emotion beats logic in the art of persuasion'. But I think increasingly that emotion needs to be clearly evidenced, or at least linked to a core truth.

Superb examples of advertising (in all its forms) for 'brands with soul' have been created by those agencies working for organizations such as Amnesty International, WWF, UNICEF, the Red Cross and Greenpeace, shown by their intelligent strategies and creative brilliance in promoting good causes, including sustainability and social responsibility, which rightly gain plaudits from those such as the annual Good Report. This is a collaboration with the renowned Gunn Report, the global index on creative excellence in advertising, which identifies the most awarded and applauded work in the world each year.

Because brands with soul, if this is done for the right reasons and implemented in the right way, also means that the saying 'Good Business is Good Business' is equally true; and in addition goes a very long way to strengthening brand engagement, ie by giving a foundation to emotionally led communication. Looking into 'brands with soul', *Adweek* magazine highlighted how they 'share a passion and motivation with their consumers, they have a clear reason for being. The brand soul is not necessarily a mission or a charitable cause, but is usually related to values and ethics, such as quality, self-esteem or integrity. The brand is a champion of those values' (Voight, 2007).

A key additional viewpoint on what people actually expect from brands is illustrated by another highly respected industry report, care of Edelman. 'People's expectations of brands and the role they play in world problems will remain high, especially among Millennials and Gen-Xers', states the Edelman 'Earned Brand' study (2017), which says that '65% of consumers buy on the basis of their beliefs and that 57% buy or boycott brands based on the brand position of a social or political issue'.

For a last word on the advertiser point of view regarding media transparency, I'll leave that to a much-repeated rallying cry from Marc Pritchard, the Global Chief Brand Officer from Procter & Gamble: 'We have a media supply chain that is murky at best and fraudulent at worst. We need to clean it up: adopt one viewability standard; implement accredited third-party measurement verification; get transparent agency contracts; prevent ad fraud. It's not rocket science, it's really just common sense' (Pritchard, 2017).

So there we have it, an advertising industry (or a complete communications industry in all its guises) that is finding that everything has changed, and nothing has changed. To state the staggeringly obvious, brands matter hugely. But primarily, it's the ones that we trust and have an emotional relationship with, and who tell their stories via powerful stories, that will gain and retain our loyalty.

It sounds so self-evident, so obvious as to be almost not worth saying, until you consider the omnipresent deluge of brand communication that consistently fails to be 'motivating, engaging and relevant'. (That's even if we notice it in the first place.) The amount of time, money and effort that the marketing world wastes almost defies belief, and it's a common complaint from advertisers.

Dynamic ways forward are being shown by a combination of approaches.

This is why I think that dynamic ways forward are being shown by a combination of approaches: from agencies creating major brand communication built on trust or via catalytic activity that generates fame, as explained by John Dunleavy at McCann's, to those like Strawberry Frog assisting brands to build 'cultural movements', whereas others like Chapter SF help to create 'brands with soul' that prove their value in our lives.

For a final example of brands that prove their value in our lives, I'll turn to the superb 'Sea Hero Quest'. This multiplatform video game, created for Deutsche Telekom, was created to assist in the global fight against dementia. Intended to help further understanding of spatial awareness, loss of which is one of the initial warning signs of dementia, the data that resulted from those playing the game were given on an access-free basis to scientists around the world. Based on the story of the son of a sea explorer who was losing his memory owing to developing the illness, this poignant and yet highly creative mobile game was a classic example of positive brand action, or in this case 'gaming for good' via empowering players. The result was the world's largest crowd-sourced database on human spatial cognition, which is a staggering achievement.

All of the examples I've mentioned give us 'headlight vision' to shine a way forward in the incredibly disruptive and challenging world of brand comms. But what they each have in common is a commitment to creating activity with meaning. And that meaning has to link with the authenticity of the brand.

Because, make no mistake, adland finds itself thrust into the spotlight, with agencies cast as post-truth businesses, where rebuilding brand authenticity and clarifying their own 'reason to be' are absolutely vital in a distrusting world.

Perhaps the last word should go to the latest Cannes Lions reports, which tend to sum up the 'State of the Nation' from an industry perspective. The one from *AdAge* states that 'Ideas that won big had sustainability woven in. Other hot topics inc diversity and discrimination. #MeToo and Time's Up. AR, VR, XR, MR. Consultancies and viewability. AI and voice. But the biggest one was anxiety' (Braiker, 2018).

The final report I'll quote is from Julian Boulding, President of The Network One, whose review is always eagerly awaited by industry strategists and creatives alike. The report describes a festival 'in crisis' whose purpose has become confused due to a range of conflicting issues, including weak content and the ever-growing power of tech companies. As the report states, 'Who'll really win the battle for the world's hearts, minds and pockets? Will it be Google, Facebook and Amazon, continually at odds with their governments and societies? Or Alibaba and WeChat, innovators to the core, but marching in step with the world's most populous nation and second most powerful government?' (The Network One, 2018).

CHAPTER FOUR

Conscious Capitalism and Brand Activism

More and more people want to feel morally good about the things they consume. Added to this are the desires of an emerging generation who state the need for finding 'meaning and purpose' in their working lives, and who are attracted to brands that reflect their viewpoints.

These are widespread social trends that grow by the day. Attend virtually any marketing conference in virtually any city in the world, and you'll hear a common desire shared by brands: the wish for an engaged and enthused community of consumers.

A backdrop to all this is that consumers are ever more informed and ever more demanding. In response, they're offered ever more choice at highly competitive price points, which is given a further twist by an always-on, always available retail environment in a world where product differentiation can be infinitesimal.

The difference between 'good brand' and 'bad brand' is becoming ever more key as a genuine differentiating factor, when the disparity between ethical brands and those that are not (ie via the dubious realities of their supply chains) is becoming easier to uncover. When a result of these 'informed consumers' taking a deeper look at the products they buy is wishing to know the 'transparent reality' of those supply chains, global businesses are taking note.

While this type of activity may historically be more associated with Western markets, the issue has been and is clearly growing on a global basis. As Nicole Fall, Founder of Asian Consumer Intelligence explained:

> Ethical branding is emergent here, for example manifesting itself in the beauty realm via the rise of independent beauty brands and other smaller brands that have more of a story around their pure ingredients or how they have been organically sourced. That is definitely not mainstream, it's for a consumer who has more money to spend, but there is growing interest. When I conduct consumer research and speak with young people, a lot of them say they are starting to vocalize that they're not happy about animal cruelty. Some people who are not Halal will seek out a brand that says it is Halal because they know that it's cruelty free. Australia is developing a reputation for having cleaner, more ethical, organically sourced foods and beauty products, so there is a bit of influence from there too. So we're probably starting to see more influences coming from those smaller Australian brands than perhaps British or American brands.

'Social purpose' is important to an emerging generation of young people, who are attracted by social commitment and enlightened business behaviour.

As outlined in the opening chapter, for companies who wish to future-proof their businesses it is key that that they think deeply about their social mission and the implications of their activities from the perspective of the 'common good'. This issue of 'social purpose' is of key importance for an emerging generation of young people, who are attracted by mission-based brands, committed to being valued for their social commitment and enlightened business behaviour. This all goes towards building up 'social capital' in addition to the standard issues by which companies are valued. They should, perhaps, have an advisory board that exists in addition to their own 'standard' board of directors, whose advice can enable the company to demonstrate how 'good business is good business'. As part of their annual report, companies should consider adding a social impact report, alongside all the usual financial information that companies are legally required to document.

In this chapter, I'll therefore explain how these themes clearly link to post-truth and authentic branding, and the types of action that brands are taking which demonstrate relevant best-practice. All of which go towards illustrating how brands need to behave in order to ensure they have credibility with tomorrow's consumer.

Community-based marketing and citizen brands

According to *Forbes* magazine, 'Human beings are programmed to want certain things. Chief among these are belonging and feeling understood. These needs are most often met through families, clubs and communities. Some of the world's strongest brands were originally built through community-based marketing: Nike, Starbucks, Google ...' (Lee, 2009).

So, while we see many of the 'accepted' types of marketing communication becoming less and less effective, aiming to play an active community role via linking with customers, partners and suppliers has become a bedrock of today's and tomorrow's brand. An increasing number of people running 'vibrant brands' realize that seeking the support and endorsement of communities validates the brand's existence by underlining its authentic credentials.

Rather than being a transient 'on-trend' piece of additional brand engagement, companies are realizing it's a core element of brand-building that's here to stay. As the *Harvard Business Review* put it: 'A brand community isn't a marketing strategy. It's a business strategy. Too often, companies isolate their community-building efforts within the marketing function. That is a mistake. For a brand community to yield maximum benefit, it must be framed as a high-level strategy supporting business-wide goals' (Fournier, 2009).

To support those business-wide goals, gaining feedback and insights from customers has been, and always will be, essential. An ever-present issue for brands is that customer needs change, trends come and go, and priorities alter over time. But consumer insights come easily to community-linked brands, as the interactive nature of community brand activity makes this ever easier, with social media obviously playing a dynamic role. A vital benefit here is that it enables claims of authenticity then to be based on genuine consumer viewpoints as opposed to purely 'wishful' corporate claims.

When done properly, and with a clear motivation to 'do the right thing' at its core, the results of community-based brand activation can be astounding. So, is there a template? Fortunately, there is. If those business goals are grounded in so-called 'humane capitalism', then everyone wins.

A key foundation for a brand seeking to undertake community-linked activity is for the team running it to clarify the 'why' that sits at the heart of the brand. This basic but utterly vital point needs setting out in terms of a clear intentional statement, one that is credible and easily understood by brand teams and customers alike.

Built on this is taking a humble and realistic look at where and how your product or service can genuinely aim to add value. Then you can establish a framework of the type of social commitments that take into account local context, needs and interests that are relevant and possible for the brand to undertake. The aimed-for end result is the establishing and building of strong emotional links with customers, something that every brand marketer knows is at the core of successful branding. Amplifying this claim with motivating, engaging and distinctive communication adds to the equation and sets up the brand for marketing while helping the brand to develop a 'citizen brand' ethos.

The issue of 'citizen brands' sums up an ethos where brands have to take care not only of their current corporate social responsibility behaviour, but also in developing long-term 'business citizenship' strategies. These in turn need to be underpinned by impactful communications that bring the brand's core values to life, via a motivating brand story that explains those values in an entertaining manner, the results assisting, of course, in the development of strong consumer/brand engagement.

This 'truth-based' dovetailing of brand intentions with product attributes and manufacturing origins goes a very long way to ensuring that the brand actually is, and will help it in being seen to be, authentic. With a dose of luck (that all brands need) it'll then get talked about as such by those who care to notice. Informed, engaged consumers do notice and pass on information about brands more than ever. Whether they do so via digital networks or face-to-face conversations, the multiplying effects of this drive things forward of their own volition.

Conscious capitalism vs purpose-washing

However, Marie Agudera, Strategy Director of the agency Fold7, points to a common issue: 'the problem is that some brands have made authenticity their marketing strategy, rather than a business one. As a result, they come across as manufactured – the opposite to authentic. This "purpose-washing" has become more prevalent than ever, as legacy businesses and start-ups alike tussle to be part of the "authentic" conversation' (Barnes, 2018).

This is a point I took up with Martin Raymond, Co-Founder of The Future Laboratory, who told me that from his point of view:

> The whole issue of truth is up for debate in a good way, because we didn't quite know what it meant because it had no opposition. I think authenticity, artisanship, seasonality, and locality, which were used as markers of honesty and of opposition to globalization, are also now being challenged, ie I'd argue if everyone grew organic seasonal vegetables we'd never be able to feed the planet. So you're getting a more pragmatic understanding. Advertising is taking us into these territories where the brand is no longer about itself, it's about extolling you to be a better person or extolling you to collaborate or to be part of a group. We're seeing the socialist colonization of advertising. If I took this out of advertising and put it down to the political staple, we'd say 'these are socialists'. It's interesting that advertising, one of the great capitalist drivers of the marketplace, has gone from being about the individual and self and creating moments of self-doubt, to one that is about fulfilment through community, collaboration and social involvement.

A superb example of a company doing it like it should be done is Falcon, who trade coffee from over 20 producing countries to roasting companies throughout the world. Their purpose is 'to build collaborative supply chains for mutual profit and positive impact'.

For them, authenticity is intrinsically linked to a core product truth, which in this instance means 'coffee as a human story, passed hand to hand, from seed to cup'. All of these issues and more were bought together in a film titled, appropriately enough, *A Film about Coffee*. This beautifully shot production follows the product-story of coffee from farms in Honduras and Rwanda to its global consumption, alongside interviews with various industry experts in Japan and the United States. It weaves a fascinating story of how the skinny cortado served up in Tokyo or Portland actually gets to be in the hands of the consumer.

In doing so, the film links authenticity, transparency, sustainability, ethics and community. A world where transparency means more than 'standard-brand' fakery, and a triple bottom line involves building wells delivering fresh drinking water for remote communities. The film shows an absolutely authentic brand conducting business in a way that illustrates 'conscious capitalism' at its finest; and if you haven't yet seen it, I really recommend that you do.

A brand that you just have to mention in any discussion relating to ethical branding is TOMS, famous for its One-for-One activity. A global 'giving company' that uses business to improve lives, their 'making a difference' idea was initially activated via the simple idea that the purchase of a pair of shoes enabled a give-away of a pair of shoes to a child in need, initially in South America. People find it easy to connect with this mission, and the ability to translate such a simple concept to consumers underlines the power of the story.

The brand has developed from purely concentrating on shoes to move into a number of different areas. The One-for One model is adapted in these contexts to mean that, for instance, buying their bags leads to the provision of birth attendants and materials to help women give birth safely; the purchase of their glasses means sight is restored to individuals through donated glasses or medical treatment; and the provision of safe-water systems is undertaken in countries where TOMS source their coffee beans. Here TOMS coffee means 'your daily ritual can help transform lives'.

Which is impressive stuff. They're not perfect, no brand is, but they try a lot harder than most to be so. They continue to be a shining example of a brand that has purpose built into its very essence. The founder, Blake Mycoskie, talks about their 'good business' brand model in detail in his book *Start Something That Matters* where he says 'giving is good business – in both senses of the word – as it helps people and makes money. It's a way to address two essential needs with an action that unifies them. More and more people are finding this out and creating businesses making giving an essential component of their model' (Mycoskie, 2012). Once again, this is 'true branding' at its finest, where the type of post-truth accusations aimed at many brands fall away. This enables consumers to feel, and actually be, part of a 'positive brand movement'.

Researching in the community

A point worth mentioning here is that, as the film demonstrates, talking with the 'right people in the right context' about a brand will soon tell you which products aren't working, which ones need revitalizing, and where the brand can add value. Conducting ethnographic in-situ research is a great way of getting to the core truth of consumption and brand attraction/rejection. That's why I recommend conducting research in the times and places relevant to social context, brand communication, brand purchase and product consumption.

The key thing is that gaining this information in the community – ethnographic style – means that you'll hear it in their terms, on their turf and in a 'brand-contextual' situation. This means talking about live music while at a festival ... the sports brand while hanging out with a local team ... the beer brand while out with a bunch of friends socializing ..., going into hotels to discuss the realities of customer service, and so on.

If brands have their own relevant locations or spaces to meet the 'brand community', that is an incredibly useful additional source of research. Setting up physical spaces for brand advocates to come together is something that few brands do well, but one of them is Vans. I gave a speech in one of their 'House of Vans' locations where the brand ethos 'Off the Wall' lives. A place where, as the publicity material on the day had it, 'imagination [is] let loose over concrete bowls, art installations, workshops and concert stages. Located in NYC and London, as well as pop-ups around the world, the House of Vans is home to the creativity that moves us' (House of Vans, 2017).

Now they're a brand that has achieved huge success, and I have to say I'm a lifelong fan, by ensuring that the consumer and the 'customer community' remain absolutely at the epicentre of their actions. From basic beginnings, they've developed their brands through a multitude of product extensions and relevant skate, surf and entertainment activities that have seen them continually reinforce their street-level credentials. You could argue that they're an ultimate example of a brand that really understands and reflects its community.

That's an issue that also resonates with the renowned trend forecaster Anne Lise Kjaer, who told me that:

one of the trends I'm very interested in is 'betterness, less but better'. Increasingly we see that trust is towards 'small is beautiful', towards the community. I think this is where it's going in the future, that we will build brand stories around taking care of the environment and people around us. This is really the premise of my 'Four P' business model. Of course 'P for Profit' is key to everything we do, but if that 'P' is casting a big shadow so you can't even see people and planet, let alone understand your brand's purpose, then it's unbalanced. I always say companies that care for people and planet with a purpose to match, those are the ones that are here to stay because their bottom-line profit is an inclusive bottom line, which feeds into the community rather than just feeding off it. That's opposed to an approach where there's only one purpose: that of profit. For me this is not where the future is going because it reduces us to little mechanical robots that are just consumers; we are no longer people in this scenario, we're just part of a system that feeds and lines the pockets of a very limited group of people. So I think brands that have a purpose beyond that of making profit will be the ones that win out in the future.

Corporate social responsibility

If an eventual aim for brands is to be in the happy position of having 'customers, fans, and advocates' then it doesn't get much bigger than LEGO, one of the world's leading brands. A core tenet of theirs is that all children have the right to fun, creative and engaging play experiences. Anyone with a knowledge of Jean Piaget (the psychologist who was an expert in cognitive development) knows that play is essential because 'the work of the child is play'.

As a global brand, they naturally undertake global activity, with their community activity including programmes in South Africa, Mexico and Denmark, along with supporting children's rights with UNICEF and as an active member of the United Nations Global Compact, via which they embedded the 'Ten Principles' in their daily operations.

Those principles include areas such as international labour rights, environmental responsibility, and ethics and transparency in business conduct. A hundred per cent of the business's leaders are trained in business ethics. Their community links have included employees conducting volunteer-based activity, working in over 180 events where they engaged with over 100,000 kids around the world via 'play experiences' along with charity partners, which involves targeted financial and product donations.

I first heard about all this when I worked on an international pitch for one of their agencies. The extent of their CSR-linked activity was really impressive, and I've always been surprised that they don't have more of a reputation linked with this work.

You could say precisely the same thing about Microsoft, albeit on a far larger scale, ie via the findings of the Reputation Institute which reports on company CSR activities by focusing their RepTrak on consumer perceptions of corporate governance, the 'Brand Positive' influence that they may have on society at large and the manner in which they treat their employees. Microsoft came second this year to LEGO. The RepTrak report said: 'Microsoft is committed to enhancing education as a highly relevant global human issue – and unlike Apple operates as an open source platform that fosters perceptions of good citizenship and good governance' (ouch) (Strauss, 2017). As reported by *Forbes* magazine, 'The company's co-founder and former CEO Bill Gates has a stellar reputation for social responsibility, due to his work with the Bill & Melinda Gates Foundation' (Strauss, 2017).

LEGO also has a well-established local community engagement programme, building and supporting local communities around the world, including involvement in summer camps in countries including China and the United States. With a mission to 'inspire and develop the builders of tomorrow', what I also find really impressive is their ambition to use only sustainable materials in their core products (Lego, 2018).

Brand communities

Go to the opposite end of the brand spectrum, and you end up with a brand like Harley-Davidson and their Harley Owners Group (HOG), more than a million of whom share an obsessive loyalty to a brand that is now over a hundred years old. With nearly 1,500 official HOG chapters around the world, each linked to an official Harley-Davidson dealer, it's an extremely successful example of a brand community, or brand movement.

When you talk with Harley owners, it soon becomes clear just how deeply the brand resonates with them, in a way that the vast majority of car brands, for instance, just don't. For them, it represents a way of life, a culture (maybe a utopian one from their point of view, but there's no bad thing in that), and it is one that can be found all over the world. If you sit down and talk with these bike owners, you will see how strongly they talk of a shared lifestyle, spirit and general attitude. The club was set up with clear aims: to enable the brand's obsessive consumer base to link with each other around a (very obvious) common theme – a genuine 'community of like-minded people with a shared interest'.

The Harley owners club is called – but of course – 'HOG'. Take a look at their site, and you'll see the ultimate Harley statement: 'We live in more than 100 countries. Our home is any road, any city, and any place we choose to gather.'

What's interesting to me in this type of brand-community activity is that a brand aura of 'Freedom' is lived and breathed by the brand's fans; and the reinforcing of this core element of the brand, once again, just as we've seen with the other examples, underlines its authenticity.

There is also a completely different angle of branded communities never actually connecting with each other but being linked purely on the basis of buying clubs. These have been around for years but have been given a contemporary twist by the likes of Beauty Pie, who have a highly vocal following and are discussed in worried tones by the major established beauty brands. (I discuss another key element of this brand in the chapter on pricing and provenance, where I look into numerous examples of, for instance, price transparency).

Offerings like this have a business model that, in this case, sees consumers join on a membership basis and then receive luxury skincare and makeup products sourced from high-end suppliers in 'image-light packaging'. The killer point here is that the producers are often exactly the same ones that supply prestige brands in countries including Italy, Germany, France, Switzerland, Spain, the United States, the United Kingdom, Korea and Japan. But the consumer pays only production-line prices for the privilege, saving about 80 per cent off regular retail prices.

This pricing strategy is what I'd call a classic example of 'hands-off' branding, done for entirely functional and pragmatic reasons, where the consumer relationship is very much product focused, and not brand image related, thus being 'image-light'; although one could argue that the brand image here is based on one where the consumer can proudly talk of her 'smart-buying' credentials to her friends.

Of course, there's absolutely nothing wrong with 'image-light' branding, and brands like Beauty Pie have an incredibly loyal following who see little reason to pay high-end prices for items where the difference between the branded product and the un-branded product may essentially come down to one that is sold with the back-up of an overblown brand image while the other is 'coldly authentic', being an item that's bought solely for func-tional reasons. In addition, of course, the Beauty Pie brand ben-efits from being founded by uber-entrepreneur Marcia Gilgore, who seems to have an uncanny way of knowing exactly what the consumer wants. That angle of 'cold authenticity' is given a twist by the way the 'smart-buying' consumer has very strong emotional warmth towards the brand, as it brings them these products in an entirely transparent and empathetic manner.

You can see the same issue being played out in a different way in Scandinavia. According to Carsten Beck of the Copenhagen Institute for Futures Studies:

if you look at the cookery scene in Denmark, the biggest success at the moment is Rema, which is a soft discounter from Norway. They have excellent ideas, on food waste, on new packaging solu-tions, new ways of doing space management from a customer perspective in-store. I'm not sure if the Danish consumer would use the word 'authentic', but if I was to ask a consumer 'ok, who do you think comes up with new ideas and is really taking an interest in both consumers and also the future?' I think a lot of them would actually point to Rema. Is that authenticity? Yes, because Rema has actually tried to tell the Danish audience that 'we are trying to come up with innovative new solutions all the time'. So for me, authenticity in Denmark is really a very complex concept.

He also says that 'the biggest hero of the moment is our EU com-missioner Margrethe Vestager in Brussels. She is a hero because she is attacking the big corporates, for instance over their tax dodging, like Apple in Ireland. Whenever she's in the media say-ing "we will go after them" the Danes cheer. They have this sense that when it comes to big global brands, something is wrong.'

Activism and the media

Moving on, and when it comes to 'hands-on' issues (sometimes in the most literal meaning of the phrase), the collapse of belief between people, institutions and governments in a post-truth world means there's an ever-shortening link between humane capitalism, brand activism and direct action. These communi-ties (pro or anti the brand in question) of 'informed consum-ers' increasingly insist that brands don't just make their profits from society, but also give something back. And that doesn't just mean paying corporation tax either, although it's an essential place to start, as those brands that have incurred the attention of the Uncut movement know to their (actual) cost, and rightly so.

I started observing and interviewing protesters at anti-corporate demonstrations way back in the 1990s and have been on many demos since. What has struck me at every one of those events is the difference between the 'ordinary' people who make up the majority of the crowds, versus the extremists who tend to dominate the resulting media reports. The key issue for busi-nesses is to understand that this type of behaviour, or action, is coming from 'ordinary people', ie the type of person – or con-sumer – at the centre of mass-market brand targeting.

I've talked with brands and agencies about the realities of consumer-activist demands many times, as these have taken in everything from women's rights to anti-sweatshop labour to ani-mal rights to non-GM food production, and just about every-thing else 'humane and reasonable' that you or I could add to the list.

But with many brands tending to act at a glacial pace, and with the number of vested interests getting in the way of change, it's increasingly down to 'citizen brands' to make the changes demanded by 'conscientious consumers' at these events, and/or via online chatrooms and other public forums.

This issue of activism stretches across multiple sectors and via multiple interpretations. Oiselle, the women's fitness apparel brand, has made activism a key part of its brand strategy where the brand 'pick our issues, take a stand, and go out in the world to do something'. According to an interview in *The Drum* with Megan Murray, their Director of Marketing, 'as socio-political circumstances polarise communities around the world, ordinary people are taking a stand for what they believe in. Subsequently, we're moving into a cultural phase that is being defined by action, by activism. It isn't enough any more to say you're for or against something; you must prove it' (Jones, 2017).

Oiselle back up their talk with social outreach action, ie projects like an after-school running programme called Girl on the Run, a programme which they describe as being 'a perfect marriage of Oiselle's passion, product, our amazing community (our Volée, Haute Volée, Muses), and our core beliefs of body acceptance and physical activity as a route to strength' (Lesko, 2017).

This was highlighted in a Union Metrics blog which noted that 'The lesson for other brands is don't try to fake it because consumers will call you out. Find what it is you honestly have in common with your audience and then how you can best communicate that not just to them, but with them' (Parker, 2017).

Nike are masters at this type of activity, where, rather than purely idolizing sports heroes, they make ordinary people the centre of attention, encouraging and empowering them the world over to be the best they can be. Once again, this linking of a global brand right down to 'genuine' individuals means they keep on reinforcing their authenticity.

But of course, Nike was a brand at the centre of the 'No Logo' debate, back when Naomi Klein wrote her incredibly impactful book *No Logo: Taking aim at the brand bullies*. In an interview titled 'Hand to Brand Combat', she talked of how 'Nike paid

Michael Jordan more in a year for endorsing its trainers than the company paid its entire 30,000-strong Indonesian workforce for making them.' That article went on to describe how 'in her opinion, this makes people angry, and why that anger's expressed in rallies outside the Nike Town superstore, rather than outside government buildings or embassies' (Viner, 2000).

The impact of this on the brand was serious. In a *New York Times* piece about the brand 'bowing to pressure from critics who have tried to turn its famous shoe brand into a synonym for exploitation', the Nike CEO Phil Knight said: 'the Nike product has become synonymous with slave wages, forced overtime and arbitrary abuse. I truly believe that the American consumer does not want to buy products made in abusive conditions' (Cushman, 1998).

The media coverage of 'brand activism' may often be one of violent imagery showing scenes of shop windows getting smashed, ie reminiscent of that famous image of Nike Town surrounded by Robocops, protecting it from demonstrators; but the more genuine interpretation of activism, in this context, is about the worlds of social interaction and community engagement where brands are being urged to take action themselves.

Or as I put it in a piece I wrote for *Sleaze Nation* magazine, about the pre-WTO Seattle, J18 protests where I interviewed environmental activists and anti-capitalist demonstrators, 'there weren't a bunch of mad conspiracy theorists rioting on June 18th, there was instead a cross-section of normal people from all walks of life, showing their concern with a system that's virtually out of control. If nothing else, at least it shows that the spirit of youthful rebellion hasn't quite been extinguished. As Hegel said, "The Owl of History Flies at Dusk"' (Sleaze Nation, 1999).

This was also something that I discussed with Martin Raymond at The Future Laboratory, who explained how:

> we're beginning to see the requirement of brands to have a political standpoint. Jeff Bates said 'if you aren't offending 50% of your

audience you aren't doing your job'. So now we understand that offence is a requirement. Social media has driven the anti-agendas, and this reminds brands that they have to demonstrate in a way where the customer can say 'this brand is like me, this brand is part of my community or part of my debating environment'. We now have a lot of brand scandal, so what happened with Volkswagen, for example, suddenly reminded people that brands lie and cheat. We now understand that data is a huge Trojan-horse in our homes that brands can access. We're beginning to question everything now, ie 'why we should hand this over, and what is it that we are giving over?'

He added:

because if you believe that a brand is a positioning, a philosophy, a mission statement and a core value, then, as we know, every value will offend someone, somewhere, some of the time. I think that is part of the whole process of where there's a new type of honesty and perhaps a new type of marketing. On the other hand, you've got lots of Procter & Gambles, Unilevers and Nestlés who for years have been kind of conning and being evasive and basically cheating by absence of information, as opposed to deliberately lying. I think most of them were doing it in a way that was keeping the truth away from you. I think that increasingly it is not about post-truth in the sense that we're back into lying, I think we're now getting to a default where a consumer will be able to check everything. We're now having to look at that and go 'so what is the next way forward?' The answer: absolute ultra-transparency.

Sustainability and the circular economy

The issue of transparency naturally links to the 'brand actions' I mentioned previously, which include, of course, activity conducted by companies when they find themselves being blamed for issues such as plastics in the oceans, chemicals in our bodies and an increasingly polluted atmosphere. As reported in an on-line petition organized by the campaigning community 38 Degrees, 'only about half of the staggering amount of plastic bottles and metal cans produced are recycled, so it's no surprise that many of these end up in our oceans. And plastic bottles take 450 years to break down, killing marine life, harming the coastal ecosystem and ruining our beaches' (Jan, 2017).

The subject of packaging was further thrust into the spotlight following the stunning social impact of the BBC's programme 'Blue Planet'. That programme reinvigorated the public's awareness of the negative impact of plastics and accelerated a demand for environmentally progressive action from packaging manufacturers. This coincided with announcements made at the World Economic Forum, where global companies stated that they'd work towards using 100 per cent reusable, recyclable or compostable packaging by 2025.

The stark realities of the absolute need for concentrating on a sustainable future gave rise to the vital concept of the circular economy. This connects brands, and brand communities, directly to an ethos where 're-use and recycle' is an alternative to a traditional linear economy of 'make, use, dispose'. As reported, 'a circular economy could bring savings of €600bn to European companies. In Finland alone circular solutions could provide €2bn–€3bn added value annually. Their government set a strategic target to become a forerunner in circular economy. The outcome is a solid plan with an ambitious vision, concrete projects and clear responsibilities' (Sormunen, 2017).

There's a stunning amount of dynamic activity taking place here, and it's interesting to see which countries are taking a lead, with, as mentioned, Finland being a prime example. This innovation sits wholly within the realm of 'authentic action', yet, while being so demonstrably fact based, those facts are constantly being undermined by lobby-groups and others with 'vested interests'. With debates about the circular economy being so (necessarily) high profile, fake news is very much part of this debate in our post-truth world and is thus an enemy to be constantly pushed back.

But, as the Finns have demonstrated, the results show the massive benefits to society as a whole of taking a circular economy approach. According to research from McKinsey, 'using and reusing natural capital as efficiently as possible and finding value throughout the life cycles of finished products is part of the answer. Such an approach could boost Europe's resource productivity by 3% by 2030, generating cost savings of €600b a year and €1.8t more in other economic benefits' (McKinsey, 2017).

We are clearly moving towards a near-future in which a circular economy is shifting from being a niche issue to one that is centre stage. This means the absolute minimalizing of raw materials, the reduction of waste and a huge increase in either the reuse or the recycling of them back into that circular, sustainable system. The most immediate implications range from the way in which the overall issues around packaging are taught on a global basis, how materials are sourced and manufactured, and the delivering of powerful initiatives from brands/retailers relating to repurposing or recycling.

A paradigm shift in consumer behaviour is clearly beginning to match their attitudes towards sustainability, with the growing rejection of single-use plastic and 'over-packaging' being core concerns. We will see brands that do not show leadership in the area of sustainability, or are perceived as ignoring it, being punished by consumers who, when faced with a viable alternative, will increasingly choose the 'better for the planet' option. The core issues to watch in this most vital of areas therefore are trust, transparency and empathy.

Activist brands and conspicuous altruism

A brand that essentially links all of the areas I've highlighted (and there are thankfully many more) is one that sets a shining example to us all: Patagonia. When the subject of 'perfect brands' comes up, if any brand is mentioned more often than 'activist company' Patagonia, then I'd really like to know what it is, because they've been talked about in this way for so long that it feels as if they really are, appropriately enough, at the tip of that mountain.

The paradox of being a hugely successful ethical and environmentally friendly brand (who describe themselves as being 'designers of outdoor clothing for silent sports'), which leads to more products being manufactured as a result of positioning themselves as 'anti-consumption', is a complex paradox that goes to the heart of this type of brand model, in what is now a highly competitive sector.

It's also, obviously, a problematic issue for Patagonia fans, who like what they produce and want to support the brand. Having a massive appeal to those that pride themselves on buying brands that are 'anti-consumption' is a Catch-22 business question in which Joseph Heller would take great delight.

> When 'perfect brands' comes up, if any brand is mentioned more often than 'activist company' Patagonia, I'd really like to know.

This was perfectly illustrated by their 'Don't buy this Jacket' campaign, which was launched to coincide with the United States' famous Black Friday annual shopping-fest that gains such massive media coverage. The results of their anti-consumerist message gained a huge amount of kudos – but resulted in consumers doing the exact opposite and buying even more Patagonia products. I've talked about that 'anti-consumption promotional messaging' in my university lectures many times, and it always goes down well!

The character of Patagonia is beautifully captured in a statement that the company's founder makes in his book about the brand, whose purpose he describes as being 'an experiment in responsible enterprise', when he says 'I've been a businessman for almost 60 years. It's as difficult for me to say those words as it is for someone to admit being an alcoholic or a lawyer' (Chouninard, 2006). I just love that quote, as it neatly encapsulates (albeit in humorous terms) the paradox of being put on an ever more extreme 'moral high ground pedestal' by consumers of a massively successful ethical brand that produces and sells its goods internationally.

While this 'conspicuous altruism' may be incredibly irritating to their detractors, who find the brand a little too worthy, those detractors are vastly outnumbered by their admirers and fanatically loyal customers who share a common love of the outdoors and their altruistic approach. This highly successful business makes a serious profit as a result of their 'responsible enterprise' via the high price points set for their sustainably produced ranges, which arrive in-store via an ethical supply chain that is very much linked to the circular economy. And good luck to them.

Years ago, every brand seemed to want their advertising agency to copy the 'empathetic approach' taken by Innocent Drinks, while over the past few years it seems that any brand with an even passing interest in community brands and ethical branding wants their brand to mimic Patagonia.

At the World Retail Congress, the annual gathering of the planet's biggest retailers, it's interesting to note just how many times their name comes up in debates, including community-branding ones about the 'dynamic selection' of retail locations utilized by leading-edge brands like them. This approach ensures that their retail spaces are community-based ones, where the physical location has resonance with that community.

Elsewhere, their approach takes an internal 'company community' aspect as well as an external community one. This is something that human resource departments often hold up as a prime example of 'doing it how it should be done'. In this instance, Patagonia seem to take the approach that if they look after their staff in the same manner that they do their customers, their staff will be happier, and that action will be noticed by the customers, which will strengthen their brand engagement – a perfect circle.

A 'brand positive' workplace culture is also incredibly important for all organizations, and on the employee activism side Patagonia have run an environmental internship programme for over 25 years, which organizes community fun-runs to raise money for the protection of wilderness landscapes, and the company volunteers donate thousands of hours of labour time to plant trees, clean up beaches and so on. As their site puts it, 'we enjoy getting dirty for fun but think it's even more important doing so in protecting the places we love'. You've just got to like that attitude. They also offer on-site childcare for staff, thus appearing to be one of the few companies on the planet to understand the challenge that childcare poses.

They were also early adopters of the movement of 'ideas lectures and thinking events' with their 'Brain Food' events where, as one employee mentioned on a Patagonia blog, she took Japanese, Spanish, investments, cooking, and knife-sharpening classes. I'd be up for doing each one of those, and they also host farmers' markets, free, for local producers to attend and sell their goods.

They also have the admiration of the trend expert Anne Lise Kjaer, who when we talked about them said to me: 'Isn't it amazing how the best case study on how to do it in the clothing industry is still Patagonia? Trying a little harder and becoming hyper-transparent, those are the stories that win out. They're such a good example of that.'

The best communities are, as we all know, ones where neighbours help each other. We essentially have to encourage local brands to behave … more neighbourly. Of course, what acts as a core foundation of a brand like Patagonia is their genuine authenticity, an issue that sits within every element of their business, ie it's not just a 'brand image' that looks great on a billboard or social media feed.

They're a brand that also interests Sarah Rabia, Global Director of Cultural Strategy at TBWA\Chiat\Day in Los Angeles, who told me that they're a brand:

> that I think are genuinely doing good and it's not just advertising. Everything from funding lobbyists, helping activists connect to organizations and drum up volunteers. They're an example of it having to be more than greenwashing. In our Pan-Activism study, one of the other things we pull out for brands is that it's become more and more tricky to do good, ie what is the right way? There is an apolitical way of doing it, that is probably the new take on being safe and neutral, and it's just about being human and decent. One of the examples we had was after the Montecito mudslide disaster in California. Ford responded to its customers with an offer of delayed lease-payment due dates, giving people more time to pay and demonstrating an empathy with what had happened. We use the language 'commercial empathy'. I think it can be very small, humble, humane behaviour that doesn't have to be overly political or activist, and we need to see more of that. Empathy is a big thing in our culture right now.

She also told me that:

> Ikea is another nice example of a brand demonstrating social engagement and commercial empathy. With the refugee crisis they started employing refugees and producing shelters for them. The shelters won a design award for it (Beazley design of the year by London's Design Museum), and I love that because it's absolutely what Ikea are as a brand, regarding their Scandinavian, social democratic roots and flatpack homewares brand DNA. It's really interesting to me why brands find it so difficult to be authentic, it just tells you that a lot of brands don't know what they stand for and how to behave coherently. That's why we often see disconnected brand behaviour, from advertising to HR. For me last year we were at a real tipping point with feminism. So many brands are doing feminist campaigns, but look at their business: how many

women are on the board? I think it's got to be much more holistic and much more business driven.

A key result of all these examples is that community branding enables brands to continually achieve and renew that brand-elixir of being authentic. They do so because from actively playing a part in communities, to purely listening to or acting upon 'always on' customer feedback, to taking a strong ethical stance; the results mean they automatically underline their brand purpose and retain brand relevance.

I discussed the issue of 'genuine internal/external 360 branding' with John Shaw, someone who has spent many years in leading agencies such as W&K, Ogilvy and Superunion.

As he said 'the idea that a brand is a veneer that you can apply over a bad company has never stacked up but increasingly it wouldn't work now, even if it ever did. In a way there is a bigger role for brands than there used to be in the past. A lot of great companies use brands as a way to manage and galvanize themselves internally, as well as just to use them to market to the consumer. Take Nike, their brand has always been very important, not as a constructed thing necessarily but almost something that kind of came from the heart of the people that built it. The guidance that that gave them as to what is Nike or what isn't Nike was quite a visceral thing and that can be the role of the brand, it's not something that is directly overlaid or just directed towards consumers, it's something that informs the whole way of doing business. The DNA of a brand can be the spirit, the character and so on. If people understand that viscerally within the organization that's a really valuable weapon because you are going to be much more powerful and nimble an organization if people understand that naturally, as opposed to having to reach for the manual. You don't really want them to have to look at the brand book, they should have internalized it.'

He went on to say, 'One of the other interesting things is the extent to which the strong brand holds you up to greater scrutiny. In *Shoe Dog*, Phil Knight's book, he talks about Nike and labour practice issues in the late 1990s. Because Nike had a strong brand it made them a big target and perhaps some people resented the criticism at first because they saw Nike as better than some competitors. But when they explored it further they might have said 'well, yes that's true but at the same time are we perfect, are we doing everything 100 per cent right, have we ever reached right down into the supply chain and made sure everything we do is as good as it could be? They came to the conclusion that it wasn't and therefore they should try and set the standards for the industry. So that became the mission for the next few years and by and large, people who know about that area now do hold them up as being a very good example of corporate behaviour. In a way that all comes out of the brand and the idea that the brand is important and there shouldn't be anything happening related to that brand that is going to cause people not to trust it. In an era where any small issue with a brand can be massively magnified now, you need to be as close to perfect as you possibly can be. One of the challenges is to retain the character of your brand at the same time as being absolutely spotless. So if you are a brand like Nike it is quite an interesting challenge because your brand image has been built in to some degree on rebellion and a counter culture, not about being spotless. They do have to co-exist now but it's an interesting tension.'

The triple bottom line and joint value creation

Another incredibly inspiring example of the way forward comes from the global non-profit organization B Lab, which was founded with the audacious idea of redefining the role of business in society and what 'success' means in business, ie as a force for good. They very deservedly have a strong media profile where their 'good story well told' lays out how they issue B

Corporation certificates to for-profit companies, who voluntarily must meet high standards of social sustainability, transparency and environmental performance plus accountability standards.

The phrase 'triple bottom line' has been used since the 1990s. *The Economist* explains how, in this context, companies prepare three different bottom lines as follows: 'One is the traditional measure of corporate profit. The second is about social responsibility. The third is a measure of environmental responsibility. "TBL" thus consists of three Ps: profit, people and planet. It aims to measure the financial, social and environmental performance of the corporation over a period of time' (The Economist, 2009).

An interview with co-founder Bart Houlahan, in the Australian magazine *Dumbo Feather*, described their thinking as they developed the B Lab idea: 'We observed there were thousands of businesses that considered themselves triple-bottom-line businesses. Those, to us, were manifestations of the same intent. Our hope was to try and bring that community together under a common identity and a collective voice which could influence all business to move towards a sustainable future' (Havea, 2014).

As it says on their site: 'B Corp is to business what Fair Trade certification is to coffee or USDA Organic certification is to milk. B Corps might turn out to be like civil rights for blacks or voting rights for women – eccentric, unpopular ideas that took hold and changed the world'. A utopian ideal? Hopefully not, which gives me a perfect excuse to use that wonderful quote ascribed to cultural anthropologist Margaret Mead: 'Never doubt that a small group of thoughtful, committed citizens can change the world; indeed, it's the only thing that ever has' (Keys, 1985).

There's also a generational issue at play when it comes to the politicizing of conscious capitalism. According to Sarah Rabia at TBWA\Chiat\Day:

Millennials in particular want brands to stand for something so you have to take a stance and you have to act on that. Every position now has been politicized; to do nothing has an implied stance, like Uber's silence in response to the Trump legislation around Muslim immigration, leading to the 'Delete Uber' campaign that happened in America. One of the things we found in our Pan-Activism study conducted by Backslash is that 85 per cent of Americans have taken some form of activism in the past year and it wasn't just one form, it was actually nine things that they did. Everything from defriending people on FB because of political stress to boycotting a brand, to buying a gun. I think one of the implications for brands is you are kind of damned if you do and damned if you don't. People expect brands to take a position, but you will probably annoy someone.

To begin to finish off, I'd like to quote from the 'Reflections from Davos' report on the 2018 meeting of the World Economic Forum, where the managing partner of McKinsey said that 'the next innovation imperative will be social innovation – business's role will be critical here'. The report went on to note that 'society is demanding that companies, both public and private, serve a social purpose' (Barton, 2018).

An acknowledgement of this was reflected by the Silicon Valley giants, when considering the impact of social media on society. For instance, Facebook now promotes the use of their platform for 'time well spent'. That strategy is reflected by Twitter, who want to enable better 'conversational health' on that particular platform.

'Social purpose' is a phrase used obsessively in modern, forward-thinking companies, and links directly to 'joint value creation' where both shareholders and society (and in cooperative organizations, the two may effectively be the same thing) benefit from business. This is exactly what can be achieved more easily, and with added credibility, when brands are able to genuinely act, as Patagonia have demonstrated, as 'responsible enterprises' with a clear and positive brand purpose at the heart of the business. This means that the leadership role in those organizations is absolutely key, in terms of laying out a clear, positive and achievable strategy to be implemented throughout the business. As mentioned earlier, being seen for having a strong social purpose is a key element of the successful future brand. 'Informed consumers' and 'active citizens' are increasingly playing their part here, demonstrating far more considered choice and intentional buying, rewarding companies that demonstrate their social commitment and rejecting those that do not.

Make no mistake, in this difficult era, linking with and enabling the community is an incredibly effective way forward in aiming for the goal that B Lab describe as 'encouraging all companies to compete not just to be the best in the world, but to be the best for the world'.

These brands and organizations live up to the maxim 'good business is good business'. In a post-truth world, their positivity and transparency are exactly what society, and responsible capitalism, needs.

CHAPTER FIVE

Price, Provenance and Transparency

Transparency has become one of the key ingredients in earning consumer trust, as evidenced by a wide range of sectors. In this context, brands that are seen to act with honesty, integrity and reliability demonstrate the way forward in our post-truth world, with 'radical transparency' being the new watchword.

Leading industry reports highlight how transparency has now moved on from being a 'nice to have option' to a 'need to have asset' (Contagious, 2017). According to the World Bank 'in the hyper-connected and ever evolving world, transparency is the new power' (Herzberg, 2014).

In this chapter I'm going to examine how issues such as pricing, provenance and supply chains have been impacted by consumer demands and innovative brand action on transparency. These are such catalytic areas, with an immense amount of conceptual and product development activity happening across a wide range of categories on a seemingly non-stop basis.

While those consumer demands are nothing new, what's changed is the strength of those demands, and the fact that they're finally being met by brands 'evidencing' their actions, which is strengthening consumer engagement as a result.

I'll cover a range of sectors, and in doing so I'll highlight key trends, clarify why these are relevant, and show some great examples of brand behaviour. I'll also explain why catalytic technological developments such as blockchain are providing a dynamic way forward to strengthen the brand–consumer relationship for future business development. I'll begin by shining a spotlight on the absolutely vital issue of pricing innovation.

According to the Boston Consulting Group, 'companies that don't tackle pricing in a strategic manner will face predators. Buyers will always seek a better price, and global trade is moving towards more open markets and fewer barriers to cross-border commerce. Technology is opening up avenues for buyers and sellers to connect wherever the companies are located' (Schurmann, 2015).

This is also where a huge amount of dynamic behaviour is being seen via the so-called collaborative or sharing economy, where consumers are evidently demonstrating that owning feels like a burden, and a notion that 'what's mine is yours – for a fee'. This is very much digitally powered, with the issue of verified trust as its core foundation. It's why we allow a stranger to rent a room in our home or get into a car late at night with someone we've never met. Essentially, this has seen the internet leverage an age-old social norm, which has shaken up an extraordinary range of established categories to massive success and apparently unstoppable growth.

A staggering statistic gained via a renowned study by Nielsen is that 'globally, more than two-thirds of people want to share or rent out personal assets for financial gain. Similar numbers want to use products and services c/o other people' (Nielsen, 2014). But their report goes on to say that 'while the sharing economy has long been associated with certain types and demographics (young, urban, middle class) perhaps those stereotypes need re-visiting'. That Nielsen survey, which was conducted in 60 countries, revealed broad support for collaborative consumption across age groups, income and geography, illustrating that we're seeing fundamental shifts in consumption patterns where access trumps ownership, ie full-ownership becomes far less valid than product utilization.

Innovative business models leveraging emerging technology mean that there's a lot of disruption in the pricing sphere. But, it has to be said, the issue of pricing is one that has traditionally languished at the rather unglamorous end of the overall brand management spectrum.

Therefore, I've deliberately chosen to look at a few highly glamorous sectors: fashion, beauty and music. Each one is a prime example of an industry where an immense amount of price disruption is taking place.

For a dynamic example of how a brand with an innovative business model goes about utilizing a dynamic pricing strategy, let's take a look at Beauty Pie, a brand I mentioned in the previous chapter, which sources the best luxury makeup and skincare from the world's leading laboratories and sells it directly to their customers. Consumers join the Beauty Pie 'club' and, in return for a monthly fee, access products directly at a fraction of the cost of buying those same products in-store, paying only the factory cost plus basic shipping and handling.

Business models leveraging emerging technology mean there's a lot of disruption in the pricing sphere.

Their transparent pricing policy is industry-leading. As shown on their website, they state that luxury beauty products often retail at up to 10× what they actually cost to produce. They then transparently break down the actual product costs. For instance, the cost of a lipstick is shown as £2.64 for product and packaging, £0.46 for warehousing and £0.16 for safety and testing, giving a total factory price of £3.86 including VAT (Beauty Pie, 2018).

According to Marcia Gilgore, founder of the brand: 'Everlane led the way with price transparency. But in cosmetics, third-party factories supply almost all luxury cosmetic brands. The difference between the products is packaging and budget. I wanted to democratize access to the best beauty products, blending the concepts of Netflix and crowdfunding, a luxury kind of beauty Costco' (Maloney, 2017).

I also highlighted Everlane in a previous chapter, mentioning their purpose-led brand. They're a company that also takes a novel and transparent approach to their pricing policy, stating that 'sometimes we love a design so much that we overproduce it. We're getting better at predicting demand, but to move overstock on selected items, we're letting consumers choose what they pay'. The pricing menu on their site shows the consumer what the implications of their price choices are; for example, paying Option A for a pair of trousers can mean that 10 per cent of the price goes to Everlane. This covers their costs for development and shipping to the warehouse. Paying more for Option B may mean covering development and shipping costs plus overhead to pay their team. Finally, Option C covers development, shipping, overhead, and allows Everlane to work on creating new products.

I spoke about this issue with the futurist Anne Lise Kjaer, who spoke about her deep interest in pricing and brand trust:

> If you think of brand trust, of course Denmark is interesting. We have a supermarket chain of brands (Fakta, Kvickly, Super Brugsen and Irma, part of coop) who never compromise on quality and they're big on ecological products. What really brings the brands together is that they are very aware of pricing as well. Therefore they have built-in trust, as everyone knows they can get a good price and good quality as well. It also fits with national branding, in that Denmark wants to be greener; they're very aware of sustainability, sustainability of the family, real social engagement. I like the Danish supermarket case study because it enables

people to feed into the ecosystem, to be part of the solution rather than part of the problem. They might not feed in at the top of the pyramid but they are part of it. That is the democratic model that the Danes are well known for. So it's not so much about prestige, its more about a good life for everyone.

PWYW: pay what you want

On the psychology of 'pay what you want' for products or services, *The Guardian* interviewed Ayelet Gneezy, Associate Professor of Behavioural Sciences and Marketing at the University of California, who researches PWYW and people's responses to it. As he told them, 'it would be more likely to work for an independent café than one of the big coffee shop chains, because customers would never feel they care about a Starbucks too much'. The system 'hinges on this notion of people wanting to do the right thing and is mostly motivated by self-image' (Saner, 2018).

An innovative example of that PWYW model from the fashion world is the French brand Maison Standards. According to *Women's Wear Daily*, the brand, which operates on a direct-to-consumer model, is eschewing the summer sale model in favour of a 'pay what you want' policy on a selection of end-of-line products. 'We're taking advantage of the sales period to talk about our model', explained the brand founder Uriel Karsenti. 'It's about putting the accent on transparency and the true value of the product' (Wynne, 2017).

However, this idea of operating a transparent 'pay what you like' pricing system is nothing new. As demonstrated by the music industry, it has links to one tried over a decade ago by the band Radiohead, when they released their album 'In Rainbows' on the band's website. The site featured an offer that allowed the band's obsessive followers to pay whatever they liked for the album. The reason behind this was to take on music piracy, where bands were seeing their music effectively stolen from them and offered to fans online to download for free.

As reported by NME, 'some people hailed it as a revolution for the industry, a model for bands to follow. Others felt they'd potentially destroyed the careers of smaller bands by making music seem worthless'. But the results spoke for themselves. Offering to give the album away didn't end up devaluing it. As NME went on say, 'it was worth a lot more to the band than previous albums when they'd been signed to a label' (NME blog, 2017).

But did it really work out like that, and was it part of some major masterplan? Thom Yorke (the band's genius singer) told *Wired* magazine that 'It wasn't supposed to be a model for anything. It was simply a response to a situation. In terms of digital income, we made more money out of this record than all the other Radiohead albums put together, forever, in terms of anything on the net. And that's nuts' (Van Buskirk, 2007).

But what's vital to note here is that it isn't the only way of doing things, in fact very far from it, and new bands should understand that instead of copying it, they should perhaps just take note of the overall principles, ie connecting with their fans and being creative in the way they try to get their music in front of them.

This approach was effectively one of the precursors of the burgeoning crowdsourcing model, albeit at different ends of the production cycle, which has had such a massive impact across a staggeringly wide range of areas in the Fintech sector.

It's an issue that also interests Emily Hare, Editor at The Honey Partnership. When we discussed the effective use of dynamic pricing strategies and tactics, she used Habito, the mortgage broker that uses artificial intelligence, as a case history:

What they found was even though there was no need for a human to be involved in that process, to actually make the sale, it had to have a human as part of the sales and support process. So it's quite interesting to see how the tech and the people go hand in hand to build transparency and ultimately trust in the brands. It's interesting to think how you can use transparency. The most obvious ways to use it include McDonald's 'Our Food. Your questions', or Southwest Airlines' 'Transfarency' campaign about their transparent pricing.

Product provenance and brand stories

As I mentioned earlier, consumers are ever more aware about making responsible brand choices, with leading industry reports stating, for instance, that 'consumers increasingly require complete and total transparency from food and drink companies; and widespread distrust has increased the need for brands to be forthcoming about ingredients, production processes, and supply chains' (Mintel, 2017).

What would have seemed an 'unrealistic' amount of information to be requested by consumers until only recently has now become the so-called #NewNormal, or should I say #NeverNormal. To quote a rather irritating old saying, things won't be the same ever again.

Provenance is a company that exists 'to empower people to change the way the global economy works'. According to them, 'we know surprisingly little about most of the products we use. Before purchase, goods travel through an often-vast network of retailers, distributors, transporters, storage facilities, and suppliers that participate in design, production, delivery, and sales. Yet in almost every case these journeys remain an unseen dimension of our possessions' (Provenance, 2015). This issue is referenced by Deloitte: 'The wealth of information available to today's consumers has created a strong desire for openness and transparency. However, food companies suffer from a lack of trust amongst consumers'. They report that 'the tendency towards distrust is most pronounced among Millennials, with a recent report stating that 43% do not trust large food manufacturers' (Deloitte, 2017).

The transparency they desire takes many forms. At the most basic level this can include: where products are made (eg trusted if made in one's own country, when relevant), ethical claims (eg 'we support local growers'), origin (eg family heritage and production location), technology (eg utilizing barcodes to learn about products).

Brands point to the provenance of their products in a variety of ways, for example simply linking the name of the brand to its local origins (eg state, city, farm or distillery), the country of origin (Nicaraguan coffee, Irish milk, Madagascan vanilla etc) the family names of producers or references to farming collectives, or specific production issues, such as grass fed, all natural, non-GMO, organic, free range, foraged and 'free not farmed', to highlight their on-pack health, ethical or social-engagement statements. (On these last issues, elsewhere in the book I've also written about the B-Corp and One Planet movements.)

According to the 'Transparency 2.0' report from Whole Foods, 'More is more when it comes to product labelling. Consumers want to know the real story behind their food, and how that item made its way from the source to the store. GMO transparency is top of mind, but shoppers seek out other details too, such as Fair-Trade certification, responsible production and animal welfare standards' (Whole Foods, 2018).

With so-called 'greenwashing' being increasingly condemned, and genuine brand action being the positive way forward, Euromonitor note that 'among consumers and business, increasing attention is paid to ethics and moral values. This translates into decisions framed by concerns about the environment, sustainability, animal welfare, production and labour practices, as well as a desire to positively impact communities and people. This trend is driven by awareness, availability and affordability' (Euromonitor, 2017). These all go towards reassuring consumers about brand claims, but there's nothing like having information authenticated directly from the source. We all know that powerful, relevant and motivating brand stories are huge enablers for brand success, and there are few things more powerful, relevant and motivating than a 'good' brand strengthening their brand engagement by providing interested and informed consumers with a transparent view of the brand.

The received wisdom for many marketers in the food industry is that most consumers appear to be completely disconnected from what they eat via an industrialized food sector. Meanwhile, a highly significant and fast-growing sector of the population want to know more about the realities of the food they consume.

Elsewhere in this book I discuss the vitality of the street-food movement, a collection of like-minded people (producers and consumers alike) joined together by a common interest. The amazing vibrancy of the street-food scene sees an almost constant stream of new ideas being brought to market, offering consumers an incredible array of brands, many of which come with interesting provenance and heritage stories, which usually have a highly personal link to the people serving those items. The information they have about supply chains and pricing strategies can also make those issues compelling, and readily understandable. Those brands demonstrate the power of authenticity (alongside some truly extreme levels of innovative product development), and they illustrate something vital that is missing from so many brands stocked on grocery shelves around the world: an inherent passion for transparency and a sharing of their story.

Retailers have been making use of product-sourcing information for years, of course. But it's those like Chinese retailer Huma, Alibaba's entry into 'New Retail', who are showing a way forward. They use technology and data to provide a more seamless and more efficient shopping experience for consumers. Everything in-store has a barcode, and when consumers scan the code using the Huma app, they then receive a mass of information on the product concerned.

Individual tech platforms have taken note and responded accordingly. An example of this is utilizing the unique point about Snapchat Stories, that they disappear after 24 hours, to demonstrate that products are fresh. In this instance, Snapcodes can be placed on the origin labels of fish. This use of technology, according to *AdAge*, 'connects the customer to the Snapchat Spectacles of a fisherman, a sales manager, and a fishmonger. The content chronicled the fish's final hours before arriving at the fish counter. It proves the story behind the origin label, demonstrating that the fish had arrived that day' (Jardine, 2017).

One question: who made this product?

I've already mentioned the fashion sector from the point of view of dynamic pricing, but the social enterprise Fashion Revolution firmly believe that transparency is a vital move to transform that industry. As they say, 'Lack of transparency costs lives. It's impossible for companies to make sure human rights are respected and environmental practices are sound without knowing where products are made and by whom' (Fashion Revolution, 2018).

Lack of transparency costs lives.

Their 'Fashion Transparency Index' reviews and ranks 100 of the biggest global fashion brands and retailers according to how much information they disclose about their suppliers, supply-chain policies and practices, and social and environmental impact. As they say, 'the results aren't surprising, the average score is 49 out of 250, proving there's lots of work to be done' (Fashion Revolution, 2018). A key issue that they focus on is supply-chain transparency, which demonstrates to consumers the full story of products, from point of production to point of sale.

The world of sustainability is, of course, vital here. The company Ecoalf integrates breakthrough technology to create clothing and accessories made entirely from recycled materials with the same quality, design and technical properties as the best non-recycled products. One of their amazing projects is to 'upcycle the ocean', where they collect the trash that's destroying our oceans and turn it into top-quality yarn to produce fabrics and products. In order to ensure 100 per cent transparency, their team manages the full process from waste collection to recycling technologies, manufacture, design and retail (Ecoalf, 2018).

A different approach is taken by the Nordic lifestyle brand Arket's 'modern-day market' where sustainability is a primary consideration, which enables consumers to choose not only the style and material of the products they require, but also the country of origin when selecting potential purchases.

So it's clear that a world where the lack of trust in brands is so unfortunately high is leading to a demand from 'informed consumers' for an end to the opaque nature of many brands' approach to communicating the details of their product manufacturing. These consumers want total transparency, where the full story of product sourcing, ingredient information, the realities of manufacturing and indeed the full supply-chain process are laid bare. The results are positive for them as individuals, good for communities and good for the planet. This connects directly with the self-explanatory 'betterness' trend that is so often an element of agency trend forecasts. It's precisely here that technology is proving to be the 'means to an answer' that consumers, brands and retailers desire.

Blockchain – the benefits are hard to exaggerate

Something that's radically impacting grocery retailers, and the brands they stock, is an empowering area of technology rarely off the business pages: blockchain. It's the technology that famously enabled Bitcoin and all those other cryptocurrencies to exist. If one thing is clear about this often opaque-sounding technology, it's that the potential to disrupt a massive variety of areas in business, society and the environment is hard to exaggerate.

In today's environment, retailers need to provide detailed information to consumers on the products they sell, and the catalytic issue of blockchain-enabled transparency is transforming that vital area of consumer engagement. As Carsten Beck, of the Copenhagen Institute of Futures Studies, told me: 'there are two main buzzwords around at the moment "artificial intelligence" and "blockchain", that's it.'

Until recently, 'Informed Consumers' who were interested in making 'intentional buying choices' had essentially been prevented from doing so unless they either had personal access to detailed information about the product concerned or they could go to the effort (often seriously time-consuming) of finding out the facts they required, over and above the 'PR-friendly' type of product information that the brand in question might choose to provide. A very real problem for those consumers was the way in which major grocery stores and big brands had found it incredibly difficult to interact with consumers consistently and effectively, in order to communicate 'nothing but the truth' transparent stories.

Blockchain gives consumers what they need and were unable to access: a 'common level playing field of trust'.

Provenance, a company I mentioned earlier, is at the forefront of this technology. Blockchain, as they say, 'enables physical products to gain a digital identity that links the flow of physical products to a distributed ledger – aiding data sharing and "proof of provenance" – through the supply chain from farmer to retailer'. Or to put it more easily, it means you can see exactly what happened when, and who handed over to whom, via a series of interlinking 'digital handshakes' (Provenance, 2017).

This gives consumers what they need and were until recently unable to access: a 'common level playing field of trust', ie a commonly accepted means of absolute proof that consumers can easily access via technology, basically acting as a base layer of truth that everyone throughout the chain can refer to in a trusted way. In everyday consumer terms, this technology enables every physical product to come with a digital 'passport' that proves authenticity (is this product what it claims to be?) and origin (where does this product come from?), creating an auditable record of the journey behind all physical products.

An interesting example is demonstrated by Whole Foods, who have 100 per cent traceability for every single albacore tuna harvested, meaning they can trace the final canned and labelled product back to the vessel that caught it. This means that sustainable fishing can be verified via blockchain technology. As noted by *Forbes* magazine, 'mobile, blockchain and smart tagging are used to track fish caught by fishermen with verified social sustainability claims. This aids robust proof of compliance to standards at origin and along the chain from point of origin to point of sale' (Hannam, 2016).

It's a similar story from the brand Leap, who say 'responsible fishing is at the heart of everything we do. We know where every fish has come from, who caught it and how. All our fish comes from Alaska, where responsible, sustainable fishing is written into the constitution. This means we can be certain our wild catch is caught sustainably and can be traced back to source' (Leap, 2018).

Blockchain also works on a B2B level when considering the 'cost of trust' from a company process perspective. That is, in business-to-business transactions, utilizing encryption to verify the secure tracking of trusted information, or, in terms of cryptocurrencies, to verify the transfer of funds, a world where 'permissionless innovation' enables any number of new entrants in the market.

Now that retailers and brands have woken up to the fact that many consumers have seemingly unending demands when it comes to brand transparency, they're being forced to act. Once one key player in a sector provides transparency via the above measures, the other competitive brands in that area have to move fast to avoid a cloud of suspicion.

So-called 'conscious consumption' is very much involved here with reference to consumers who choose to make 'mindful choices' about their attitudes and behaviour around brand adoption and rejection. These are key issues for those who require reassurance about community impact and environmental claims.

The non-profit 'Feed the Truth' organization seeks to improve public health by making truth, transparency and integrity the foremost values in the food system. Talking about why he established the company, Daniel Lubetzky, CEO and Founder, says: 'My intent was to elevate reputable science, bolster the voices of the nutrition community, and improve the guidance and information offered to consumers. As a business owner, I understand the importance of prioritizing your bottom line, but it's equally as important to think about the long-term impact on the community' (Feed the Truth, 2018).

But to be blunt, and for those who may not be convinced, just how much of a big deal is this? In her excellent book *Who Can you Trust?* author Rachel Botsman states that 'a decade from now, we'll wonder how society ever functioned without it. Blockchain will transform how we exchange value and who we trust' (Botsman, 2017).

That's a level of societal impact that the strategy consultant Don Tapscott appears to agree with, as according to him, 'what if there were not just an Internet of information, but a native digital medium for value? For the last 40 years we had the Internet of information, a medium for publishing information. I think that blockchain will change every institution, in some ways more so than the first generation' (Tapscott, 2018).

Alexa, buy me something ... good

What about the implications of voice-activated technology for e-commerce and in-home buying? Arguably, this is where the 'ease of purchase' that has so far eluded ethical retailing becomes a simple task.

The massive growth in voice-enabled tech (which I highlighted in the chapter on privacy), brought to us via the likes of Home, Echo and DingDong, clearly shows that this technology has a seemingly incalculably important role to play in people's lives around the world. That is a seriously huge issue, if you just consider the implications of a report from ComScore, who stated that half of all searches will be voice searches by 2020 (Bentahar, 2017), while Ovum noted that there'd be 'more digital assistants than humans on the planet in 2021' (Ovum, 2017).

So now that 'Alexa talks to Cortana', we can effectively demand that we require our shopping to be done via proven 'good brands'. Essentially, 'ticking a virtual box' means that by the simple act of demanding best-practice from our online buying partner, technology will do the hard graft for us. And so, with one simple move, the barrier between, for instance, the wannabe ethical buyer and the 'good brand' with the ethical supply chain is removed.

This is where, via the abilities and buying power of the technological power-companies, those same brands that are so often held up to be 'public enemies' are now being cast in a light that they prefer, ie enablers and providers of 'good consumption'. This is because of the abilities they now have with the blockchain-enabled 'trust sourcing' of the types of brands we require in each area of our shopping. This means, in this instance, that our ethical-purchasing desires can be met, with all the hard work done by the retail-tech giants. All of which is a huge step forward for consumer power, ethical sourcing and sustainable production.

However, this all comes with an inbuilt serious problem for brands, when those brands are going to be chosen by virtual assistants. A situation where the consumer-brand purchase selection is intermediated by voice-active software will, according to a Mindshare report, mean that 'algorithm optimization will become the new SEO'. This is because 'while we have seen many smart speakers with integrated visual interfaces, voice technology works best when there's only one answer, according to 80% of global regular voice tech users' (Mindshare, 2017).

But how deep does technology really go in people's lives on a day-to-day basis? According to research from WPP, '45% of global smartphone users are interested in the idea of chatting with their fridges' (Mindshare, 2017).

Now the idea of lonely singles sitting at home with only a fridge for conversation might sound like a particularly tragic and dystopian future that JG Ballard might have forecast. But the relationship between consumers and their voice-activated smartware does indeed seem to be a deeply, dare I say it, personal one, and the opportunities for brand engagement evidently seem to be extensive.

Go figure, as the Americans say.

We want control of our health

It's not just grocery shopping where the impact of blockchain will be felt, of course. The ramifications range from the health sector to ethical diamond mining to the second-hand car industry.

It's the health sector that I'll look at now. It's an area that has seen an incredible amount of innovation over the past few years via artificial intelligence, augmented reality, virtual reality and so on, and it's a rate of innovation that appears to be speeding up in an unrelenting manner. For instance, we're now seeing more and more doctors recommending the use of apps, and a whole realm of health-related technology. Only a few years ago, it seemed that the most trend-forward thing was noting how tech-obsessives interested in the 'Quantified Self' movement were utilizing data relating to their sleep patterns alongside records of park runs noted by their fitness trackers.

Now this is a sector that is as future focused as any other, and it's an incredibly interesting one to analyse. This is partly because, as noted by the World Advertising Research Centre

(WARC), 'Technology is enabling a shift to value-based care, which achieves and maintains consumer health as measured through "quality outcomes". Products need a trigger for use i.e. via advertising or word of mouth, which turns into action i.e. tech use, followed by a reward and ending with an improvement in well-being' (WARC, 2018).

This is a point taken up by JWT Intelligence, who report that 'tech companies are turning their attention to myriad areas of healthcare, from diagnosing cancer to shaking up the insurance system. As life expectancy continues to increase, these innovative approaches to tackling health problems are surely set to proliferate with the relationship between tech and healthcare providers drawing ever closer' (JWT, 2017).

But what role does blockchain actually play in all this innovative activity?

On the core issues of trust, the health industry has an immense amount to gain from the world of blockchain. For example, an individual's encrypted health information could be utilized by various health providers, such as clinics, hospitals and insurers, without the risk of privacy breaches.

A common consumer complaint about healthcare is that they lack knowledge and control of their personal medical histories. Access to that data is key, because once they're finally enabled to share and distribute that information with trusted medical staff, insurers and so on, the situation changes radically. Having mentioned earlier how voice-activated technology is impacting the food and drink sectors, where Amazon is aiming to rule supreme, the potential impact on the health sector is just as important.

Deloitte believes that blockchain technology 'has the potential to transform healthcare, placing the patient at the centre of the healthcare ecosystem and increasing the security, privacy, and interoperability of health data. This technology could provide a new model for health information exchanges (HIE) by making electronic medical records more efficient, disintermediated, and secure' (Deloitte, 2018).

Where large-scale innovation is taking place, a certain brand is never far away. According to a *New York Times* report looking into how a deal between the biggest retailer in the world (Amazon), the biggest US bank (JP Morgan Chase) and Berkshire Hathaway (Warren Buffett's holding company) might disrupt that sector, 'Amazon could assume drug distribution. They could start to use voice platforms, like Alexa, to help discuss symptoms and get feedback, to coordinate hospital post-op care through voice-activated A.I.' (Hsu, 2018).

Who could you trust more than 'Doctor You'?

Monitoring our own health is a really big deal. Technologies such as the smartphone are key enablers in this area, and Apple is set to ask organizations to let patients use their iPhones to download personal medical records. This will, in effect, enable patients to turn their phones into medical devices. In what the industry refers to as the #DigitalTherapeutic or #DigiCeutical trends, we can, for instance, utilize sensors built into the phone to measure our body fat, blood pressure and heart function.

This issue of empowering individuals via smartphone technology was covered in a 'Doctor You' report, which stated that 'Apple's Health app brings together medical data from participating hospitals and clinics, as well as from the iPhone, giving users direct digital control of their own health information for the first time. Alphabet, Google's parent firm, Facebook and Microsoft are all preparing to add health to their core business' (Economist, 2018a). So, the potential to give patients access to their medical files, whenever they want and wherever they are, changes the game.

If we concentrate purely on transparency as opposed to efficiency and control, it's a similarly huge issue. According to McKinsey, 'interest in public-sector transparency is growing. The governments of 46 countries recently joined together to form the Open Government Partnership, committing themselves to promote fuller sharing of information. Their rationale is simple: evidence is emerging that transparency may be a key precondition for service improvement and productivity' (McKinsey, 2011).

Summing up the impact of all this ongoing innovation from the technology giants, and the effect on the profits of the healthcare sector, is staggering. 'Healthcare costs make up about a tenth of any country's GDP on average', states *The Economist*. 'Apple and Alphabet have the potential to generate or enable valuable health insights for hundreds of millions of users, collecting a slice of that value in return' (Economist, 2018b).

And finally …

In the sectors I've described, and in many more, the vital issue of transparent information goes a long way to enabling consumers to make informed decisions, and thus puts them in far more control of the brand–consumer relationship. In doing so, technology, particularly in the form of blockchain, is helping to protect workers, manufacturers and others right along the supply chain, until we the consumer consider the purchase of the product concerned.

This is because in blockchain we see 'end to end' transparency being offered up for consumer inspection. According to a think-tank blog, 'blockchain enforces the transparency, security, authenticity, and auditability necessary to make tracing the chain of custody and attributes of products possible. Which in turn allows customers to make more informed choices' (Happycius Blog, 2017).

This is not to suggest that 'mainstream consumers' are suddenly going to be interested in the company's operational details of 'how they do it'. They are, of course, far more interested in the 'why' and the 'what' of branding.

How this is done, from an internal company technology point of view where all things AI related currently rule supreme, is of little or no interest to them. So, while this is precisely the type of industry-disrupting technology that will be endlessly discussed in corporate boardrooms, it'll rarely be discussed anywhere near the home of a consumer; or should I say 'real person'. It is the effects of transparency that consumers desire when it comes to their brand adoption/rejection viewpoints in a world of multiple choice in virtually every sector, not the minutiae of how this transparency is achieved.

That issue was put into stark relief by the techno-sociologist Zeynep Tufekci, referring to the abilities of Google Assistant that were highlighted at its launch. She wrote about it 'making calls pretending to be human not only without disclosing that it's a bot, but adding 'ummm' and 'aaah' to deceive humans, with the room cheering it … horrifying. Silicon Valley is ethically lost, rudderless and has not learned a thing' (Tufekci, 2018). She'd previously given a very well-regarded TED Talk where she'd stated that 'we're building an AI-powered dystopia, one click at a time' (Tufekci, 2017).

This illustrates, albeit from a giant organization, the prime importance of trust for brands when people are increasingly making their brand choices on the basis of 'Good Brand vs Bad Brand' (or 'Trusted vs Untrusted Brand'); something that is of stark importance to brands in any 'normal' sector where they don't enjoy a virtual monopoly. As I note numerous times in this book, this is due to the essential fact that genuine brand differentiation is so rare.

Bluntly put, being a 'more trustworthy, nicer and better' business than your competitors, which includes utilizing the type of transparent strategies and tactics I've highlighted, is a better way of doing business for all concerned. Leveraging transparency to gain and retain consumer trust goes a long way to providing a solid foundation of this brand reality.

Because, as *Contagious* magazine put it so succinctly, 'Today, being open and honest is an effective way of building trust. Tomorrow it will be an essential means of boosting your bottom line' (Contagious, 2017).

CHAPTER SIX

Makers, Innovators and Outsiders

This chapter outlines a range of individuals, brands and organizations who define the truism that 'maker' brands are often cited as being the most authentic, building strong emotional connections as a result. When this bumps up against disruption, markets can be revolutionized.

At one end of the 'maker' spectrum we have technology brands, discussed at places like the SXSW festival in Austin, where this culture can, according to *The Guardian*, 'seem dangerous and edgy to the uninitiated, like all good subcultures. Maker culture can be thought of as a technology focused form of DIY. Those immersed in the subculture don't refer to themselves as DIYers. Instead, they prefer to be called hackers or makers' (Northover, 2014).

However, rather than focusing on tech-hackers such as Palmer Luckey of Oculus Rift fame, instead I'll concentrate mainly on a range of 'maker and innovator' issues (and the personalities behind them), from the street-food movement to that of singer-songwriters and those like the craft-beer independent producers, who have collectively brought so much collective disruption to local and global markets. Passion, purpose and identity tend to shine through these types of brands, where the common denominator seems to be the celebration, or enablement, of 'artisanal autonomy'.

It's in the very act of making that the notion of authenticity shines brightest. Unfortunately, in many countries we've seen the 'connection gap' between maker and consumer widening across a multitude of sectors for decades, and it's only in recent years that the desire for this gap to be closed has really taken off, at scale.

A major part of the blame for the fault of that widening gap can most obviously be pointed at hyper-efficient production methodologies and globalized distribution where, to take things to their logical conclusion, the ultimate targets used to be uniform consumers with uniform tastes. Theodore Levitt, a professor at Harvard Business School whom many associate with coining the term 'globalization', wrote a massively influential piece years ago for *The Harvard Business Review* (which he edited) where he argued that owing to the effects of globalization, 'gone are accustomed differences in national or regional preferences... commercially, nothing confirms this as much as the success of McDonald's from the Champs Elysées to the Ginza, of Coca-Cola in Bahrain and Pepsi-Cola in Moscow, and rock music, Greek salad, Hollywood movies, Revlon cosmetics, Sony televisions, and Levi jeans everywhere' (Levitt, 1983).

This article, and the debates around it, became a pillar of the '10-brand world' strategy that trend forecasters and scenario planners developed, where hyper-efficiency would lead to a winner-takes-all situation, meaning the last brands standing would win the day. This might have sounded great in the corporate boardroom and looked even better on a graph, but it proved to have little enduring appeal for discerning consumers – and consumers appear to be getting ever more discerning.

Over the past decade, consumers have begun to turn away from so many of those identikit brands (in a multitude of sectors), presented to us in identikit locations, promoted via identikit stories. Far from seeing the world that Theodore Levitt suggested (and yes, I know he was exaggerating for effect), the precise opposite has happened. It appears that 'one size fits all' actually means that no one gets what they really want.

At the opposite end of Theodore Levitt's theory of hyper-efficient markets lies the growing interest in the localism movement. This global trend is all about people wanting brands, products and services to be more real, more human and more empathetic; where brand touchpoints are quite literally just that. At the heart of this trend are the makers. 'The power of making, from the height of luxurious freedom to the depth of deprivation,' is, according to Professor Daniel Charny, 'something people can do. While for some people making is critical for survival, for others it is a way of learning, or defying conventions, enjoying life or for solving its problems' (Charny, 2011)

I talked about trends in artisanal culture in Asia with Nicole Fall, Founder of Asian Consumer Intelligence, who told me that:

> it's definitely growing in South East Asia. In North East Asia there has always been an appreciation, particularly in Japan and maybe South Korea and to some extent China, although it's just too big a place to generalize about. There's an appreciation around masters of a trade or a craft, and it's growing in other places. Of course, it's enabled by technology. The fact that you can have these smaller e-commerce sites where anyone can set up a business, make things and put them online to sell them, means they're able to reach consumers in a way that they've never been able to in the past; when it was just the preserve of the big brands with their huge marketing spends who could reach the consumer. Now with these bespoke e-commerce stores, everyone's making little candles and soaps on the side, which is really big out here. People are able to indulge in that, support it and buy those products. People have

always been makers in this part of the world, that's a typical Asian story, people made things and sold them. That farmer culture and market culture are still very strong, we live in these big cities but get outside of them and go into rural areas and very quickly you realize just how different it is. So, yes there is a sense that anything that is artisanal is to be appreciated.

This movement is all about empowerment, equality, resilience and creativity: a movement where the act of consumption can effectively move from being a passive to a highly active one in regard to the holistic benefits that follow on as a result of buying from the maker. Those who are the 'informed and interested, demanding and unpredictable' consumers of these brands, products, services and experiences are becoming a powerhouse of early-adopting and opinion-forming customers, eager to seek out the maker that directly links them to the 'Made By', reflecting their need for 'intentional buying'. This issue of intentional buying is absolutely intrinsic to this movement, where consumption is considered and deliberated.

Consumers are eager to seek out the maker that directly links them to the 'Made By', reflecting their need for 'intentional buying'.

Once they've found what they're looking for, these people are highly vocal on social media and in face-to-face conversations about their latest discoveries. This word-of-mouth activity is nirvana for marketers, who understand that in a world where fewer and fewer corporate messages are believed, and where 'real' has become a consumer obsession, authenticity is the ultimate goal.

That makes this modern consumer incredibly important to the modern business. It's a point I discussed with Emily Hare, Editor at The Honey Partnership, who said:

There's definitely a rise in people moving away from massproduced things to having fewer possessions and buying objects that they really care about and want to invest their money in. It is natural to want those fewer possessions to be high quality. If you've got a story that could be woven into it, which lots of craft-produced items do, ie it's something created lovingly and thoughtfully, and you can maybe trace the individual person that made it. I think that companies like Everlane and Honest Buy are trying to build trust into their supply chain – not so much a beautiful craft story but a very transparent presentation about their products and where they are sourced from. I think buying products that you care about and feel like you know something about them, the story, the craft and the heritage is definitely something that is going to stick around.

The human touch in the smart city

Talk to any metropolitan architect or urban anthropologist and you'll soon hear of a common problem with the modern city: people are living in smaller and smaller spaces, hence a corresponding need for public spaces in which they can congregate and socialize.

In a world where streets from Tokyo to Toronto are lined with the same outlets offering the same tired brands and products, we increasingly seek spontaneous experiences care of brands with meaning. This

Whether it be in Williamsburg or Shoreditch, the street-food scene has radically changed the way urbanites are eating.

is where the latest dynamic breed of street-food operators are providing a needed service, bringing a wide variety of affordable products to a public that are rejecting the offerings from mainstream outlets and allowing them to 'spontaneously socialize'.

Whether it be in Williamsburg or Shoreditch, Kreuzberg or Fitzroy, the street-food scene has radically changed the way urbanites are eating around the world. Outfits at the top of their game include those such as the Street Feast and Kerb Food organizations in London, or those like the Food Truck Park, Welcome to Thornbury, or Hank Marvin's pop-up mess hall in Melbourne; or Hard Times Sundaes in Brooklyn, King of Falafel in Queens, or indeed DF Nigerian who started by selling food in New York City from the boot of his car. (If I really wanted to go on highlighting the great operators out there, this book could very easily be filled several times over with an ever-growing list.)

This is an incredibly vibrant sector, which has consequences far beyond the simple act of eating a gourmet burger or that bao bun that you may be imagining. Many seem to assume that it's simply a case of 'what you see is what you get', but it's much more than that. So I'm going to explain why I think it's so multi-dimensional and inspiring, and where the sum of the parts really is more than the whole.

What the street-food scene seems to share is a collective, co-operative and collaborative ethos, which means that the group is stronger than the individual, and that everyone involved – producer, maker and customer alike – benefits from this approach. By combining personal autonomy, pooled creativity and a shared experiential offer, the modern street-food scene has created the seemingly 'perfect combination' that so many of us seek. I say 'modern street food', as the general concept is as old as society. One of the current prime examples is the Time Out Food Court at Mercado da Ribeira in Lisbon, which has essentially been in existence for over a thousand years, but after its recent revamp into an 'affordable gourmet paradise' is now Lisbon's No 1 tourist attraction.

Key to their world is taking a community approach, where numerous producers gather together and where more can 'bolt-on and connect-up' as the local scene develops. This offers both a greater a sense of collectiveness to the participants and a greater range of choice to customers, both in price and variety. We've all suffered from trying to agree an acceptable price range and cuisine type that'll suit everyone involved when looking to eat out as a group. What marketers would describe as the 'key value proposition' of street food is that wildly different tastes and wallets can be satisfied, but all at the same time and in the same place. This collectiveness issue is as opposed to lone operators who can operate purely as solo players. These lone wolves may gain a greater sense of absolute autonomy but lose on the benefits of co-opetition (cooperative competition) and collaboration.

The fact that this whole scene lends itself to being highly flexible in the spaces within which it operates means that, very often, it's in the run-down or 'spare' urban places where street food seems to work so well. This reinvigorates sometimes dubious or perhaps just overlooked areas and enables the vital element of urban reinvention to be leveraged.

Closely linked to this area is that of supper clubs and alternative-use retail spaces, which sees independent teams and individuals providing innovative dining experiences or reinvigorating otherwise empty cafés or shops. An example is the Disappearing Dining Club, whose founders, combining long and varied careers in restaurants, bars, festivals and clubs in New York, London, Stockholm, Ibiza and Melbourne, 'have been throwing dinner parties in lighthouses, launderettes, abandoned music venues, antiques shops, department stores, churches, salvage yards, railway arches, photographic studios, film sets, galleries, fashion stores, recording studios, private homes, stately homes, car parks, beaches, rooftops, street-food markets, gardens, and countless warehouses of all shape and sizes' (Disappearing Dining Club, 2018). Quite a list, the point being that this illustrates the extraordinary variety and vibrancy involved in the scene.

Shop small and shop local

In producer terms, local suppliers can benefit from enabling a consumer desire to 'eat local' while makers benefit from being able to sell direct to the public with few overheads involved, and the consumer gains by being able to access a wide variety of quality items made 'just for them' at a reasonable price. But another ingredient to this mix is absolutely crucial: the makers are often those who've turned their backs on corporate life to concentrate on their individual passion as a means to try to make a living. This passion may not work on a spreadsheet, but it works on the basis of a personal reinvention as a 'free entrepreneur'. This links the ethos of the self-taught chef in Helsinki directly to the app developer in Hanoi, where a start-up mentality requires the vital ingredients of agility and passion.

I discuss the issue of 'brands as story-tellers' in more detail in the chapter devoted specifically to communication trends, but what I would say here is that this key issue of storytelling is an incredibly powerful tool, and one that links individuals, communities and societies around the world.

But what I also find fascinating with this scene is that they don't see corporates as the enemy. Instead, there are many links between them and big business, particularly in the creative industries, which see linking with the street scene as giving them added authenticity and credibility, hence the number of advertising agency and record-label events that have their catering supplied care of street-food suppliers.

Big corporates have also made strong moves to support smaller non-competing brands over recent years, with 'Small Business Saturday' sponsored by American Express being such a great example. This sees the macro and micro business communities linking together, enabled by the bigger partner, for the greater good. As part of their mission 'to help businesses to do more business', this initiative encourages people to shop small and shop local. Small Business Saturday quickly proved to be so successful for the US economy that the US Senate declared it an official day, after which it went international, to enormous success. The vital point here is that the retail news is often full of information about the latest staggering statistic from Alibaba about the Singles Day/Global Shopping Festival, or the Cyber Monday and Black Friday shopping mayhem, events that mainly benefit major brands. But it's the SMEs that benefit most from

Small Business Saturday, making it a massively useful occasion for localized, grass-roots players.

Underlining the 'brand action' issue here, from the perspective of American Express, it's worth noting a comment from Tom Goodwin in his excellent book *Digital Darwinism* where he reminds us that 'a brand is what a brand does. It lives in the minds of people, not in the brand onions of agency strategists. A brand is now linked more to ratings online than to what ads tell people to think' (Goodwin, 2018). In this context, a finance company that encourages and enables people to 'shop small' clearly understands the triple bottom line benefits and the positive resulting impact for brand, customer and community.

Intentional buying

This small-business ethos links to the movement for 'intentional buying' I've already briefly mentioned, which sees people considering their purchases more carefully. It also links to the circular economy, where 'reuse and recycle' is an alternative to a traditional linear economy of 'make, use, dispose'. A really interesting approach conducted recently was the 'Wasted' series of events run in the United States and the United Kingdom. As *The Wall Street Journal* put it, 'in one of the year's most influential moments in dining, chef Dan Barber served food waste to eager gourmands. It was a bold gambit to prove that an entire menu worthy of the highest critical acclaim could be built from ingredients that most restaurants would toss into the trash' (Schwaner-Albright, 2015).

On the other hand, it may also nudge them towards natural products, for instance for consumers particularly wanting to connect more closely with nature. This has added benefits for urbanites who may feel increasingly removed from the countryside, and where 'sensory purchases' mean that they gain deeper satisfaction from knowing more about the provenance from the manufacturing story behind the product. Additional pleasure is gained from knowing that their consumption may directly benefit the maker, for reasons of fair trade or support for the vulnerable, where making and selling their own products is a vital means of income and where the simple act of purchase plays a directly positive part in the maker's life, with no inbuilt concerns over dubious supply-chain issues. The pride that this also brings to 'the maker, the person' can be typically seen by the maker at a market stall, or the participants at Open House movements, where local artisans sell direct to the public via their or a friend's home. I'd also point towards the 'Slow Movement', which sees a key link with handmade items being the simple fact that they are low production items, ie a fault-line in the business model (a solo maker can typically produce only limited amounts of what they make) means that product runs often cannot be scaled large enough to make a high turnover possible. On the positive side, it means that, for the purchaser, what they're buying is often, by definition, literally 'limited edition'.

To state the stunningly obvious, essential points of enablement in this instance include social media, e-commerce and ease of one-off distribution. Or to put it another way, the modern context is an omnichannel mix of Instagram and Twitter, buy-buttons and websites, Etsy and Amazon, ad infinitum. This all goes towards reinforcing the mindset of the entrepreneurial creator/maker/producer as being a micro-corporation, based on the well-worn but entirely justified phrase that you are 'The Brand Called You' and where a sort of mass-autonomy seems to work just fine for all concerned.

Part of the new breed of magazines that has reinvigorated the publishing scene is also linked to this world, for example Hole & Corner, Selvedge, Kinfolk or indeed the retailer New Craftsman which has also built dynamic links with Harrods. Overarching this are official government-funded creative arts organizations. All have championed craft and effectively repositioned it into something that has clearly lifted its overall 'sector image' from its somewhat dated overtones and helped to reinterpret it into something imbued with a modern aura of respect and coolness.

But another issue needs highlighting further: that of the maker and the customer being able to meet and discuss the product created. The mixture of pride, pleasure and interest that it gives producer and customer alike is seriously powerful. If a key issue is that it allows the customer to see and experience the process, then let's not forget that the world of luxury is never far away. Handmade, or bespoke, has historically been clearly linked to the realm of luxury. Meeting the atelier, or briefing the atelier or artisan or creator (call them what you will), has historic associations, most readily with the worlds of fashion and art. In those instances, ownership is by definition a privilege for the moneyed elite, and of course the world of high-end price points is still there and shows not the slightest signs of going away. But we're now seeing a modern reinterpretation where handmade is being made more accessible.

It's been interesting to watch the way that Burberry, for instance, invites customers to join workshops where they can interact with artisans and therefore see craftspeople at work, gaining a greater understanding of the production process as a result. This means they have a deeper appreciation of the products created, understanding the skills involved, which goes towards reinforcing that brand's high-quality credentials. This links an age-old bespoke approach taken for high-end customers, for example by the likes of Dior, to the 'of the moment' one taken by leading winemakers such as Nyetimber, Rathfinny or Wiston where the public can meet the winemaker as part of a vineyard tour.

Anarchic branding

I hope we can agree that among the key reasons people like products associated with 'the hand of the artisan' is that these are seen to be genuine, real and human. They come with a story built into the very essence of the product, because the real-life background to the product is the story itself. 'You can't fake reality' is the way the thinking goes here, and if the brand takes off and becomes successful, retaining a clear and unbreakable link to that core story is fundamental to its ongoing success.

Over the past decade, the drinks industry has been through an incredible period of disruption. I've worked on plenty of trend research and consumer insights projects, either helping to develop the next big thing or trying to help strengthen the brand–consumer relationship. One of the key disruptors in the brewing sector has been the rise and rise of the craft-beer market. Decades of research from a wide number of agencies, telling clients that drinkers were losing interest in 'same old same old' product offerings which were felt to be lacking in taste and personality, appeared to fall on deaf ears at many a Big Drinks Co HQ. The sector seemed to be hurtling towards a Theodore Levitt-style situation where a small number of beer brands utterly dominated key international markets, but did so in a manner that actually seemed to suck all the life out of the market – until the public fought back by increasingly 'refusing to consume', particularly in bars and clubs where the products were both bland and very highly priced.

Cue the appearance of a huge number of independent operators, keen to offer consumers something that they kept asking for, and which the drinks companies seemingly refused to action. As business fails go, this is quite startling, and will give future MBA students plenty of case histories on which to base their essays.

So, at the opposite end of the drinks-industry spectrum from the glamorous world of fine wine, the craft-beer market has completely disrupted an industry seemingly settled in its ways. Those craft-beer brands, just like the street-food operators I've mentioned, have a deep sense of authenticity that runs right through them. A great example of this disruption is BrewDog. A small-town brewer from Scotland has grown into an international giant, seemingly without losing its core 'punk' credentials. (There's always been something of the counterculture linked with the 'rebels' of craft ale.) It's been fascinating to watch how the big drinks-industry brands have finally woken up to the threat and attempted to muscle in on the craft-beer market by buying up these specialist players. The response to this has been strong, with media reports that craft ale is not a standard market, and drinkers have been furious at the intrusion of big business into their territory.

James Morgan of Truman's Brewery said in an article highlighting the moves from big brewers onto the craft ale turf: 'It's one of the pre-eminent instances in recent years where Joe Public has managed to force a huge change onto a multinational industry dominated by two or three major players. I can see why it then sucks to find that those major players are buying up the beers you love' (Moulds, 2017). Independents that do give in to the financial inducements of a mega-brewer often find themselves on the receiving end of irate social media complaints from committed customers. When Camden Town announced its sale, one drinker tweeted: 'What's the going rate for a soul these days?' A bit harsh maybe, but you know where they were coming from.

Unlike the unfortunate Camden Town, the two founders of BrewDog were reported as sharing £100 million from the sale of equity in the business but still retain their 'punk ethos' by being, or certainly appearing to be, almost entirely unchanged by the sudden windfall of such a staggering amount of money. Which, as they say, calls for a beer. It helps that they built what they describe as 'a radically new type of business' by giving 10 per cent of the company profits to staff and another 10 per cent to charity via their Unicorn Fund. The co-founder James Watt said in an interview for *The Scotsman*: 'We want to create a blueprint for a completely new type of 21st century business and use craft beer to make the world a better place. Giving away 20% of profits, for ever, is not about altruism. It is about impact. It's not about profits. It is about purpose' (Mackie, 2017). That's about as 'real and authentic' as you can get; there's not a hint of post-truth waffle or lies anywhere near that kind of statement.

Beavertown is another great brand doing it 'for real'. They also run international events where the finest beers known to man (probably) are sold at gatherings that also feature talks, break-out sessions and seminars curated by industry experts. To illustrate the links between these types of brands and street food, at the 'Beavertown Extravaganza' Kerb Food provided the catering.

From 'normal' to 'insane'

As I mentioned at the start of this chapter, while it's the low-tech (or no-tech) brands and products that most readily lend themselves to association with authenticity, this isn't always the case, in fact very far from it. Particularly when they're clearly linked to the 'aura of the originator', who therefore has a very clear association with the brand image, some of the planet's most exciting brands can also define authenticity. And so, far from the worlds of street food and craft beer, let's move to the other end of the maker–brand spectrum, and to another leading-edge operator, Tesla. In this strand of autonomous making, a highly futuristic product has made one person, in particular, very famous and amazingly wealthy, while also retaining his authenticity. That is quite a feat.

Low-tech (or no-tech) brands and products are not the only ones associated with authenticity.

Tesla achieved staggering fame via its electric vehicles. But what's even more extraordinary about this 'disruptive technology' brand than the products it makes is that it actually exists. If you consider that not only did Ford start before the First World War, and that there hadn't been another successful new car company in the United States between Ford being established and Tesla getting set up, it points towards the difficulties faced by new motor brands. Even more so, when in this case a new independent outfit that was made up of people with zero experience of the motor industry sought both to take on that industry and effectively to create a new market by trying to make electric cars. A classic example of the difficulties linked to this problem was shown by GM (who reportedly spent over US $1 billion testing and developing their own electric vehicle, the EV1) as highlighted in the (pre-Tesla) documentary film *Who Killed the Electric Car?* which suggested that the market failure of that vehicle may not have been all that it seemed ...

In a story that has become folklore to entrepreneurs, when commenting on what he saw as the 'killer app that the auto industry had missed' Tesla co-founder Marc Tarpenning noticed that 'We kept running across these articles that would say the reason why electric cars will never succeed is that battery technology has not improved in a hundred years. Literally, articles would say that, and it's true of lead acid batteries. But it's not true of lithium-ion batteries ...' (Baer, 2014). Or to put it another way, everyone was looking in the wrong direction when it came to one of the biggest breakthroughs in decades.

Talking of decades, it must have felt to the founders as if they had endured many of those, as they had to surmount seemingly endless design, production, manufacturing and distribution problems before the company achieved the recognition they deserved. Elon Musk, who from a public perspective effectively is 'Mr Tesla' (and of course Mr SpaceX), made a fantastic speech for the launch of the Tesla Model D, which has the same acceleration as a McLaren F1 supercar, where he told the audience that driving the car 'was like taking off from an aircraft carrier. In the option selection you can choose between three settings: normal, sport, and insane', as reported by *Forbes* and highlighted in the Tesla Forums blog (Just an allusion, 2014).

I will always remember the first of my numerous stays at the Virgin hotel in Chicago, Virgin being another classic example of a brand where the image of the maker underlines the authenticity of the product or service. One of the main reasons I've stayed there is that, apart from the great location, guests also have use of a complimentary Tesla for use when zipping around the city. Yes, it did feel insane the first time I had a go. (On the consumer response, Mashable reported that the 2017 Consumer Reports Annual Owner Satisfaction Survey saw them top that survey for the third year in a row.)

But back to this amazing organization, and Tesla has gone on to become one of the world's most dynamic and disruptive brands, doing so from a position of being an 'outsider' company whose brand purpose is effectively to break our addiction to fossil fuels, helping to create a truly sustainable world – which is staggeringly worthwhile and not at all insane. The issues of a strong brand image reinforced by a dynamic brand purpose, brought to life in emphatic 'living and breathing' terms, are phenomenally expressed by this quite extraordinary and entirely authentic brand and the people behind it.

Brand fans – getting up close and personal

The final 'authentic brand' that I'd like to focus on here is a true individual, but about as far from Elon Musk as I think you could possibly get. I mentioned the 'punk brand' BrewDog earlier. Punk was all about DIY music, for and about the streets. Just like grime, you might say. This individual brand, or 'autonomous maker' if you like, reflects that ethos of DIY music, where the giant corporate entertainment brands are held at arm's length in favour of a more real, organic and humanistic approach. This is where the gap between artist and audience is kept as minimal, or even non-existent, as possible. This is of course an aim for many street-level, authentic musicians, who just want to make a living by playing music and being genuine artists, far removed from the fakery of stardom.

The inspiring example I'd like to highlight here is the musician Lucy Rose, and specifically the incredible tour of South America she did, where she epitomized the 'authentic artist'. Lucy had never played South America, in fact her music hadn't even been released there, yet she had fans contacting her via her website and social media, pleading with her to do some gigs in the region.

She wanted to, but there were a couple of key problems: she didn't have the money to afford such a trip, let alone find a way to either organize or pay for any live-music venues. What she and her fans came up with was an ingenious way of dealing with the situation: they would pay for her flights, she'd stay with them in their own homes and play a free gig, organized by them, the intention behind all this being to spread some positivity.

She linked up with about 40 people, and she visited eight South American countries. But what transpired was a completely different situation from what she initially expected. While she'd presumed that she'd be playing to a handful of fans and families, what actually happened was that these fans had booked venues and had been hugely active on social media, the result being that she ended up playing packed venues in Ecuador, Peru, Chile, Argentina, Uruguay, Paraguay, Brazil and Mexico. Not only that, but the crowds that turned up knew every word of her songs, singing along, despite her being a supposedly 'unknown' artist.

There's a great video of the 'fans tour' on her website, where she talks about the trip being the happiest days of her life, as she stayed with people who had very few material goods but a wealth of love. The common bond was simply that these people felt comforted by her very personal songs. The confidence that they gave her, that what she was doing really struck an emotional chord with them, gave her added inspiration to write and record more work. As it says at the end of her video, 'to every fan that I now call a friend, thank you for giving me the experience of a lifetime' (Rose, 2017). The key issue here is that she used the 'freedom to live authenticity' and understood that the human touch, and human connections, are everything.

What this range of brands, products, services and experiences that I've mentioned have as a common connector, the golden thread that runs through them, is a mixture of absolute integrity, passion and authenticity. This demonstrates one of the oldest truisms in marketing, that without a core foundation of authenticity any brand is weaker as a result.

This doesn't mean that brands have to be small and that once they've succeeded they lose their grip on authenticity. When brands make continual efforts to connect and re-connect with consumers by showing that their story and positioning are real, and that they are on the consumer's side, strong connections result.

What this range of brands, products, services and experiences have in common is a mixture of absolute integrity, passion and authenticity.

These issues are as key for the artist as they are for the street-food operator or super-cool craft beer or futuristic car brand. The lessons they give us and the example they demonstrate show that there isn't a brand out there, in any sector, that can't do with a healthy dose of authenticity in a post-truth world.

CHAPTER SEVEN

Reputation Capital and National Branding

As the old saying goes, 'Heaven is where the police are British, the cooks are French, the engineers are German, the administrators are Swiss and the lovers are Italian. Hell is where the police are German, the cooks are British, the engineers are Italian, the administrators are French and the lovers are Swiss'.

Depending on your nationality, that quote may annoy or please you in equal measure. But something that anyone working in marketing can surely agree on is that national stereotypes have enormous implications for consumer brands. This is because something that's 100 per cent guaranteed to crop up regularly in the life of a marketer is linking consumer brands to national brands via referencing the nation in which their brand was created.

The ways in which brands can link to the positive narratives and myths about their country of origin cuts across virtually every sector, as it enables them (when done properly) to leverage incredibly powerful emotions. As emotions are what we increasingly base our decisions on in a post-truth world, the issues of truth, trust and authenticity as they relate to national-branding messages cannot be overstated. Put simply, when it comes to branding, as it does in life, 'nation of origin' affects us all whether we like it or not.

In this chapter, I'll therefore highlight leading-edge and award-winning examples of national-branding campaigns, using these to illuminate a way forward for readers who may be about to embark on this type of activity, or who simply wish to remind themselves of the core principles.

According to a report from Superbrands, 'when we express a preference for French holidays, German cars or Italian opera,

When it comes to branding, 'nation of origin' affects us all whether we like it or not.

when we instinctively trust the Swedish government, comment on the ambition of the Japanese… admire the heritage of China and India, we are responding to brands in the same way as when we're shopping for clothing or food' (Anholt, nd). What has massively increased the emphasis of all this in recent years has been the incredible impact of globalization, which means that Country A has to compete with Countries B, C, D – and many more – for consumer or media attention and for the tourist or student or investor budget. In doing so, they're having to utilize exactly the same armoury of marketing communications tools as consumer brands.

In an 'always on' globalized and digital media environment, who we are and how we present ourselves to others has rarely mattered more. This connects directly to all things 'post truth' because every country naturally wishes to tell a good story about itself in public diplomacy terms. This leads immediately to the issue of 'soft power', a term coined back in the 1990s by Professor Joseph Nye to explain how modern states can use positive attraction and persuasion to achieve global influence. *Monocle* magazine describe it as: 'while military and economic muscle can yield the most dramatic change, a nation's soft power can achieve more worthwhile outcomes' (Monocle, 2017). (Their annual survey puts a spotlight on nations that use their gentler sides to gain influence.)

If you look at a range of surveys, you'll have noticed that a fairly small number of nations always seem to make the 'Top 10' in respected polls that measure global soft power. As the United Kingdom has led those lists numerous times, I often reference it as an ideal case history, and it'll be fascinating to track the impact of Brexit on the UK's standing in future polls, although this currently appears to be recovering after taking a downward turn following the referendum. The World Economic Forum assesses nations on six measures of reputation and influence :'Government, Culture, Education, Global Engagement, Enterprise, and Digital' (WEF, 2015), using data from Facebook on governments' online impact, and from ComRes, which runs opinion polls on international perceptions of countries.

From the point of view of governance, and enabling democracy, in Jamie Bartlett's excellent book *The People vs Tech* he put forward the notion that 'there are six key pillars that make this work: active citizens, a shared culture, free elections, stakeholder equality, competitive economy and civic freedom, and trust in authority'. The last of those points is that 'a sovereign authority that can enforce the people's will, but remains trustworthy and accountable to them' (Bartlett, 2018).

But there is also 'sharp power', of course. This term was invented by a US think-tank, the National Endowment for Democracy, whose aim is to support freedom around the world. They describe authoritarian regimes using sharp power abroad via leveraging 'authoritarian influence' in order to shape public opinion and perceptions in those countries in the way that they 'pierce, penetrate, or perforate the information and political environments. These regimes are not necessarily seeking to 'win hearts and minds', the common frame of reference for 'soft power' efforts, but they are surely seeking to influence their target audiences by manipulating or distorting the information that reaches them' (NED, 2017).

In our post-truth world, the inclination to smooth over 'an inconvenient history or an awkward present' into something more palatable for the modern day means that many national-branding initiatives often find themselves 'creating their own realities', to put it politely ... very politely. The past and the present also often clash when the 'governmental wishes' of national brands bump up against the 'transparent reality' of consumer brands. This is because nation branding is a concept often misunderstood by political leaders and used as a magic wand via which marketing techniques (effectively amounting to 'historical airbrushing') can be utilized to re-create the tarnished image of a nation through the prism of a political viewpoint.

Any marketer worth their salt can easily point this out to their political clients, so it's really interesting to see the same old mistakes being made around the world, shown via the resulting ineffective national branding campaigns. What the 'political clients' generally seem to forget is that any brand story (of any type) needs to engage the audience and communicate something genuinely interesting and motivating. It's about storytelling, the building of emotional bonds – not merely highlighting rational facts, or post-truth 'facts'.

The wrong history – and which truth?

Many of you reading this will know all about the perils of working on consumer brands that have clear links to a national brand. An easy way to illustrate this is via US ones, simply due to the number of successful US brands in global markets. However, what can really trip consumer brands up if they're closely aligned to the national brand is when 'major news' becomes intrinsically linked to brand image.

This is illustrated by a classic industry example. Just after Gulf War II, one of the biggest ad agencies in the world warned its clients that the war in Iraq had fuelled anti-Western feeling. In particular, it had sparked a surge of global hostility towards the United States for which their branded figureheads took the hit in terms of global consumers (temporarily for most, terminally for some) turning to alternative brand options.

As a result, the agency advised their clients they should not 'wrap their brands in the national flag'. Instead, they needed to emphasize their 'strong community roots'. Of course, some products are more exposed than others: as the *The Daily Telegraph* reported, 'while technological products such as IBM tend to be viewed as "politically neutral", brands such as Marlboro, Disney or Coca-Cola – once described as "the sublimated essence of all that America stands for" – are cultural icons irredeemably associated with the West' (Born, 2003).

This again links back to stereotyping – which is great when the stereotype is positive, but an absolute nightmare for marketers when the brand – or brand link – in question becomes tainted by association. The book *Nation Branding* highlights this issue because 'it is essential for countries to understand how they are seen by publics around the world; how their achievements and failures, their assets and their liabilities, their people and their products are reflected in their brand image, and that image reflects on brands linked to the nation concerned' (Dinnie, 2015).

One of myriad ways in which countries are viewed is in how 'technology-forward' they are. This was illustrated by Nicole Fall, Founder of Asian Consumer Intelligence, who, when I interviewed her, told me:

> When you're in a city like Singapore or Tokyo or Seoul, it's very easy to believe you are in one of the most developed places on the planet and you can see how technology is enabling everyday life. Regarding China, in places like Shanghai I do actually feel that the rest of the world is so far behind. As far as most places in Asia are

concerned, technology enables, technology is the solution, technology will provide the way forward, for instance when looking for solutions to the environmental issues we're seeing, there have to be solutions in technology.

But choosing the most relevant and attractive 'bit of the truth' that the country wishes to base its storytelling on is the key issue here. The question is 'whose truth?'

In the introduction to this book, I noted a range of famous philosophers who are naturally referenced whenever the subject of 'truth' is debated. However, in this instance I prefer to mention another philosopher obsessed with the truth, Gottfried Leibniz, who defined two logical types of truth in terms of two kinds of statement: 'the first is true (or false) within its own terms – the second is only true or false depending on facts outside it' (Braun, 2004).

So, in the context of this chapter, a tactical national-branding message may reflect a travel theme and say something like 'Saudi Arabia has huge deserts to explore' or 'Travelling around friendly Saudi Arabia is a relaxing experience for the family'. In the first example, the truth can be established by analysing the statement. (It's self-evidently true.) This kind of statement therefore became known as an analytic statement. In the second example, the statement requires us to consider further information – and philosophy refers to this type as a 'synthetic statement'. What Leibniz's work does is to force a distinction between these two different kinds of truth with a view to avoiding the trap of self-delusion – something that national brands in particular are prone to do in wildly overblown terms. This is a constant threat posed by brand managers, who often become blinded by their own vision of how things might be even when they may be working on fairly 'unemotional' brands, let alone national ones that are incredibly emotive.

This puts them right back in the frame when it comes to classic examples of post-truth communication. Furthermore,

Leibniz felt that 'necessary and eternal truths' were understood by reason, but 'truths of fact' were contingent and empirical. Consumers – being driven by emotion and experience – clearly fall into the latter definition.

A pity then, that a lot of advertising is still created around rational statements even when most consumer–brand relationships are based heavily in emotion. This is a subject discussed in great detail in a separate chapter, you'll be delighted to hear.

Branding nations – key approaches

Once you've decided to do so, how do you go about branding a country – or how do you take lessons from country branding and apply them to your consumer brand when positive 'national linkage' is what you're after?

Step forward the national-branding experts – the whole point of whom is to use classic consumer marketing to enhance national reputations on the international stage. I'm concentrating on two examples, showing how the 'Cool Britannia' and 'Britain is Great' campaigns were done from different perspectives and with differing results. I choose those examples not just because I'm English (honestly) but because they really are prime – albeit alternative – examples of national branding that benefited UK consumer brands enormously. The first of these examples was a widely reported 'cultural moment' captured and reframed by a political think-tank – and then widely reported again and widely reinterpreted; the second was a national-branding initiative formally organized and promoted on a global scale by government.

The book *Diplomacy in a Globalizing World* (Kerr, 2013) describes the branding of a nation-state and the successful transference of this image to its exports as being 'just as important as what they actually produce and sell' – also referred to as 'country of origin effect'. As already mentioned, the overall aim is to leverage the national brand image, as the reputation of a nation can massively influence its success in a wide range of areas, from cultural attractions such as music, theatre and the arts to the influence of its political leaders.

Key implications of a positive national brand image can be demonstrated by the resulting magnetic effects of pulling in holidaymakers, financial investors and international students, and of attracting the type of skilled workforce required for future-proofing modern economies.

What is required in a marketing context is an ongoing series of engaging, interactive and informative communication that is 'evidence based'. This needs to motivate the viewer/reader/listener and lead to an enhanced image of the country concerned. Sounds spectacularly obvious, doesn't it? Now try to think of several great examples.

A country should concentrate on what it does and what it makes, rather than obsess about what it says or how it looks.

It's in those 'national brand stories' where we, of course, see post-truth rear its head in these globally turbulent times, as nation branding grows in importance and influence. But when the national brand in question finds itself portrayed in a bad light, normally (fairly obviously) for reasons of either domestic issues or foreign policy, then things become a little more difficult when it comes to 'honestly' shaping imaginations from the point of view of media management, and in particular 24/7 social media.

So what's the secret? One of the world's most famous national-branding experts, Simon Anholt, had this to say when interviewed about the role of image and identity from a national brand perspective: 'the message is clear: if a country is serious about enhancing its international image, it should concentrate on what it does and what it makes, rather than obsess about what it says or how it looks. There are no short cuts'. He summarized this process as 'strategy, substance, and symbolic actions' (Anholt, 2010).

Something that's increasingly being seen here is the deliberate muddying of the water with irrelevant stories being seeded into media streams and used as deliberate distraction techniques to blur news and national brand narratives. By the way, I deal with the issues of distraction techniques and fake news in the chapter devoted to those areas.

Let's look at some examples of best-practice in the world of national branding.

Cool Britannia: linking with culture

I sat in a think-tank meeting a while ago, just over the road from House of Commons in London, surrounded by a usual mixture of political journalists and policy wonks that you get at these events – plus hangers-on like me. I was there to hear about the latest insights from Demos, an independent cross-party think-tank who were launching a key edition of their quarterly journal of political and social ideas. 'Post-truth' was mentioned time and time again at the meeting, but as that edition of their journal marked the 20th anniversary of the 'Cool Britannia' era, against the backdrop of Britain's decision to leave the European Union, it seemed like a good moment to return to the questions of how politics and culture collide, and how when a recognizable collective experience is clearly shaping and reflecting the public zeitgeist, it's time to act …

'Move it along, Granddad, you're getting in the way of The Scene! The London Scene, that is! From Soho to Notting Hill, from Camberwell to Camden Town, the capital city of Dear Old Blighty pulses anew with the good vibrations of an epic-scale youthquake!' (Kamp, 1997). I'm quoting from *Vanity Fair* magazine, which published a famous and highly influential issue that loudly proclaimed 'London Swings Again!' The cover showed Manchester uber-lad Liam Gallagher and blonde bombshell Patsy Kensit lying together in the ultimate British bed, complete with Union Jack duvet and pillows. That issue had a 'How London Got Its Groove Back' report featuring personalities du jour Damien Hirst, the Spice Girls, Terence Conran and Tony Blair.

A couple of months later, New Labour (the political party Tony Blair led, for anyone unaware) won a national election landslide. This was swiftly followed by a desire to 'Rebrand Britain', which, in possibly the least cool thing ever, involved a government 'Committee for Cool' called Panel 2000, set up to advise them on, well, you can guess.

The Cool Britannia 'cultural moment' seems suspended in time now. Luck played its part, of course; the coming together of a multi-industry creative explosion was set in a city that was (perhaps for the last time) affordable for young people to live, work and socialize in. More than that – it was all set to a soundtrack that was uniquely British and summed up the moment: Britpop. (This rebranding effort employed an age-old marketing trick of leveraging surprise. People around the world thought they knew Britain (basically 'dull old Britain'), and Cool Britannia was an attempt to prove them wrong and to completely reframe the 'national brand debate'.) For a while it worked brilliantly.

Pretty quickly, however, Britpop's early sense of freedom and 'anything goes' was replaced by an obsession with wildly conspicuous consumption. This is where the brand managers and advertising agencies got really excited because here was a cultural moment that had branding at its very core. Cue endless campaigns by brands mirroring the cultural mood of the day, with many of them plastered in Union Jacks, while (alongside a music industry gone berserk in its attempts to sign any group of young men who could hold a guitar and look at a camera) the worlds of fashion, art and film fell over themselves to be involved.

The most memorable image that sums up that moment for many people is of the famous Downing Street reception held a couple of months after New Labour gained power. According to *The Guardian*, it was intended as 'a celebration of a modern, outward-facing Britain with a new kind of industry, and a new kind of workforce', where new Prime Minister Tony Blair was photographed with Noel Gallagher of Oasis. 'We saw it as a chance to redefine what the UK's economic future would be about', recalled a government special adviser on culture (Campbell, 2017).

I digress – back to the Demos evening, and according to Philip Collins (who was supposed to be chairing the session, but had to go off to interview President Macron, as you do), 'culture exerts a seductive appeal to politicians. The company of the stars of popular music, television, theatre and film seem to confer, strangely enough, not radicalism but respectability. For a political movement, it seems like a vindication and an assurance that it really is new, cool and of the moment' (Collins, 2017).

Take a look at that famous shot of Blair grinning like a Cheshire cat and Noel Gallagher getting stuck into the free champagne at No 10 (only a short time before he could afford to buy a vineyard), and the danger of that approach becomes self-evident. Nothing dates faster than fashion. Blair looks like a used-car salesman and Noel Gallagher is wearing a really, really horrible shirt. Seen from today, and if you didn't recognize the characters or know the cultural significance of the photo, it might strike you as portraying a couple of 'new relatives' meeting for the first time at a slightly improbable wedding.

Fast-forward to the present and, in the *New Statesman* magazine, John Harris asked where it all went wrong, and if the patriotism and triumphalism of Cool Britannia sowed the seeds of Brexit. As he said in his excellent article, 'just as Bill Clinton had framed his challenge to George Bush Sr in terms of a watershed generational shift, so Blair portrayed New Labour (the British political party) as the epitome of everything fresh and new, fully in tune with a popular culture that was suddenly brimming with infectious confidence' (Harris, 2017).

As London got hip and self-reverential British music became the latest thing, Blair managed also to fashion himself a self-reverential 'lead-singer' role in what you might call the cultural festival of 'Cool Britannia' that captured that era. (I have to say, from the stark realities of today, how innocent and very far away those days now seem.)

Storytelling goes for gold

Why does all this stuff about bands and parties from another era matter for brands today? Because in the present, a culture and society that is awkward and troubled, and faced with growing challenges, is not one with which brands are overly keen to associate themselves. So we have to look backwards again for an example of a time when the stars aligned, and national branding could once again rear its head. In a nice way ...

For as I had to point out at the Demos event, the most recent cultural high-water mark for 'Britishness' wasn't actually 'Cool Britannia' (a hugely powerful cultural moment though it was), but instead something that happened years later. The Cool Britannia party was always destined to be a single point in time, as it was so closely aligned to a sound (Britpop) that was incredibly specific – if you look at the key bands most closely associated with it. (Elastica and Pulp were the sharpest of the lot and still sound great.) A decade (and a bit) down the line, and the moment that most contemporary culture-watchers tend to agree on as being 'Peak-Brit' was the London Olympics.

I have to say that 'Britishness' was of even more interest to me during the Games, as I spent a long time researching the subject for a number of brands. More specifically, I was asked to look into the cultural and social foundations of the Britishness of their brand and strategy for the biggest sponsor of the London Olympics.

A key issue for an extraordinary number of brands at that point was how to interpret their links with the national brand in a way that felt appropriate for the consumer brand. Most effectively did nothing else apart from filling their TV ads with, or covering their packaging and branding efforts in, the national flag. This was all possibly (or probably) due to a lack of clarity about what the national brand meant, ie having something clear that consumer brands could utilize in a way that felt authentic, relevant and motivating.

In terms of motivation, when I interviewed James Harkin (then head of talks at the ICA, and who later achieved acclaim for his amazing journalism covering the Syrian conflict), he told me: 'what the country needs is a positive vision, clearly communicated'. Telling 'positive visions ... clearly communicated' is something that the advertising industry has been (fairly obviously) obsessed with for years.

So when the curtain rose on the London Olympics, what we saw in the opening ceremony rather underlined many of the points made by branding experts at the time (with myself at the bottom of that pile) about some of the most positive (and internationally welcomed) elements of 'Brand Britain' that we could and should highlight. The genius work of Danny Boyle was 'a celebration of Britain from our days as a green and pleasant land. The mood of the nation that it was said to capture was pioneering, inclusive, influential, multicultural, creative, welcoming; looking not back to days of Empire and war but forward to connectivity, care for all and youthful optimism' (Tyers, 2016).

The beauty of this for brands was that the sheer breadth of cultural, social, geographical and historical issues covered meant that those with a genuine brand story to tell were given renewed impetus to reference this staggeringly powerful national story. The extraordinary variety of national heritage and cultural issues referenced meant that every brand strategist watching could find a creative angle to link with any British brand for which they might be responsible. The resulting brand stories were thus given a fresh breath of life, and a massive dose of authentic narrative was delivered up for the modern day. As reported by *Forbes* magazine, this was, as ever, the case at their annual rosé-wine-fuelled extravaganza, the Cannes Lions Festival, where 'storytelling was a central theme, featuring in the title of at least eight main stage seminar presentations'(Sachs, 2014).

Of course, opening ceremonies are always judged against the ones that they follow, and China's stunning efforts at the previous Olympics had set an incredibly high standard. But as *The Guardian* reported, 'Although Boyle said that he consciously avoided trying to compete with the scale of Beijing, there were moments of jaw-dropping wit and invention' (Gibson, 2012).

From superhumans to stereotypes

Brands were all over the Olympics, as they always are, with marketing initiatives naturally planned and created far in advance. A famous British Airways commercial showed a plane taxiing through London, with a soundtrack featuring The Clash's epic 'London Calling'. Channel 4's 'Meet the Superhumans' was a truly incredible piece of communication, enabling positive change when the Paralympic Games presented themselves as the perfect platform to challenge established views. Stella McCartney designed the Team GB kit for Adidas, and also put on an Olympics party where The Stone Roses played.

This was all about 'positive branding', ie brands proactively involving themselves in a beneficial manner for consumer and company alike. (By the way, elsewhere in this book, I delve deeply into the issue of brand purpose and community branding.) Finally, here was an event that bought us a truly amazing moment: Jessica Ennis and Mo Farah proudly holding their Union Jacks aloft, when 'Britishness' seemed to crystallize and clarify for a short period around a shared set of values and opinions that were almost entirely positive. Happy days. (Similar intentions, of course, would have related to 'Brand Russia' and the outstanding 2018 World Cup that they hosted.)

Still, back to stereotypes as the easiest way of linking the national brand to consumer brands, and some things never change.

A couple of years later, *Marketing Magazine* reported that 'national stereotyping was alive and well in the campaigns of official Euro 2016 sponsors, with the English, French and Germans getting the caricature treatment by Mars, Carlsberg and Lufthansa respectively' (Gwynn, 2016).

These featured 'If Carlsberg did revolutions' with the appropriate line 'Let them drink beer', while a film about an English fan on a Lufthansa flight saw him enduring a mixture of lederhosen and cuckoo clocks. Meanwhile, 'Super Harry Kane' was seen swimming the Channel, along with other Premiership players, in an ad for Mars, before he emerged on a French beach.

Britain is ... GREAT

The national-branding research that I mentioned conducting earlier also referenced the Commission for Racial Equality, who commissioned two parallel, wide-ranging surveys: one of white Britons, the other of non-white Britons, via YouGov. They included a simple open-ended question: 'what does Britishness mean to you?' The responses revealed something highly significant. Broadly speaking, most answers fell into one of two categories: Geography/tradition (eg place of birth, monarchy, pride in British achievements) or Values (eg democracy, fairness, free speech).

That was, perhaps, predictable. What was striking was that by two to one, white respondents opted for geography/tradition. Non-white respondents, also by two to one, opted for values. (Years later, these issues would be referenced in a highly influential book *The Road to Somewhere* by David Goodhart, which I also mentioned in a previous chapter).

So, with 'brand storytelling' being key, after that Britishness research project I was asked to share my thoughts from both that project and a mass of other social/cultural research among various advertising, PR and media agencies. I therefore found myself taking planners and strategists through a range of issues that summed up, in my eyes at least, a contemporary view of Britishness seen through the eyes of a wide range of experts and 'ordinary people' from various urban, suburban, rural and 'bits in the corner' parts of the United Kingdom. It was therefore brilliant to see, a while afterwards, some superb work created for the government – the 'GREAT' Britain campaign – led by the Department for Culture, Media and Sport.

I went to see a person at the centre of that project, Alex West. As he said:

> The Great Britain campaign captured the best of all that is familiar about the UK but also what's new and surprising about the country. We're global leaders in the creative industries like music, fashion, design and film. We can offer visitors unforgettable experiences, breath-taking landscapes and iconic attractions. Our aim was to encourage people around the world to think and feel differently about the UK – what we needed to do was create a campaign, showcasing the best of what GB offers.

The government's most ambitious international promotional campaign ever, it united the efforts of the public and private sectors to generate jobs and growth for Britain. As the prime minister said in a speech in New York City, 'This campaign is simple. There are so many great things about Britain and we want to send out the message loud and proud that this is a great place to do business, to invest, to study and to visit' (Gov.uk, 2011). (Later, in the run-up to the Olympics, the government, backed by the Foreign Office and UK Trade and Investment, hosted a global investment conference in London on the eve of the Olympics and set up a 'British business embassy' showcasing the country's innovations, creativity and entrepreneurship.)

The multifaceted and creatively flexible campaign has so far highlighted concepts such as 'Culture is Great … Food is Great … Creativity is Great … Bond is Great … Shakespeare is Great … Entrepreneurs are Great … Innovation is Great … Exporting is

Great ... Love is Great ... Music is Great ... Education is Great ... Heritage is Great ..., etc'. Each of those topics was backed up with an impressive depth of information on their specific links with 'Brand GB'. In terms of financial returns, at the time of writing, the campaign had already secured confirmed economic returns of nearly £3 billion for the United Kingdom.

Authentic branding

The annual 'Best of Britannia' (BoB) event is a celebration of British manufacturing founded by Antony Wallis. I set up the trend talks at the event, years ago when it started, and something that always stands out to me is the amazing range of exhibitors. Britain has an astonishing range and depth of high-quality artisans and craftspeople at the core of our manufacturing industry, and many have an incredibly interesting 'brand story' based on a core truth. Not a 'post-truth' but a 100 per cent transparent honest story, based on fact – and vitally on a core 'why' as espoused by Simon Sinek, who famously talked about how 'Very few people or companies clearly articulate why they do what they do. We say what we do, we sometimes say how we do it; but we rarely say why we do what we do' (Sinek, 2011).

This issue of cutting right through to the 'why' is a really powerful example of pushing any notion of post-truth aside in the quest for an authentic core truth, to then be told in a motivating and engaging manner, be it linking national brands to consumer brands or otherwise. Perhaps that type of leveraging a 'cultural moment' has passed us by in Britain for the moment, particularly in an era when defining a contemporary view of 'Britishness' is seen as a highly divisive topic.

Brexit, of course, is a massive issue, and one that's causing immense problems for those on either side of, or indeed anywhere near, the argument. What does all this mean for the countless brands that trade on their British heritage and use it as a key branding and marketing tool, and want to do so in an authentic manner? A report by marketing agency The Partners claims that 'British brands are experiencing an identity crisis' in the wake of Brexit. It argues that the referendum result is a 'compounding factor' within a longer-term trend that has led many brands to underplay their Britishness (The Partners, 2017).

However, there's no reason why this branding approach shouldn't be utilized by other countries seeking to clarify and promote their national brands around vibrant issues, particularly when seen against the youth demographics in (for instance) many Asian, African and Middle-Eastern countries. Even more so when one looks to recent reports by the World Economic Forum when they announced that the 'Top Ten most dynamic cities in the world' include Bangalore, Ho Chi Minh City, Silicon Valley, Shanghai, Hyderabad, Hanoi and Nairobi. As the WEF report mentioned, 'A city's capacity to embrace rapid change determines its ability to compete in the world – today and in the future. The overriding factors that characterize the world's most dynamic cities are technology and innovation – and cities that best absorb, adapt and leverage these drivers come out on top' (Kelly, 2017).

The impact of cities on the regions around them is naturally of huge importance. Carsten Beck, of the Copenhagen Institute for Futures Studies, talks about that: 'while some global Danish brands link to the national brand because we are high in the national-branding charts for happiness and welfare etc, there's also a trend for localism'. He points out that in Denmark (a leading country in soft power terms), 'there's a lot of attention given to spreading creative activities in Copenhagen out into the countryside. Localism is very high on the agenda here'. When it comes to the United States and the US national brand, he says 'it has obviously declined, if you look at the news stream from the States it's pretty much all negative: it's the shootings, it's the Trump administration, it's the trade war, that's it basically'.

Future brand stories

In an era when we're feeling more divided, do the issues of nationalism and identity politics really link to a consumer brand that's linking to a national brand? I believe this is clearly the situation in which brands find themselves. As I've highlighted, any cultural-marketing campaign must be judged against geopolitical realities – and at the moment country brands are set in a context that includes nationalistic and protectionist 'walls not bridges' going up around the world, alongside huge demographic change.

But, and with reference to how quickly things can change, it's interesting to note the results of the Anholt–GfK Nation Brand Index study, which reports that 'while Germany had reclaimed top "nation brand" the USA had dropped to sixth place'. The report went on to say that 'the USA's fall in the "Governance" category suggests that we are witnessing a "Trump effect", following President Trump's focused political message of "America First"'. (Their report also noted that France was second, the UK third

The soft power of Europe is recovering, and while that of North America reduces, the influence of Asia grows.

'having regained the ground lost back in 2016', while Canada and Japan were fourth equal (Anholt-GfK, 2017).)

This stands slightly at odds with the latest 'Soft Power League Table' announced by the World Economic Forum in a study conducted by Portland, which saw France gain top spot followed by the United Kingdom, United States, Germany and Canada. WEF coverage of the findings pointed to issues such as France's huge diplomatic network, its cultural hinterland. Noting the decline in the ratings of the United States, they suggested that this could be due to the 'America first' policy of Donald Trump, which has not gained the United States many favours internationally, irritating old allies and causing global diplomatic problems.

This all comes at a time when, as is frequently reported, the soft power of Europe is recovering, and while that of North America reduces, the influence of Asia grows. This is clearly illustrated by China, as reflected by the study's polling data, which 'suggests a more favourable view of its role on the world stage'. The report also notes the way that power is shifting 'away from traditional institutions, such as governments, and into cities, multinationals and even individuals. This is in large part due to the digital revolution, which has eroded national borders, creating challenges and opportunities in equal measure' (Gray, 2017).

It's worth repeating a note of caution here: politicians, marketers and agencies have to be careful when attempting to assimilate cultural, social and historical stories as a way of creating national-branding campaigns. Cheapening a national brand by being seen to be twisting the truth can have disastrous knock-on effects, for both the image of that national brand itself and also for the many consumer brands that are seen to link to that national brand via their 'nation of origin' links.

An everyday example of the power and relevance of the way national brand impacts consumer brands, regarding national reputation and therefore product provenance was pointed out by Nicole Fall, Founder of Asian Consumer Intelligence, who told me:

> Provenance is super important in a lot of markets in Asia. A great example is Vietnam, where quite frankly if a product is made in certain other Asian countries, people are suspicious. We're even seeing cultural shifts happening where people are hesitant to eat street food, because they are suspicious about where the oil is from; has it been reused, are some of the ingredients from farms elsewhere that don't have quality assurances? So for sure, provenance is a massive driving factor. For example, people will trust a beauty brand if it says Made in Japan, Made in Singapore, Made in France etc. The provenance of where something is from is a huge driver and it shapes a lot of consumer behaviour in this part of the

world. It's important for national brands to tell clear stories. Japan is widely reputable, whether it's Japanese food or beauty, it's generally highly regarded across APAC (Asia Pacific). So, if it says Made in Japan there is a perception of higher levels of safety and standards around it, and it is perceived as being of better quality.

The trust issue here is reflected in the latest global 'Trust Barometer' report from Edelman, which notes as part of its 'Polarization of Trust' findings about institutional trust that, for instance, while China and the UAE are the countries which have seen the most extreme 'trust gains', those at the bottom of that list are the United States followed by Italy.

Remember, a nation brand is the sum of our perceptions of a country across key areas of national competence: Tourism, Culture, People, Investment, Immigration, Exports and Governance (VisitBritain, 2017). And in telling stories about all of these ... truth matters.

I'll finish by quoting Jay Wang, Director of the USC Center for Public Diplomacy (and author of *Shaping China's Global Imagination*), who explored the nation branding concept through the instructive case of the Shanghai World Expo. For him, an absolutely key issue in the pursuit of soft power via marketing communications is 'Storytelling as the Foundation'. This means that shaping perception through branding 'is less about making good arguments than sharing a compelling and relatable story about a nation's image' (Wang, 2013).

Endeavours to brand a nation are a hugely delicate task that requires deep knowledge of a place and its people. Telling an impactful, engaging and motivating story is key for those undertaking nation brand exercises, just as it is for consumer brands. But doing so in a way that has an authentic truth at the heart of that story is absolutely vital from the perspective of national-branding campaigns – because who wants a national brand story built on lies?

CHAPTER EIGHT

The Marketing of Culture

This chapter illustrates how brands often seek added authenticity by leveraging culture, with many doing so incredibly badly, and why there are clear lessons for businesses in a post-truth environment.

This is becoming ever more important, as 'brand behaviour' on a cultural and social level is growing in importance from the vital perspective of brand adoption or rejection, when a distrusting world demands ever-higher standards.

Doing this for the 'right reasons', ie when the brand in question links their 'marketing of culture' from a joint value creation perspective, essentially giving something back and adding to – rather than hijacking – the culture or cultural event in question, can mean everyone wins. But when it's done for the wrong reasons, the results are usually ineffective (or worse) for the brand and, more seriously for the rest of us, can negatively impact the culture involved.

To quote Baudrillard: 'We live in a world where there is more and more information, and less and less meaning ... where we think that information produces meaning, the opposite occurs' (Baudrillard, 1994). Or to put it in a different way – and in the context of this book – we live in a world where there's more and more branding of culture, but less and less genuine cultural connection; where we think that most cultural marketing produces connections between people and brands, the opposite occurs.

The marketing of culture and the culture of marketing

Public Enemy No 1, when it comes to an area most traditionally linked to the 'marketing of culture', is the specialist one of youth marketing. Unfortunately for brands, it's one in which virtually everyone interested in the culture involved seems to either ignore or detest most of the marketing activity that results.

We live in a world where there's more and more branding of culture, but less and less genuine cultural connection.

Advertising agencies have always been obsessed with chasing two things: authenticity and cool. It's attempting to wrap those up and then selling 'culture + brand' back to us that gets companies into such trouble. Any fan of *Mad Men* will remember the famous advertising leveraging of counterculture, as done via the 'Buy the World a Coke' campaign, just as fans of the film *Withnail & I* will remember Danny the Dealer complaining about 'the sale of hippy wigs at Woolworths' (Robinson, 1998).

I discussed this issue with Martin Raymond, co-founder of The Future Laboratory, who told me:

> Authentic in itself should mean something real and essential, that isn't open to equivocation or debate. But in fact what happened is that authenticity became about beards and hipsters. So, because of that, a lot of people who would be nominally described as hipsters disengaged with, and pushed back against, brands that were

claiming authenticity, on the grounds that authenticity had become fake and questioned and suspect.

A typical example of this heavy-handed approach of linking brands to culture was a campaign produced for an international breakfast cereal. With the big budgets that come from working on a major brand, this particular campaign gave us the heart-warming story of how a Northern Soul obsessive, who had to give up clubbing when he had kids, ended up going back to his favourite all-nighter accompanied by his son when he was old enough. Even more wonderfully, in the wonderful world of advertising, their bonding over a shared love of cereal made the whole thing possible owing to the product's energy-providing ingredients.

Now I don't know how much effort the creative team put into researching the brilliant and dare I say it 'authentic and cool' world of Northern Soul (and before anyone at the agency gives me a hard time, yes I understand that the strategy was based on 'looking after your heart'), but one thing that everyone wasn't taking to get them through all-nighters at clubs such as the Golden Torch or the Twisted Wheel was cereal. As a Northern Soul obsessive blogged on the Soul Source forum, 'Someone should tell them that the wide eyes and fast chewing wasn't excitement at being offered breakfast …'.

To state the obvious, music has an amazingly deep emotional resonance. But when it gets used to advertise culturally irrelevant brands, it can embed those in our minds alongside 'chosen' memories linked with that track. This constitutes what you might call 'personal collateral damage'. Basically put – stuff in which we have zero interest weaves its way into our minds.

This may appear fatuous, but on a wider industry level the issue of 'memory theft' annoys an incredible number of people, and researchers have been reporting it for years, with respondents in focus groups often complaining about 'Track X that used to remind me of a happy time now reminds me of a washing powder' and so on. In marketing terms, the results may mean a high ad-recall score, but unfortunately the emotions linked to that recall are seriously negative. In this context, the culture of marketing has the opposite effect of the Midas touch when it comes to the marketing of culture.

In a post-truth environment where authenticity is all-important, the increasingly disconnected world of advertising, which in this context simply links brands with 'any' music culture without pausing to reflect on the wider impact, irritates more and more of us.

Fortunately, you might say, it's getting harder for adland to link with culture, particularly on a large-scale basis, because the speed at which the cycle of cultural production and societal adoption now moves, especially when it comes to fashion and music, is so much faster than in the early days of Northern Soul. In those days, culture essentially built up slowly, steadily moving through the old cycles from opinion formers, early adopters to mainstream consumers. Those young consumers were themselves far more easily identified via their strong allegiance to, and shows of, 'youth tribalism'.

A key issue, of course, is that teenagers today are, according to *The Guardian*, 'more interested in constructing an identity online than they are in solely making an outward show of their allegiances and interests. It's a lot easier to adopt personas online that cost you absolutely nothing apart from demonstrating certain types of arcane knowledge, that the ethnographer Sarah Thornton termed "subcultural capital"' (Petridis, 2014). (But just to put in a caveat here, I'm fully aware that there's plenty of 'subcultural capital' going on in the world of brands such as Palace, Patta, Thames and Supreme.) Unfortunately for adland, this is essentially the opposite of what they need in order to copy that culture and then attempt to sell it back to us via major advertising campaigns.

Northern Soul had an obsession with the obscure and the hidden built into its DNA. Massive and yet seemingly hidden, for a long time it was referred to as the only remaining youth subculture yet to have been exploited. The last thing it needed was adland trying to elbow its way onto the dancefloor and make friends with everyone.

Because, as nobody ever said at an all-nighter in the Wigan Casino, 'Shredded Wheat – Keep the Faith'.

#Adfail

Another example of the pitfalls of attempting to link with 'real' culture was illustrated by one of the all-time advertising #fails, when a brand that really should have known better aimed to gain kudos by linking itself to the culture of protest. Step forward Pepsi and Kendall Jenner with their disastrous activism-themed commercial. Just to remind you in case you've somehow forgotten, in the ad, which drags on from one appalling moment to the next, Jenner sticks it to The Man by walking off a photoshoot to join in with a load of typecast Millennials engaged in a suspiciously bland protest.

She also got a nod from a guy in the street, a male model type with a goatee beard who'd been playing a cello (while enjoying a can of Pepsi) before he also joined in the demo. The ad featured loads of other annoying people, variously enjoying an al fresco lunch on the street where the protest was taking place (as you do) along with the world's most irritating band. I actually just watched the ad again, and have to say that I thoroughly enjoyed it, as it was so jaw-droppingly terrible.

Kendall naturally gets on incredibly well with the equally incredibly friendly protesters, who are carrying banners saying stuff like 'Join the Conversation' (which no doubt sounded great when discussed in the company boardroom, before being signed off by committee). I don't know about you, but that's unlike any march that I've ever seen. Anyway, this being adland, she finally manages to make everyone get along by handing a policeman a can of Pepsi. Job done. Or perhaps not.

The intended brand communication, according to *Wired* magazine, was crystal clear: 'all those Women's Marches, Black Lives Matter protests and demonstrations outside Trump Tower would be much more effervescent, and effective, if someone had just bought some soda' (Watercutter, 2017).

To put it mildly, it seemed that everyone in the world who didn't work for Pepsi disagreed. Twitter and Facebook nearly imploded with people putting up pastiches of the ad, alongside a torrent of abuse. In other chapters I talk about how divisive the internet is getting, but this was a rare occasion on which seemingly the entire planet agreed on something. And that thing was that this was an #adpocalypse.

Pepsi certainly achieved the first rule of advertising, ie being noticed, but seemed to forget about other fundamental issues, such as relevance. Let's not even go there when it comes to likeability. Having said that, brand owners love an ad with strong recall, the only problem in this case being that no one who saw it is ever likely to forget that epic fail.

The issue that seemed to mystify just about everyone on the planet was how the ad was made in the first place. Jill Avery, a senior lecturer at Harvard Business School, explained: 'By brand managers not doing their cultural homework – relying upon surface-level understandings of the cultural phenomenon featuring in their marketing communications and not understanding the deep well of emotions, identity politics, and ideologies that their ads trigger' (Pinsker, 2017). It just shows the problems that can arise when a brand's communication, particularly when attempting to link with culturally sensitive issues, is done in an inauthentic way, and points to many people's problem with the whole issue of 'Brand Purpose' done badly.

What mystified a lot of people in the industry was how Pepsi, which has linked with youth culture for many years, got this so catastrophically wrong. In this instance, apparently utilizing that adland equation to making 'youth' ads, ie celebrity + youth + a standard music video approach, had the opposite of the effect intended. According to Aimee Drolet Rossi, a professor of marketing at UCLA's School of Management, 'It just seems like they were going through the motions' (Pinsker, 2017).

That point about 'going through the motions' was given a twist that delighted an ad industry (which was initially/naturally blamed for the fiasco) when it was soon revealed that the ad was produced not by an outside agency, but rather by Pepsi's in-house Creators League studio. High-fives no doubt broke out in ad agency boardrooms across the world, soon followed by every New Business Exec in the business contacting Pepsi to offer their agencies' services....

Away from adland, *The Atlantic* also quoted how the United States' favourite late-night TV host Jimmy Kimmel told his audience that 'the fact that this somehow made it through – I can't imagine how many meetings, edits and pitches, and then got the thumbs-up from who-knows-how-many people is absolutely mind-boggling.' According to NBC News, 'Jimmy Fallon seamlessly linked it with news about North Korea. 'I saw that today North Korea conducted a missile test, which escalated tensions in the region', he began. 'But don't worry. Things settled down when Kendall Jenner stepped in and handed them a Pepsi' (Variety, 2017). *The Hollywood Reporter* noted remarks from Late Show host Stephen Colbert, who said: 'So far we don't know what has caused all of America's hot extras to take to the streets. But I'm guessing it's a protest for Attractive Lives Matter'. He also had a problem with the 'Join the Conversation' banners I mentioned earlier that were being waved. As the article also noted, he said: 'That's the most corporate thing of all time. They might as well hold up a sign saying "We are all the core demographic"' (Rahman, 2017).

Pepsi pulled the ad in what can only be politely described as a 'global meltdown' shortly after its release, claiming it 'missed the mark', which is one of the great understatements of all time. A corporate spokesperson said it 'did not intend to make light of any serious issue' with the ad and apologized to Jenner for 'putting her in this position'. In a trailer for a series of Keeping Up with The Kardashians that followed the campaign, *The Drum* noted that Jenner talked about the commercial and said 'it feels like my life is over' (West, 2017).

A completely different example that illustrates where brands have aimed to embed themselves with a cultural issue involves the fashion industry, which quite frankly does this on a fairly non-stop basis. A famous case is Tommy Hilfiger, a brand basically created around its links with music.

But in this case, the marketing of culture seriously backfired. As *Rolling Stone* magazine notes, in the early years of the company 'Hilfiger sponsored music tours – making his one of the first fashion brands to do so. It was ties with hip-hop that cemented his status. Rap at the time was seen as somewhat counterculture – but Tommy thought it was hip' (Indvik, 2017).

Hilfiger fell out with the hip-hop world, dogged by a rumour that he had told Oprah Winfrey he didn't want black people wearing his clothes. The rumour spread, and because of it the community soon turned their backs on the brand. But in his autobiography Hilfiger says he never said those words, and the only mistake he made was not denying it sooner. 'I thought it was nonsense', Hilfiger writes in the book. 'I'd never been on Oprah. If I just ignore this I figured, it'll go away. The opposite happened ...' (Hilfiger, 2016).

The issue here is that if you're to link with culture, you have to treat that culture with respect and be seen to be actively engaged in supporting it. Fortunately for them, everything in fashion is cyclical and – many seasons on – the brand is back in fashion, as demonstrated by their links with Gigi Hadid via the 'Tommy X Gigi' New York Fashion Week activity.

Cultural icons and Parisian chic

What about authentic cultural looks and icons that endure, and what are the key lessons that brands can note from an ultimate example of cultural branding? A classic case is illustrated by the way in which women the world over show not the slightest sign of losing their obsession with the supposedly timeless style that is 'Parisian chic'.

To understand the extent to which this is such a readily identifiable and yet endlessly argued-over issue, it's necessary to go back to the person who 'laid down the tablets' – the grandmother of Parisian chic, Coco Chanel. For an expert view on her, I went to see an old friend, Nilgin Yusuf, Creative Director of the London College of Fashion, where I've enjoyed being a visiting lecturer for years. She told me:

> Coco's whole philosophy was about this idea that women should be independent and free in what they wear, 'in charge of their own bodies and not trussed up like dolls just for men's pleasure'. A lot of her ideas were about borrowing things from her boyfriends' wardrobes and those sorts of things have become part of the language. Fast-forward to today, and there's a direct link between her and the rise of 'relaxed style', which goes in and out of fashion on a rolling basis. She also believed in simple pieces that don't need to be invented every six months, and so in many ways she was actually very anti-fashion, perhaps the original promoter of 'slow fashion' in that you invest in key pieces that work with you, your body and your lifestyle and they last you ideally for a lifetime.

So, Chanel laid that down and established a whole modern, easy 'style language' that is ageless and works across all boundaries, more to do with an attitude and a mentality rather than being a certain type of person.

A perfect example of this is gloriously imperfect: when you think of the famous art-house film *Breathless* by Jean-Luc Godard, starring the American Jean Seberg, who in an iconic scene sold the *New-York Tribune* in her branded t-shirt, which totally embodied the idea of Parisian chic. I explored this idea with Nilgin Yusuf, who talked about 'the idea of not very much make up (or no make up), a very natural beauty with short hair, an easy look and being very comfortable in her own body. This idea of being comfortable in your own body and being completely relaxed with yourself; it's very, very attractive and French women are very sexy because of that.'

As Nilgin went on to tell me:

the jeans, denims, sailor pants – that was a Chanel thing, from yachting with her rich friends in the South of France; so she adopted the stripy top, the sailor's trousers and that's become an absolute classic. The men's shirts reinterpreted, repurposed for a woman's body. There's a nonchalance to Parisian style which I think is really important. You have to look like it's all been thrown on together and you've just picked stuff up and you really haven't spent that much time thinking about how you look, it all works effortlessly. Comfortable too, with your clothes enabling you to get on without having to think too hard about them. Sometimes when you see images on Facehunter, all these people dressed up in pantomime clothes because they want to make an image, to be seen, to be noticed, to be in the spotlight ... Parisian chic is the opposite of that, it's just 'ignore me if you want to, it's fine, I'm just getting on with my life' and that's really attractive. Not caring is an attractive trait!

After chatting with Nilgin, I also went back to see several other experts about this, following a study I'd done into the subject. One of them was the fascinating Navaz Batliwalla, author of *The Modern Gentlewoman*. So I asked about her views:

For me Parisian style is about the everyday girl, the more accessible market, especially led by the Instagram influencers; or the Caroline de Maigret kind of person, who is very cool and wears her Sandro shirt, her APC jeans and Ray Ban sunglasses and looks really effortless. What's she's wearing could be from Isobel Marant or APC or Zara or mixed up together. When I picture the chic Parisian woman I picture someone who is really confident and comfortable in herself – you never feel that they are wearing a look or trying to get the look or copy someone. There are people who inspire them and they admire in terms of style icons, but you never feel that they'll copy them head to toe. There's also lots of dualities, so mixing old and new; you wouldn't necessarily go out and buy a whole new outfit. Whereas the idea of French Chic in the '80s maybe '90s was the Chanel suit, high-heel stilettos and red lipstick and everything very 'done'. I see that as very old fashioned and mature now.

'Parisian chic' today means contradictory things; it's all about attitude and combining the classic with a 'twist' to make your own look. So, a combination of the old and new, the impact of jarring a 'quality classic basic' with one's own confident 'individual edge' is what makes this work today; and it's about not appearing to be trying too hard.

The issue for brands here is that it moves this forward to the present, as opposed to the look that was prevalent a few years ago when more and more brands began to pile into the area, trying to exploit 'Parisian chic' for instant commercial success. The problem was that in their efforts to 'brand' a culture and a fashion, what many brands ended up doing was simply losing the authenticity of this culture by turning it into a stereotype, basically a formulaic uniform.

They thus illustrated the problem area that trips most brands up when aiming to 'market culture'. In this case it's really all about an authentic attitude; and getting 'attitude' right is something that brands find incredibly hard to replicate without simply going for the most obvious version of that trend. A brand that understands how to do this the right way and has made great gains as a result is Claudie Pierlot (which brings to life classic 'Parisian chic' staples, and strangely enough is run by sisters who are also the creative directors of two other great French brands, Maje and Sandro).

Another brand I have to mention is every Parisian woman's favourite – Sézane. French fashion brands were, it's reasonable to say, fairly slow off the mark when it came to e-commerce, but Sézane are renowned for making it the key element of their business model. They offer regularly updated capsule collections, make brilliant use of social media, send out their products with surprise gifts (which customers then Instagram – hence effectively doing their marketing for them) and have standalone 'Apartment boutiques' in Paris and New York which act as 'cool hangout places that bring the brand to life'. (I discuss their advertising stance in more detail in the communications chapter.) Very clever, very creative, and very 'Parisian chic'. Key points here are having a genuine intent to start with ... ensuring that there's a clear brand fit, the right influencer models, and using the right tone of voice across every form of communication utilized.

Alternative culture vs the Burning Man

For a completely different example, let's take a look at a cultural icon that's gained almost mythical status by being an ultimate example of its attempts to be 'pure' in the unbranded sense of the word. The Burning Man festival is the supposedly ultimate 'unbranded event' whose ultimate goal is to encourage the culture of creativity and which has 'decommodification – unmediated by commercial sponsorships, transactions or advertising' – as a core principle.

The festival, which started in the late 1980s, moved to Black Rock a few years later – not what you might think of as an ideal location for a festival at first glance, as that bit of Nevada is basically uninhabitable, baking hot, flatland desert, although apparently Larry Harvey saw deep parallels between the desert and cyberspace. A decade on, cutting-edge magazine *Sleaze Nation* commented that 'rather than droning on about corporate sanitation of festivals, we point you towards Burning Man. In 1986 Larry Harvey went down to Baker Beach and set fire to a wooden effigy. A small crowd formed, Harvey found the incineration a cathartic experience and decided to make it a regular thing' (Enrail, 1999).

The word spread, and now Burning Man attracts people from around the world. The site, a 'sprawling counterculture settlement where people are encouraged to push boundaries', is genuinely unique, resembling something out of *Blade Runner*. Incredibly cinematic, and unbelievably apocalyptic, it stretches for miles across the desert and even has its own temporary airport. As for numbers, around 70,000 fans attend, paying about $425 each for the privilege.

Key to Burning Man is that, unlike other festivals, everyone attending is expected to do more than just stand around and watch the acts, and to actually do something useful. People talk a lot about the 'festival spirit' of other events around the globe, particularly when the weather turns bad. But at Burning Man, this is actually not a vague expectation but something of a demand; owing to nothing being sold on site, everyone has to depend on what they've brought along to make in situ. Burners are encouraged to 'push boundaries' and cultural norms, although, as many of them just make the trip from San Francisco, breaking cultural norms is presumably something of a daily routine.

However, the original 'diehard Burners', as they like to call themselves, don't overly appreciate newcomers flying in to blend an alternative culture experience with luxury camping. The first wave of these was the original Silicon Valley tech start-up lot, which may have been vaguely acceptable to the rest of the crowd. But now many think things have gone seriously awry, care of celebrity attendees such as Paris Hilton.

Fred Turner from Stanford told the *Financial Times* that he believes Burning Man's ideals about building a common, project-based artistic labour have helped 'shape and legitimate' the collaborative processes key to Silicon Valley. But, noting the growth in power of Silicon Valley that's taken place since the festival first began, the newspaper stated: 'rather than shaping the tech industry, Burning Man now legitimizes it, reinforcing the myth that technology is all about the pioneering spirit and doing it yourself. Festival-goers embrace it – before they return to their offices for endless meetings and the tweaking of algorithms' (Kuchler, 2017).

What seems key to keeping the cultural legitimacy and thus the 'brand authenticity' of the event alive, in this context, is for attendees to embrace the original 'core principles' of Burning Man, and to embed those principles in their working lives and the brand strategies and marketing tactics that they then utilize. Otherwise, what's it actually for anymore? It would be a nice touch if they also did so in memory of Larry Harvey, who died in 2018.

On a global level and looking at 'cultural marketing' in its broadest sense, the agency Added Value's 'Cultural Traction' report ranks brands based on what it terms 'VIBE', those perceived to have the most Visionary, Inspiring, Bold and Exciting attributes, via research conducted among more than 62,000 respondents in 10 countries covering 160 brands and 15 sectors. According to Added Value, 'brands with the greatest cultural vibrancy are more likely to hit the trifecta of delivering purposeful and compelling visions for positive change; establishing truer, deeper, more lasting connections with people; and enriching brand experiences to be more open-ended and ongoing' (Added Value, 2017).

In a *Forbes* article covering one of their reports, Maggie Taylor, CEO of Added Value North America (noting that tech brands topped the list), explained it wasn't that technology necessarily equates to brand vibrancy, but 'tech connects us in better, deeper, broader ways – the product experience is much more in tune with culture' (Rooney, 2013).

A brand that also did notably well was Ikea, apparently owing to its ability to connect with consumers. 'A brand that's not just about diving into the cultural conversation; it's all about refreshing the brand in a way that is culturally relevant – but doing it in a way that stays true to who you are', stated the report. Ikea tapped into the cultural zeitgeist by acknowledging how people are increasingly interested in design and fashion. Its brand experience is a much more connected one; Ikea 'lives it' in everything they do. The takeaway for marketers – according to Added Value – is to look at your brand from the outside in and not just the inside out. That's the key according to Taylor: 'looking at the hidden meanings in everyday culture and making sure that brands keep fresh and relevant. For a marketer, there's nothing more critical than that' (Rooney, 2013).

The search for authenticity

What these examples show us is that the search for authenticity, at the heart of culturally based brand activity, is an 'always on' endeavour that requires the brand to get as close as possible to the core of that cultural issue. That helps them to genuinely understand it and therefore enable the brand team to work out where they can add value to the culture or cultural event, or learn from and reference it, in a way that is relevant to the brand itself. Only then can the result-

Mass advertising can help build brands, but authenticity is what makes them last. If people believe they share values with a company, they will stay loyal to the brand.

ing brand activity be done in a manner that has authenticity running through it, and therefore legitimizes the collaboration or learning. Integrity is all. Lose it and little of real value remains.

So what do these examples tell us about the foundation of 'successful brand reality'? That in a post-truth world, authenticity is absolutely key. To quote Howard Schultz: 'mass advertising can help build brands, but authenticity is what makes them last. If people believe they share values with a company, they will stay loyal to the brand' (Schultz, 1998).

This matters everywhere, from the major corporate statements about supply chains, through annual accounts and sustainability indexes, across consumer- and trade-facing communications, in day-to-day press relations and right up to long-term brand strategy thinking and the outputs of scenario planning.

Brand differentiation

Authenticity sets 'Brand A' apart from 'Brand B' where seeking clear differences between the product, packaging, pricing and so on may actually be fairly difficult. In an endless quest by brands to connect with consumers, key themes emerge time and time again. Those themes are headed by two key points:

1 Don't just say it, do it and be it. What I mean here is that too many brands rely on their communications to simply claim a point of difference, often utilizing what one can only refer to as 'truth-stretching claims'. That was fine about 50 years ago when consumers weren't so marketing savvy and sectors weren't so packed with 'me-too' brands. This explosion of choice from what are essentially identical brands has led to what Barry Schwartz terms 'The Paradox of Choice'. In his book of the same name he says: 'We assume that more choice means better options and greater satisfaction. But while the modern world does indeed offer us more choice, ironically, we get less satisfaction. In the long run, this can lead to decision-making paralysis, anxiety, and perpetual stress' (Schwartz, 2005). What's needed is for brands to 'Be the Change' and then talk about the impact of what they've done and why it is that they do this – not purely talking about vague notions of 'what they believe in' and doing little or nothing about it, which is effectively just virtue signalling.

2 Real people trust real people. What I mean here, for instance, is that sports fans are motivated by athletes or experts in

their chosen sport. Travel obsessives are motivated by people who've been there and done it. Those interested in wellbeing are motivated by specialists in or users of leading-edge and meaningful health products and practices. And so on. What all of the above have is authenticity as a golden thread that runs through their own lives and areas of relevance to the particular audience. Basically, they mean what they say and say what they mean. Of course, leveraging the 'influence of the influencers' has become a seriously big business. *Campaign* magazine noted in an interview with uber-influencer Xenia Tchoumi – a UN Ambassador, digital feminist and a fashion influencer with over eight million fans – that 'when authenticity is the most over-used, yet difficult to attain goal in marketing it is easy to see why influencer marketing is in the midst of such a rise in advertising spend' (Kemp, 2017). According to data from YouTube, 70 per cent of teenage subscribers trust influencer opinions over traditional celebrities. It is a shift that makes understanding and connecting with influencers an area of massive growing importance to brands.

It's a very short jump from the decline of trust in institutions and figureheads of all types to a world where brands are increasingly finding themselves held under a spotlight that seeks to highlight their product/price value in 'customer' terms and social/cultural values in 'people' terms. This combination of 'value and values' is an intrinsic part of the modern brand–consumer relationship.

What a hugely increasing number of people want is for a company to be both dynamic and innovative on one hand – and trustworthy and empathetic on the other. What underpins these is what I refer back to time and time again in this book: brand purpose. As any marketer knows, that is built on the 'why' as opposed to purely the 'what' of corporate manufacturing and the 'how' of business operations. On what Raj Sisodia, research scholar in conscious capitalism at Babson College, refers to as 'purpose beyond profit', this is epitomized by that 'good business' mantra, 'Purpose should impact every aspect of the firm. Brands with a purpose do better and make the world better' (Sisodia, 2014). What underpins brand purpose, and goes to the absolute nucleus of the brand, is authenticity.

In their 'Authentic Brands' survey, Cohn and Wolfe gained the opinions of over 12,000 consumers in 12 markets and found that nearly 90 per cent of global consumers felt that it was important for brands to act with integrity at all times. Their analysis found that this was more essential than innovation and product uniqueness when asked what they valued most in a brand. That's why I so admire socially conscious brands such PARK Social Soccer Co. Their 'One for One' ethos links to that of TOMS Shoes, but in this instance, for every one of their (massively stylish) footballs purchased, an identical ball is passed on to a kid in need. As their website says, 'soccer promotes community spirit, gender equality, teamwork and a sense of belonging. It reduces social exclusion, discrimination and the risk of players focussing on negative influences such a drugs and alcohol. It's also a global sport that nurtures and promotes understanding and inclusion of different cultures and beliefs' (PARK Soccer Social Co, 2018).

In their report, Cohn and Wolfe identified a number of 'authenticity anchors', business behaviours important to consumers, and found that 'characteristics such as communicating honestly about products and services and being open about environmental impact and sustainability measures are more important to global consumers than product utility, brand appeal and popularity among peers' (Cohn and Wolfe, 2014).

I talked about this with Emily Hare, Editor at The Honey Partnership, who told me:

> From a brand point of view this has always been something that's been relevant, but I think now it's become critical rather than nice to have. It's because of how society is changing, people are starting to question a lot of established factors, like media and brands, questioning sources; but also the tech tools that are available that

make it much easier to get to ask questions and find information. A lot of brands coming up set out to be transparent from the word go, they don't have to introduce transparent ways of operating to filter legacy systems, that is just how they are run. If you're an established brand competing against that, it's more of an overhaul; it's a big effort and something that a lot of brands struggle to do.

But how do you define authenticity in everyday branding terms? Is it being honest in your marcoms, running a transparent business, having integrity built into the DNA of your organization? The answer is essentially a tick to all three points, but the key is to actually implement these (fairly standard) industry buzzwords, which most of us hear repeated ad infinitum in meetings.

What's vital is also the level to which organizations live and breathe these terms. This connects closely to an increasing consumer desire to know why a brand was set up in the first place and what it (still) stands for.

Keep it real, live the change, build momentum, stand for something, and don't be short-termist.

So you need to think about cultural relevance – but from a meaningful long-term partner perspective, not a 'turn up and take over' angle. In terms of activation, 'be local and act local' is a great way to think and act. You need to be consistent, which is where adherence to an agreed brand plan and brand playbook is so vital.

A piece written about brand reinvention by the agency Fold 7 put this really well when their strategy partner wrote that 'brands that reinvent themselves because they have to, are significantly more likely to get it right. With a tangible business problem to solve, the stakes are high and there's no room for half-measures'. She went on to outline some key principles, which were to 'keep it real, live the change, build momentum, stand for something, and don't be short-termist (Gaufman, 2017).

If you want an example of a staggeringly powerful piece of social and cultural commentary that does the above, then

'This is America' by the supremely talented Childish Gambino (aka Donald Glover) illustrates 'how to do it' in the most emphatic way. His video, which gained global attention with its message about race and gun violence, became an overnight media obsession and was viewed over a billion times in one week on YouTube – which is about as impressive a stat as you're likely to witness. And he's an artist who does indeed 'keep it real, lives the change, builds momentum, and stands for something'.

So, brands that are genuine, have integrity, talk in honest terms, play a role in the society that provides their consumers, respect the culture within which they operate and demonstrate commitment via purpose-led branding to show that they're essentially 'on our side' are the ones that will continue to grow – because if you're not authentic then you're not genuine. In a post-truth world, linking with culture must be about adding value and being authentic.

CHAPTER NINE

Truth, Lies and Advertising

Here's a question for you – in corporate terms, can you think of anything more 'post-truth' than the tobacco industry? An industry whose promotional activity is steeped in deceit and deception to an astonishing degree. Post-truth communication works really well for autocrats and bullies alike – and the tobacco industry certainly acts like both whenever it can.

In this chapter, I'm going to talk about how and why one of the most successful marketing campaigns of all time – that's saved thousands of lives along the way – came into being. A truly brilliant bit of communication, and one in which by an amazing coincidence I played a very minor part, linked adland to a truly great purpose-led campaign, in this instance involving a powerful leveraging of 'real' youthful rebellion. It had a huge impact on me and has influenced the approach I've taken to research ever since.

The death industry and youth marketing

First some context: the tobacco industry is the only industry that gets away with selling a product that kills its customers when used as intended. Cigarette smoking is responsible for nearly 500,000 deaths per year in the United States alone, alongside staggering financial costs. The products they sell kill more people than terrorism, AIDS, murder, suicide, fires, alcohol and all illegal drugs combined. According to the Centers for Disease Control and Prevention, 'tobacco use remains the leading cause of preventable disease, disability and death in the US' (Centers for Disease Control and Prevention, 2017a).

A key issue, or a 'killer issue' you might say, is that the tobacco industry has an endless requirement for new consumers, because it keeps killing so many of its current ones. So it targets young people, endlessly trying to connect with the world of youth culture and 'teenage cool'. By a not so astonishing coincidence, it also effectively wrote the youth marketing handbook. Virtually every element of major youth culture has in some way been linked to tobacco money. Tobacco brands make every effort, leveraged by their enormous financial power, to make themselves attractive to youth.

In the film industry, a cigarette hanging out of the mouth of the anti-establishment hero in (place the name of any of your favourite old films here) has seemingly for ever been associated with 'nonchalant cool'. According to the Centers for Disease Control and Prevention, 'tobacco use in big films rose by 80% in recent years'. They state that 'the amount of smoking was particularly alarming in films with a PG13 certificate, the highest US rating for films that children can watch without being accompanied by an adult' (Centers for Disease Control and Prevention, 2017b). Their report cited findings by the US Surgeon General that concluded that 'exposure to on-screen smoking in movies causes young people to start smoking' (Surgeon General, 2014).

The deliberate coercive genius of all this has been duping young people for years. A key film that the CDC report cited was *Hail Caesar* in which, as reported by *The Times*, 'all the stars smoke, and Scarlett Johansson's smoking is supposed to look glamorous, and appealing. When she seduces a flustered studio fixer, the scene evokes the classic Hollywood sirens of the 1950s in which the film is set: Marilyn Monroe perhaps, or Lauren Bacall' (Hoyle, 2017).

CNN also reported a public health analyst at CDC's Office on Smoking and Health as saying: 'We know that the more you see smoking on screen, the more likely you are to see youth smoking cigarettes in real life. There's a causal relationship between the two'. They also quoted a film historian and communication professor from Pepperdine University, who stated that 'there's so many iconic images of cool associated with smoking that it's a hard habit for actors and directors to break' (Knight, 2017).

However, the use of powerful icons to generate brand recognition works both ways, as Sergio Zyman (former Chief Marketing Office of Coca-Cola) pointed out in his book *The End of Advertising*. When discussing this issue he noted that 'Joe Camel was an incredibly popular icon, but he generated a huge amount of bad press for Camel when it became clear that Joe, who was one of the most identifiable characters among young kids, had probably been responsible for getting millions of them to start smoking' (Zyman, 2002).

Leveraging the issue of 'working both ways', the team at *Adbusters* magazine subverted the Marlboro Man (as they had when redrawing Joe Camel, placing him in a cancer ward) with images of a tough-looking cowboy standing in front of a gorgeous sunset with a droopy cigarette hanging out of his mouth. The caption read 'Smoking causes impotence'.

After the conquest of cool, the fightback begins ...

Taking on the tobacco brands was incredibly difficult, and dauntingly expensive, owing to the litigious behaviour of that highly powerful industry. However, an important success was noted by Kalle Lasn in his book *Culture Jam*, where he mentions how in Alabama, the only state in the union where a private citizen can file a legal petition to dissolve a corporation, Judge William Wynn did exactly that. 'Acting as a private citizen and comparing his actions to making a citizen's arrest, Wynn named five tobacco companies that, he asserted, had broken state child-abuse laws and should be shut down' (Lasn, 1999).

Then the really epic event happened. To cut a very long story short, the largest civil litigation settlement in US history had a vital output: the recovering of vast amounts of money spent on caring for sick and dying smokers via Medicaid. This resulted in tobacco companies being forced to provide US states with billions of dollars to run activity which included advertising aimed at decreasing youth tobacco use.

So, it was in this context that one of the edgiest ad agencies in the United States (Crispin Porter + Bogusky) were briefed to create a hard-hitting anti-tobacco campaign for the Florida Pilot Program on Tobacco Control. (It went on to become effectively a pan-US campaign, still running today.) The task they'd been set was to change social norms and reduce youth smoking.

Truth is not anti-smoking. Truth is anti-lies, anti-manipulation and anti-secrets.

A big ask, particularly when, as any agency who's ever worked on anti-tobacco comms knows, the first issue that you run into is that while young people know all about the standard perils of smoking, there are also plenty of 'positives'. Most of those have, as mentioned, deliberately arisen as a result of decades of tobacco-industry cultural marketing, very much including the positioning of smoking as an act of rebellion and social bonding.

A quick note here on the world of cool. As Alex Wipperfurth pointed out in his book *Brand Hijack*, when talking about cool being indefinable and unquantifiable, 'cool is temporary, attitudes are ever changing. Think of the 'In/Out' and Hot/Not' lists that appear in magazines on a monthly basis. Even when marketers can figure out what they need to do to make a brand cool, most find that cool moves too fast for them to keep pace' (Wipperfurth, 2005).

The goal of the CP+B campaign would be to counter the misinformation and subterfuge used by the tobacco industry to sell its products to underage smokers. The core strategy that was created, which came in large part via Jen Urich, their Head of Planning, and Graham Hall, Head of Informer Research, was: 'Truth is not anti-smoking. Truth is anti-lies, anti-manipulation and anti-secrets'.

So, the 'big idea' was to counter the appeal of cigarettes by encouraging teens to rebel against the duplicity and manipulation of tobacco companies. Essentially, the key thought was 'Their brand is Lies – our brand is Truth'. The campaign that resulted, 'Truth – a generation united against tobacco', did indeed change social norms and massively reduce youth smoking.

Of course, the Truth campaign couldn't be found to be playing the same game as that of the tobacco industry, if it was to have rock-solid credibility in exposing their overall industry image as being 'based on lies'. But this obsessional focus on truth couldn't be seen to be a 'worthy and dull' fact-checking exercise, and would resonate years later with the fight against fake news, as per my earlier chapter. This point would be highlighted in an excellent *Guardian* article which quoted complaints by both Clay Shirky (during the 2016 US presidential campaign), 'that we've brought fact-checkers to a culture war', and Hussein Kesvani (in *Vice* magazine), who said 'fact-checkers are terrible at telling stories', whereas 'the neo-Nazi "alt-right" movement is great at building and maintaining a narrative' (Belam, 2017). So the agency created an impactful and motivating series of rock-solid 'true propositions' as portrayed and articulated in a manner that the audience would associate with a cool best friend, ie independent, appealing, self-assured, and credible.

> *Their brand is Lies – our brand is Truth.*

I was part of a research team conducting campaign-development with US 'SWAT teams' (Students Working Against Tobacco). This activity clearly highlighted that these young Americans didn't like being manipulated by brands, because that is not cool. Therefore, clarifying that they were being treated like fools by pseudo-cool tobacco company advertising became a clarion call, along with leveraging the insight that young people believed that tobacco use would be a hindrance to them achieving their potential, and thus had potential inbuilt life-altering consequences.

Getting the consumer on your side, via anti-consumerism

The resulting campaign included a series of Adbusters-esque messages essentially built around a theme of 'Don't be a walking target market, don't be coerced into being replacement smokers in a market where one in three consumers dies'. As we'd pointed out to teens in research, 'if you and two friends are smokers, one of you will probably end up dying from it. But the tobacco industry needs young smokers to replace the dying ones, that's why they market to teens'.

There was also plenty of work done to make sure that, from a demographic point of view, 'no one was left behind'. As with many other health-related issues, an unfortunate fact about tobacco is that the people with the most money, access and education exhibit healthier behaviour than those lower down the demographic scale.

As reported by *AdAge* at the time, the first Truth campaign was so good that Philip Morris USA actually threatened to stop its funding for the hard-won anti-tobacco settlement (Teinowitz, 2000). (This campaign was via good old TV-led, guerrilla-marketing-supported activity, back before Twitter, Facebook *et al* existed.) It helped that, to get the campaign off to a truly impactful start, it was based in Florida, as the advertising laws in that state allowed for far more aggressive messaging than elsewhere in the United States.

The ad agency was thus taking an approach that the late great Bill Bernbach of DDB would presumably have approved of, as in an anti-advertising stance. In his highly influential book *The Conquest of Cool*, Thomas Frank talked of Bernbach being Madison Avenue's answer to Vance Packard: 'His agency had ... the uncanny ability to speak to the scepticism of advertising ... appealing directly to the powerful but unmentionable public fears of conformity, of manipulation, of fraud, and of powerlessness. He invented what we might call anti-advertising: a style which harnessed public mistrust of consumerism to consumerism itself' (Frank, 1997).

Whenever you mention leveraging 'anti-advertising', it is a given that you also have to mention the staggeringly talented comedian Bill Hicks, who so tragically died far too young. As he used to say in his stage shows (I saw him in London), 'If anyone here works in advertising... kill yourself. Seriously. Oh, I know what any marketing people here are thinking right now: "You know what Bill's doing? He's going for that anti-marketing dollar. That's a good market. He's very smart. And the righteous indignation dollar. Huge in times of recession. Giant market"' (Hicks, 2004).

The key point here is that the CP+B Truth campaign really tapped into something that Bernbach and Hicks (which sounds like the greatest agency in history) would instantly recognize. Although Bill Hicks hated advertising, I like to think he would have approved of what the campaign was trying to do.

The ability of advertising to massively boost the power of brands doing good is a story that needs to be told more often. The Truth case history is a real example of this type of activity. According to *The Telegraph*, 'By lending glamour and reach to campaigns for better behaviour, healthier living and more active citizenship, brand owners can make a real social contribution and generate brand loyalty. Businesses can be even better if they adopt pioneering environmental policies, encourage their employees to do voluntary work, and fund charitable foundations' (Vander Weyer, 2002).

That original CP+B 'big idea' went on to be utilized by the American Legacy Foundation (a non-profit health organization, itself now rebranded as the 'Truth Initiative') across the United States. Generally consistent with Florida's campaign, Legacy's version of 'Truth' featured hard-hitting messages highlighting the deceptive practices of tobacco companies, and stark facts about the deadly effects of tobacco.

Fairly obviously, a key element to all this was the use of media planning. As the agency pointed in an official strategy report, 'If we wanted youth to really embrace our anti-tobacco effort, it made sense that we should deliver it just like other successful youth brands' (Hicks, 2001). The launch of the campaign included a 'Truth' magazine distributed in record stores and surf shops, a public relations tour called the 'Truth train' and a 'Truth truck', which became a fixture state-wide at concerts, beaches and raves.

Other countries committed to reducing youth smoking might look to these principles, and to the experience of 'Truth' to help design effective youth-focused tobacco control campaigns.

How a Vietnam Vet made things personal

Personally, the next stage in all this for me was when I also played a bit-part in some of the later work created in other US states. Which was why a couple of months later, I caught a late-night flight from Houston up to Jackson, Mississippi, where I met a truly remarkable man: Purify Johnson. Every researcher conducting cultural and social research swears by the 'instant update' offered by taxi drivers. I've been given incredibly useful insights from taxi drivers from Melbourne to Riyadh to Helsinki to Portland, since I started in work in the industry.

Purify was hanging around in his cab outside Jackson Airport at about 0100 hrs when my late flight got in. I asked him to tell me about himself, expecting a quick chat about his week, but what I got was an epic life story that plugged me straight into Mississippi. I'm writing this years later, so forgive me if the details are slightly rusty, but what it essentially came down to was him growing up in the Southern states, where his parents had been born and worked all their lives, as had his forefathers, back to the hideous days of slavery. Purify went on to tell me about joining the airborne forces of the US Army and going off to fight in Vietnam, where he took part in a battle that became infamous: Hamburger Hill.

When his tour of duty had finished, he returned to a very different United States, one where the race riots were in full flight, and within a few months found himself in jail having got involved in the civil-rights demonstrations. Post-jail (and I'm cutting a few corners here) he got married, had kids and one of his daughters went to Jackson State University, one of the first universities that admitted African Americans in the United States.

He told me all this as we were driving into town, along with a whole load of really interesting stories about how the lives of people in the 'Mississippi of today' had changed and been impacted by the societal changes from only a few years previously. All this was incredibly useful anecdotal stuff that I referenced in my conversations with the various people I was later to meet in my research fieldwork.

I remain ever grateful that he ended up driving for the Deluxe Cab Co, and that I was therefore lucky enough to meet him. (Of course, I massively recommend those Deluxe Cab Co 'kings of the road' should you ever find yourself in Jackson, MS. If you meet Purify, please say hello from me.)

I then conducted research around urban and rural Mississippi with a great bunch of people from a local agency called Maris, West & Baker. When it came to creating anti-tobacco work, they were raring to go. So, I ran a load of (segregated) ethnographic research with black and white teens and parents in Jackson, Meridian, Vicksburg and the wonderfully named 'Yazoo City'. The campaign that MWB created was another highly successful one in the roll-call of hard-hitting anti-tobacco communication, and it was a real pleasure to link up with them on that initial 'Question It' campaign. Their work was really impactful and needed to be, as they'd won the account in a pitch against other hotshots, including Spike Lee's company.

As a postscript to that project, when I found myself presenting the findings of my research to the Attorney General, Mike Moore (who, for all you trivia fans, would later also be featured in the story of the anti-smoking film *The Insider* starring Al Pacino), I mentioned Purify Johnson to him, and how I thought they should really get him involved, as he was such an inspiring guy.

Adweek described the Truth campaign as 'an attempt to turn the movement into something like a Human Rights campaign'.

Looking back on all that work (and I returned to conduct more research in later years), probably the most standout bit of communication, for me at least, featured hundreds of body bags being piled onto the pavement outside a tobacco company c/o of CP+B, to illustrate in a graphically hard-hitting manner what the 'real life' daily statistic of 1,000+ tobacco-related deaths looks like.

From gesture politics to collective action

The campaign has been through various developments, including a really hard-hitting one that referenced the Occupy movement, an approach that 'Adweek described as 'an attempt to turn the movement into something like a Human Rights Campaign' (Coffee, 2014).

Throughout all of its iterations, the Truth campaign changed the way that an 'anti' message has communicated with both potential and existing smokers. As shown back in the early CP+B strategy development days, what wasn't needed was a parent, teacher or other authority figure pointing at or lecturing 'youth'. Instead it's been about things such as it being cool for young people to realize that a tobacco industry strategy is to treat them like fools and try to trick them into smoking.

Earlier, I mentioned the campaign tactics that were used in the days before social media existed. Bringing this up to date, Fast Company more recently noted that 'Truth spends about 40% of its marketing investment in digital and social. The "Left Swipe Dat" campaign featured YouTube stars talking about how unappealing smoking pics were on Tinder' (Beer, 2015).

'Truth' was and remains massively successful – and via its latest iteration (#FinishIt, care of that excellent agency 72andSunny) is still going strong nearly 20 years after it was first created. But, while the original 'Truth' campaign was designed for a generation renowned for being naturally rebellious, 'Finish It' was developed to suit the desire of the latest crop of youth to be agents of social change. (This, of course, has obvious resonance with campaigns including #LikeAGirl.) Today's teenagers are less interested in 'mere' protest and more interested in driving positive collective action via community collaboration.

According to a report in *The Guardian* on the tactics of Big Tobacco using 'intimidatory tactics to suppress health warnings' in Africa, 'Multinational tobacco firms have threatened governments demanding they axe or dilute the kind of protections that have saved millions of lives in the West'. The head of the government's Tobacco Control Board in Kenya stated: 'BAT has done as much as they can to block us' (Boseley, 2017).

Truth – the legacy

Developing campaigns via a laser-like concentration on a core 'human insight' to cultivate meaningful relationships with consumers is vital. In this instance, leveraging a genuine brand purpose founded entirely on truth, while the opposition has a standpoint based on lies, was and is both a correct and incredibly powerful position to articulate.

At a time when adland is under an onslaught of criticism, it's worth giving plaudits to a campaign that has genuinely improved the health, and thus extended the lives, of countless people. 'Truth' is part of the reason that teen smoking has dropped from about 25 per cent before the campaign started, to 6 per cent today (Beer, 2015).

In *AdAge*, the CEO of Legacy said the US Surgeon General had 'recently reported that 5.6 million youth alive today will lose their lives to tobacco if we don't continue to step up with game-changing solutions. Truth has been one of the most successful social norm-shifting campaigns ever. It must be to end this epidemic and create Generation Free: the first smoke-free generation' (Morrison, 2014).

It's quite a thought that, as I pointed out in a speech at the European Youth Marketing Summit and as reported in *Contagious*, huge numbers of the teenage youth that 'Truth' targeted way back in the 1990s have gone on to have their own kids – who will now be targeted by an updated version of the same anti-tobacco campaign, one that will go on to also improve their health and help them to life longer lives. In doing so, CP+B created a truly amazing brand years before the industry became, quite rightly, obsessed with 'brand purpose'.

It's hopefully worth repeating a quote from Alex Bogusky (then Creative Director at the agency) in *The New York Times* after we'd both been at an Anti-Tobacco Summit in Florida where the campaign's big idea was originally fine-tuned. 'Teens are very brand-conscious ... we hope "Truth" will ultimately be a brand as cool as Camel and Marlboro' (Elliott, 1998). As anyone who's ever tried defining cool (from a branding perspective) will know, having a brand with authentic foundations and an ethical stance, which is then communicated in a culturally relevant way, goes a long way to achieving that elusive goal.

The CP+B team achieved their aim, yet to a level they probably didn't realistically anticipate. They created an absolutely superb piece of communication that has stood the test of time. By leveraging one core point, a key insight, they took something vital back from the pseudo-cool world of corporately infiltrated youth culture and allowed that insight to shine brightly again.

Truth is cool.

CHAPTER TEN

Summary

The Post-Truth Brand Manifesto

Businesses want to have strong and long-lasting relationships with their consumers. The brand–consumer relationship, like all relationships, is built on trust.

Yet, as mentioned throughout this book, in a post-truth world brands have a serious challenge when so much of modern life is defined by mistrust, and people are increasingly asking whom can we really trust? As explained, we need faith and confidence in the people, institutions, ideas, objects, technology and systems around us, in order to trust in them. Society would face collapse if trust disappeared, and that is why being trustworthy is so crucial. For brands, the situation is no different, and is therefore not an optional extra. Why would consumers feel confident in choosing a brand that they didn't trust?

When you have trust, everything is simple. When you don't, things get complicated.

To reinforce that point, I'll quote a famous saying by the CEO of Alibaba, the business magnate, philanthropist and investor Jack Ma, who said, 'When you have trust, everything is simple. If you don't have trust, things get complicated' (Kim, 2014). As *The Economist* put it in a statement that's endlessly referenced in company boardrooms, 'Consumer trust is the basis of all brand values, so companies that own brands have an immense incentive to retain it'. That article went on to say, 'The dependence of successful brands on trust suggests that consumers need more of it, and therefore brands will need to be ethically robust and environmentally pure' (Leader, 2001). Those words could have been written right now, as the 'trust issue' is inevitably an essential element of brand presentations created by, for instance, consumer insight teams, trend-forecasting agencies, scenario planners or strategy consultants.

Consumer trust is the basis of all brand values, so companies that own brands have an immense incentive to retain it.

Over the time that it took me to write *The Post-Truth Business*, social media companies, which play such a dynamic role in our lives, were exposed for a shocking misuse of personal data. Alongside this were seemingly endless examples of corporate malpractice, on a truly global basis. I could have very easily written a book about nothing but these issues. This toxic environment is a real problem for businesses, as it also includes 'image contagion' where even innocent brands are impacted by the effect of guilty ones. Therefore, brands must realize that ignoring the situation in the hope it'll go away is not an option.

This impacts brands of all descriptions, from political parties to health services, international food companies to charities, innovative start-ups to major financial institutions. For all of them, the trust agenda is a vital underpinning of their brand foundations, just as a truthful evidence-based world view is so vital for a healthy and progressive society.

However, I firmly believe that while 'reputation capital' is an absolutely vital foundation of successful and enduring brands, this purely tells us about their past actions. The future is where brands must focus. This means leaders of companies taking deliberate and definitive action to ensure that their businesses demonstrate 'corporate social leadership'. Along with making reputable products, providing employment and returning dividends to shareholders, corporations can and should endeavour to make the world a better place, contributing to and engaging with society. If nothing else, fear of regulation relating to Silicon Valley brands, for example, should make them reconsider their civic duties.

Fortunately, there are, as ever, superb examples of brands doing things the right way. Their honest, competent and reliable brand values reaffirm our faith that there are inspiring people and great organizations out there, showing us all 'how to do it better'. The actions of these 'positive brands' concentrate unrelentingly on building a reputation built on trust, transparency and authenticity. They understand that these values have to exist throughout the company, in every facet of its business.

With good leadership at the core of these businesses, every member of the organization is enabled to understand and demonstrate 'why they do it, how they do it, and what they do'. The end result, from a customer point of view, is that these brands are then seen by the consumer as being on their side, standing with them and matching their own values in an inspirational manner. Because in a post-truth era, we want, and need, to believe in something, and increasingly, brands that really do 'live it like they say it' are some of the few things that we can actually believe and rely on.

A huge number of other brands need to take action to rebuild their authenticity. A key lesson I've learnt over 20 years of conducting research in Europe, Asia, Russia, Africa, the Middle East and North America is that a great deal of the accepted thinking within client-side marketing teams and their agency partners appears to be incredibly unrealistic, perhaps owing to not being properly 'reality-checked'. By that I mean as opposed to genuine consumer beliefs about, and experiences of, brands in the real world. This is often where the famous 'credibility gap' comes into play, and a brand with weak credibility is a weak brand. To reconnect that gap, I believe that ethnographic research is the best way to start.

Drawing together the interlinked issues that I've identified throughout this book, I'll summarize the key lessons for brands in what will be termed, somewhat grandiosely, 'The Post-Truth Brand Manifesto'.

Just prior to doing that, of all the areas that I mention in the manifesto, there happens to be one issue not directly highlighted, which goes to the heart of the erosion of trust: fake news. Or, perhaps to give it a more relevant term considering the seriousness of its impact, the 'weaponizing of lies'. This issue sees the subversive acts of those conspiring against democracy doing so with a clear intent to 'Dismiss, Distort, Distract, Dismay'. The end result is a divisive mix of lies and false equivalence, which is outrageous, immoral and damages us all.

While it's enormously encouraging to see a rising level of trust in individual journalists who provide the honest, high-quality reporting that underpins democracy, it is of the upmost importance that from a media perspective, social media platforms (in particular) are forced to act with a high level of responsibility, which seems to have eluded them over the past few years. The 'open and honest' communication of political messaging in particular needs to be held under a media spotlight on an unrelenting basis, with those who create it seeking to provoke and divide society being held to account. As 'engaged citizens' I believe we're obliged as active members of society to be far more questioning of the trustworthiness of the news on which we rely. We should always remember that the perspectives of those who hold political viewpoints opposed to our own deserve to be listened to and debated. Because, in so many societies, the centre-ground isn't holding, and this destructive situation is often being deliberately manipulated. It's therefore critical that, as individuals, we need to build more bridges, as opposed to the walls being constructed around us.

Why do these issues, which are usually political in nature, matter so much to consumer brands? Because when confusion and mistrust are so prevalent in our daily lives, and in a 'hyper-normal' world where nothing appears quite right, a continual decline of societal trust combines with an already sceptical consumer sentiment to undermine institutions and brands of all types. The future for brands without trust is bleak.

So, here is my manifesto.

The Post-Truth Brand Manifesto

Be authentic

- Brands are built on trust, but in a post-truth world they're faced with a serious credibility challenge when so much of modern life is now defined by mistrust. As an indispensable element of the consumer–brand relationship, consumers will reject brands that they don't trust when they have a choice. They're also increasingly likely to communicate either positive or negative things about brands, and this word of mouth has an immensely powerful impact.
- To rebuild their authenticity, brands must engage with 'informed consumers' who make 'intentional buying choices' and who often want to engage more with the brands that they select. Truly authentic brands obsess over their heritage and origins, and highlight their individuality and distinctiveness.
- Fakery isn't a part of an authentic brand's image or business practices. These brands earn and keep our trust by 'living it like they say it'. Their high levels of credibility assist them in achieving more persuasive levels of impact via their brand stories, and therefore help build stronger levels of customer engagement.

Be transparent

- From car company lies about environmental standards to fashion companies using child labour, banks creating chaos in the financial system, to concerns over sinister digital mass persuasion and psychological manipulation, brands keep being found out and levels of trust have fallen so dramatically that disconnection and rejection are the result.
- Brand statements that reference 'good behaviour' have to be truthful, and these claims need to be substantiated. This behaviour needs to be communicated in a transparent manner, for public scrutiny. Otherwise, brands will be found out in an era when distrusting consumers and an ever-watchful media shine an unrelenting spotlight on brands, and on the businesses and people behind them.
- For brands to thrive, businesses need to find a way to regain and retain the confidence of consumers. In this instance, actions may range from transparent pricing policies to corporate sustainability practices to animal welfare standards to blockchain-enabled product information. Proving the honesty behind the myriad claims made by brands and businesses starts with transparency.

Respect privacy

- Privacy is a fundamental human right that must be protected. The use and abuse of private data is causing enormous concerns over issues such as civil liberty and personal privacy re: Article 19 of the Universal Declaration of Human Rights. However, it must be noted that cultural sensitivities towards privacy vary widely around the world.
- Hence, while many people are increasingly concerned about how much of, and why, their personal data is being utilized, more and more are also willing to trade privacy for things that clearly benefit them. This is where choice of use, clarity

of purpose and the implications of effect are key issues that brands must both understand and then demonstrate their actions and ethical behaviour.

- The levels of antipathy engendered towards brands that are seen to be profiting from 'surveillance capitalism' must be understood and deliberated by companies involved in this area. The implications for brands that abuse our privacy are deeply serious and far-reaching.

Demonstrate empathy

- More and more people want to feel morally good about the things they consume and are attracted to brands that reflect their viewpoints. For those brands that wish to have an engaged and enthused community of consumers, acting in an empathetic manner and demonstrating that empathetic behaviour is vital in order to build up their social capital.
- To connect with those who identify with like-minded brands, these brands 'tell it like they do it' when it comes to the beneficial social impacts of their business. They also own up to their mistakes, when and if they're made, in a clear and open way. From a behavioural perspective, they negotiate with us, as opposed to purely aiming to impose themselves on us.
- Brands that wish to engage with these consumers need to substantiate their social empathy and positive corporate ethos. To illustrate this, they should publish a social mission statement along with an annual social impact report setting out the effects of their 'brand positive' ethos.

Be trustworthy

- The truth is ever-harder to find and 'whom to trust' is a question that we're asking with increasing urgency. Brands, in all their forms, need to earn our trust and work hard to keep it in order to consolidate their 'reputation capital'. When there is seemingly never-ending choice in virtually every sector, it has never been easier or less stressful to switch our brand choices, meaning that when choice increases, mistrusted brands lose and trusted brands win.

- An industry-wide obsession with the 'why' while apparently forgetting the 'how' and 'what' needs to be radically updated. 'How' people and businesses do things and 'what' they do are just as important as 'why' they do it. A crucial point is that this is a business-wide issue, not just a marketing one; therefore leadership is vital, and leaders must ensure that they involve every facet of the organization. Companies have to be consistent and trustworthy in their behaviour, from top to bottom, and right along the supply chain, from the 'first hand of production to the final hand of the consumer'.

- Brands that are trusted most tend to have a legacy which has enabled them to clearly demonstrate their 'good business' and/or 'reliable product' credentials, or are those which are clearly connected to the 'hand of the maker or innovator' or indeed have transparency built into the core of their business model. They have brand stories that we find compelling and meaningful. Thus, their 'trustworthiness' is built on matching what the brand actually does to what its communication claims it does, along with demonstrating their positive business strategy and brand behaviour by being seen to act in an honest, competent, reliable and empathetic manner.

Owing to the confusion and doubt that we experience around us, there is a golden opportunity for brands to take a more positive approach: re-engaging with consumers, building stronger connections and gaining more committed loyalty.

This book has aimed to demonstrate that, from a business perspective, there is a positive way forward, summarized by my Post-Truth Brand Manifesto. That checklist is intended to assist those who are aiming for the type of reputation and degree of trust that strong and successful brands require, if they're to engage with increasingly informed consumers, on both an emotional and functional level.

As highlighted throughout this book, for companies that wish to future-proof their businesses, it is also key that that they think deeply about their social mission, and the implications of their activities from the perspective of the 'common good'.

I hope that the brand activity shown via the wide range of sectors and areas covered in *The Post-Truth Business* has illuminated and clarified some inspiring examples of best-practice, and some unfortunate examples of worst-practice. There are many superb types of the former out there, which are unfortunately rather outweighed by the latter. But I'm given hope by the deeply impressive activity demonstrated by the former, ranging from start-ups to legacy brands.

To finish, I strongly believe that the number one issue for brands is trust. In a post-truth world so badly impacted by mistrust, brands need to take action to deal with the situation in a positive and progressive manner. For brand owners and their agency partners who genuinely believe in, and act on, the range of values highlighted in this book, the future is bright.

References

Chapter 1

Aaronovitch, D (2017) [accessed 5 April 2018] Social Media Zealots Are Waging War on Truth, *The Times*, 30 November [Online] www.thetimes.co.uk/article/social-media-zealots-are-waging-war-on-truth-8l0nrkjgq

Achan, C and Bartels, L (2016) *Democracy for Realists: Why elections do not produce responsive government*, Princeton University Press, Princeton, NJ

Attila, A (2017) [accessed 3 April 2018] Populism and Climate Change in the Era of Post-Truth, *3rd International Populism Conference in Prague*, 22 May [Online] www.academia.edu/33061955/Populism_and_Climate_Change_in_the_Era_of_Post-Truth?auto=download [accessed 3 April 2018]

Badawi, Z (2018) [accessed 4 April 2018] Davos: The Fake News Challenge to Politics, *BBC News at WTO Davos 2018*, 28 January [Online] www.bbc.co.uk/programmes/w3csvvdy

Barber, L (2017) [accessed 5 April 2018] Fake News in the Post-Factual Age: Lecture to Oxford Alumni Festival, *Financial Times*, 16 September [Online] www.ft.com/content/c8c749e0-996d-11e7-b83c-9588e51488a0

BBC (2017) [accessed 5 April 2018] Washington Post Uncovers Fake Roy Moore Story 'Sting', *BBC News*, 28 November [Online] www.bbc.co.uk/news/world-us-canada-42150322

BBC Newsnight (2018) [accessed 20 April 2018] Mark Zuckerberg Answers Congress, *BBC Newsnight, iPlayer*, 10 April [Online] https://www.bbc.co.uk/iplayer/episode/b09zbf11/newsnight-10042018

Belkina, A (2018) [accessed 5 April 2018] Davos: The Fake News Challenge to Politics, The World Debate, *BBC*, 28 January [Online] www.bbc.co.uk/programmes/w3csvvdy

Bennetts, M (2018a) [accessed 1 June 2018] Pro-Kremlin Media Turns Up Heat on West after Arkady Babchencko's Fake Murder, 31 May [Online] https://www.thetimes.co.uk/article/8fc7ef26-64c1-11e8-9092-dbb5f656af2a

Bennetts, M (2018b) 'I Hid in Mortuary... to Convince World I Was Dead', Says Arkady Babchenko, 1 June [Online] https://www.thetimes.co.uk/article/456f1c04-64ff-11e8-aeba-dfc3db1a69eb

Blight, D (2017) [accessed 4 April 2018] The Civil War Lies on Us Like a Sleeping Dragon: America's Deadly Divide and Why It Has Returned, *The Guardian*, 20 August [Online] www.theguardian.com/us-news/2017/aug/20/civil-war-american-history-trump

Boot, M (2017) [accessed 3 April 2018] Trump is Commander-in-Chief of the War on Mainstream Media, *Foreign Policy*, 29 November [Online] http://foreignpolicy.com/2017/11/29/trump-is-commander-in-chief-of-the-war-on-mainstream-media/

Botsman, R (2017) *Who Can you Trust? How technology brought us together – and why it could drive us apart*, Portfolio, London

Bridge, R (2018) [accessed 6 July 2018] Facebook Switches from Tech Firm to a Publisher, *The Times*, 5 July [Online] https://www.thetimes.co.uk/article/6e82fe5c-7fe5-11e8-af03-7edc8dc9d023

Brown, T (2018) [accessed 20 April 2018] Social Media and Online Platforms as Publishers, *House of Lords Library*, 8 January [Online] http://researchbriefings.parliament.uk/ResearchBriefing/Summary/LLN-2018-0003#fullreport

Collins, D (2017) [accessed 5 April 2018] Damian Collins: Combatting Fake News, *Sleeping Giant Media*, 7 June [Online] www.sleepinggiantmedia.co.uk/posts/fake-news-damian-collins/

Collins, D (2018) [accessed 3 May 2018] Restoring Trust: How Do We Tackle the Crisis in Public Information? (Audio) 2 May [Online] https://soundcloud.com/lsepodcasts/restoring-trust-how-do-we

Cooke, K (2017) [accessed 30 April 2018] 'Fake News' Reinforces Trust in Mainstream News Brands, *Kantar*, 31 October [Online] https://uk.kantar.com/business/brands/2017/trust-in-news/

Davis, E (2017) *Post-Truth: Why we have reached peak bull**** and what we can do about it*, Little Brown, New York

Deacon, M (2016) [accessed 20 April 2018] In a World of Post-Truth Politics, Andrea Leadsom Will Make the Perfect PM, *The Telegraph*, 9 July [Online] https://www.telegraph.co.uk/news/2016/07/09/in-a-world-of-post-truth-politics-andrea-leadsom-will-make-the-p/

DFR (2017) [accessed 3 April 2018] Fake News: Defining and Defeating, *Digital Forensic Research Lab*, 15 January [Online] https://medium.com/dfrlab/fake-news-defining-and-defeating-43830a2ab0af

Diakopoulos, N (2018) [accessed 21 May 2018] Machine Reality, Deepfakes, Misinformation, *Columbia Journalism Review*, 15 May [Online] https://www.cjr.org/tow_center/reporting-machine-reality-deepfakes-diakopoulos-journalism.php

Dorsey, J (2018) [accessed 20 April 2018] We Have Witnessed Abuse…, *Twitter*, 1 March [Online] https://twitter.com/jack/status/96923427932 1419776?lang=en

Economist (2017) [accessed 4 April 2018] Do Social Media Threaten Democracy? *The Economist*, 4 November [Online] www.economist.com/news/leaders/21730871-facebook-google-and-twitter-were-supposed-save-politics-good-information-drove-out

Edelman (2018) [accessed 3 April 2018] 2018 Edelman Trust Barometer Global Report [Online] https://cms.edelman.com/sites/default/files/2018-01/2018%20Edelman%20Trust%20Barometer%20Global%20Report.pdf

Edgecliffe-Johnson, A (2017) [accessed 2 April 2018] Can Journalists Ever Regain Americans' Trust? *Financial Times*, 17 November [Online] www.ft.com/content/955f7d84-c60e-11e7-a1d2-6786f39ef675

Financial Times (2018) [accessed 30 April 2018] OpEd: The Dangers of a Global Fake News Backlash, *Financial Times*, 8 April [Online] https://www.ft.com/content/135836ac-3b32-11e8-b9f9-de94fa33a81e

Fischer, S (2018) [accessed 5 April 2018] Facebook Can't Guarantee Its Platform Is Good for Democracy, *Axios*, 22 January [Online] www.axios.com/facebook-good-for-democracy-1516614297-6d7f49a0-4bce-46bc-a682-857b22253150.html

Ford, M (2017) [accessed 3 April 2018] Trump's Press Secretary Falsely Claims: Largest Audience Ever to Witness an Inauguration, Period, *The Atlantic*, 21 January [Online] www.theatlantic.com/politics/archive/2017/01/inauguration-crowd-size/514058/

Garton Ash, T (2016) [accessed 29 May 2018] What to Do When the 'Truth' Is Found to Be Lies, *Financial Times* [Online] https://www.ft.com/content/631d6b58-c3b5-11e6-81c2-f57d90f6741a

Giles, K (2017) [accessed 4 April 2018] Countering Russian Information Operations in the Age of Social Media, *Council on Foreign Relations*, 21 November [Online] www.cfr.org/report/countering-russian-information-operations-age-social-media

Groll, W (2018) [accessed 20 April 2018] Zuckerberg: We're in an 'Arms Race' with Russia, But AI Will Save Us, *Foreign Policy*, 10 April [Online] http://foreignpolicy.com/2018/04/10/zuckerberg-facebook-were-in-an-arms-race-with-russia-but-ai-artificial-intelligence-will-save-us/

Halper, E (2018) [accessed 20 April 2018] Senators Vented at Facebook CEO Mark Zuckerberg – But May Leave It at That, *Los Angeles Times*, 10 April [Online] http://www.latimes.com/business/technology/la-fi-tn-zuckerberg-testimony-20180410-story.html#nws=mcnewsletter

Haynes, D (2018) [accessed 5 April 2018] Spy Unit to Stop Foreign Fake News Campaigns, *The Times*, 24 January [Online] www.thetimes.co.uk/article/spy-unit-to-stop-foreign-fake-news-campaigns-5q0tfxs3p

Hern, A and Pegg, D (2018) [accessed 11 July 2018] Facebook Fined for Data Breaches in Cambridge Analytica Scandal, *The Guardian*, 11 July [Online] https://www.theguardian.com/technology/2018/jul/11/facebook-fined-for-data-breaches-in-cambridge-analytica-scandal

Ingram, D (2018) [accessed 5 April 2018] Facebook Says It Can't Guarantee Social Media Is Good for Democracy, *Reuters*, 22 January [Online] https://uk.reuters.com/article/uk-facebook-politics/facebook-says-it-cant-guarantee-social-media-is-good-for-democracy-idUKKBN1FB13Q

Insight Team (2018) [accessed 30 April 2018] Exposed: Russian Twitter Bots Tried to Swing General Election for Jeremy Corbyn, *The Times*,

29 April [Online] www.thetimes.co.uk/edition/news/exposed-russian-twitter-bots-tried-to-swing-general-election-for-jeremy-corbyn-zffv8652x

Ipsos MORI (2017) [accessed 5 April 2018] Veracity Index 2017, *Ipsos MORI*, November [Online] www.ipsos.com/sites/default/files/ct/news/documents/2017-11/trust-in-professions-veracity-index-2017-slides.pdf

Jaffe, A (2017) [accessed 3 April 2018] Kellyanne Conway: WH Spokesman Gave 'Alternative Facts' on Inauguration Crowd, *NBC News*, 22 January [Online] www.nbcnews.com/storyline/meet-the-press-70-years/wh-spokesman-gave-alternative-facts-inauguration-crowd-n710466

Jefferson, M (2018) [accessed 25 May 2018] Fighting Fake News: Facebook Unveils New Initiatives, *Mediatel*, 24 May [Online] https://mediatel.co.uk/newsline/2018/05/24/fighting-fake-news-facebook-unveils-new-initiatives

Johnson, A (2017) Orwell, G (2017) Orwell on Truth (Preface), Harvill Secker, London

Kahneman, D (2012) *Thinking, Fast and Slow*, Penguin, London

Kempe, F (2018) [accessed 21 May 2018] Atlantic Council DFR Lab Partners with Facebook to Combat Disinformation in Democratic Elections, *Atlantic Council*, 17 May [Online] http://www.atlanticcouncil.org/news/press-releases/atlantic-council-s-digital-forensic-research-lab-partners-with-facebook-to-combat-disinformation-in-democratic-elections

Kennedy, B (2016) [accessed 5 April 2018] Most Americans Trust the Military and Scientists to Act in the Public's Interest, *Pew Research*, 18 October [Online] www.pewresearch.org/fact-tank/2016/10/18/most-americans-trust-the-military-and-scientists-to-act-in-the-publics-interest/

Khan, J (2018) [accessed 5 April 2018] World Economic Forum, Davos 2018 'Fake News' Debate, *BBC*, 24 January [Online] www.youtube.com/watch?v=-rMYjUyLaGo

Kiefer, B (2018) [accessed 20 April 2018] Vice Dares Facebook users to Burst the Filter Bubble by Liking Posts They Hate, *Campaign*, 10 April [Online] www.campaignlive.co.uk/article/vice-dares-facebook-users-burst-filter-bubble-liking-posts-hate/1461691?bulletin=campaign_

agencies_bulletin&utm_medium=EMAIL&utm_campaign=eNews%20
Bulletin&utm_source=20180411&utm_content=Campaign%20
Agencies%20(11-04-2018)::www_campaignlive_co_uk_ar_9&email_
hash=

Klaas, B (2017) [accessed 5 April 2018] @brianklaas American Efforts
to Promote Press Freedom in Authoritarian Regimes Abroad
Have Been Destroyed by Trump's Tweets. Imagine Trying to Press
Myanmar to Release Its Jailed Journalists from the State Department
While the Myanmar Government Screams 'Fake News!' & Cites
These Tweets, *Twitter* [Online] https://twitter.com/brianklaas/
status/955796380236308481

Kuchler, H (2017) [accessed 5 April 2018] Start-ups Scent Opportunity in
Tackling Fake News, *Financial Times*, 10 December [Online]
www.ft.com/content/ddc1f4e6-da16-11e7-a039-c64b1c09b482

Levien, M (2018) [accessed 2 March 2018] Read More, Watch More,
Listen More: The Future of Journalism Is Up to You, *Medium*, 2 May
[Online] https://medium.com/@meredith_levien/read-more-watch-
more-listen-more-the-future-of-journalism-is-up-to-you-23c14d1d80bb

Lucas, E (2018) [accessed 1 June 2018] Ukraine Should Beware Copying
Russia's Tricks, *The Times*, 1 June [Online] https://www.thetimes.
co.uk/article/82fb88de-6507-11e8-9092-dbb5f656af2a

Macintyre, B (2017) [accessed 4 April 2018] Orwell's Prophecy of Our
Fake-News World, *The Times*, 4 November [Online] www.thetimes.
co.uk/article/orwell-s-prophecy-of-our-fake-news-world-ss3lq7vhb

Manthorpe, R (2017) [accessed 5 April 2018] This Start-Up Wants to Fix
Fake News. But Will It Do More Harm Than Good? *Wired*, 29 June
[Online] www.wired.co.uk/article/fake-news-ai-factmata-fullfact

Marr, A (2017) [accessed 4 April 2018] Anywheres vs Somewheres: The
Split That Made Brexit Inevitable, *The New Statesman*, 17 March
[Online] www.newstatesman.com/politics/uk/2017/03/anywheres-vs-
somewheres-split-made-brexit-inevitable

Marshall, T (2018) *Divided: Why We're Living in an Age of Walls*, Elliott &
Thompson, London

Mascarenhas, H (2017) [accessed 5 April 2018] Twitter Suspends 45
Russian Propaganda Accounts That Shared Messages on Trump,
Merkel and Brexit, *International Business Times*, 25 November

[Online] www.ibtimes.co.uk/twitter-suspends-45-russian-propaganda-accounts-that-shared-messages-trump-merkel-brexit-1648858

Matsakis, L (2018) [accessed 1 June 2018] Why a Russian Journalist Faked His Own Murder – and What Happens Now, 30 May [Online] https://www.wired.com/story/russian-journalist-arkady-babchenko-fake-murder/

McCarthy, J (2017) [accessed 5 April 2018] How Media Brands Are Turning Accusations of Fake News into Page Views, *The Drum*, 23 November [Online] www.thedrum.com/news/2017/11/23/how-media-brands-are-using-marketing-turn-accusations-fake-news-page-views

Midgley, N (2016) [accessed 20 April 2018] Word of the Year 2016 Is Post-Truth, *Oxford Dictionaries* [Online] https://en.oxforddictionaries.com/word-of-the-year/word-of-the-year-2016

Mohan, M (2016) [accessed 4 April 2018] Do Your Favourite Brands Show How Divided Brexit Britain Is? *BBC News*, 10 August [Online] www.bbc.co.uk/news/blogs-trending-36970535

Mosbergen, D (2017) [accessed 5 April 2018] Russian Warns US: Don't Meddle in Upcoming Presidential Election, *Huffington Post*, 28 December [Online] www.huffingtonpost.co.uk/entry/russia-us-election-meddling-putin-navalny_us_5a449174e4b06d1621b6d98f

Naughton, J (2018) [accessed 21 May 2018] As Facebook Becomes Better Policed, Bad Actors Are Moving to WhatsApp, *The Guardian*, 20 May [Online] https://www.theguardian.com/commentisfree/2018/may/20/as-facebook-becomes-better-policed-bad-actors-are-turning-to-whatsapp

Neiwert, D (2017) *Alt-America: The rise of the radical right in the age of Trump*, Verso, London

Nicas, J (2017) [accessed 5 April 2018] Facebook Plans to Let Users Know if They Followed Russian Pages, *The Wall Street Journal*, 22 November [Online] www.wsj.com/articles/facebook-plans-to-let-users-know-if-they-followed-russian-pages-1511370767

Nimmo, B (2018) [accessed 4 April 2018] Russia's Full Spectrum Propaganda: A Case Study in How Russia's Propaganda Machine Works, *Atlantic Council's Digital Forensic Research lab c/o Medium*, 23 January [Online] https://medium.com/dfrlab/russias-full-spectrum-propaganda-9436a246e970

Noble, J and Lockett, H (2016) [accessed 20 April 2018] Post-Truth Made Word of the Year by Oxford Dictionaries, *Financial Times* [Online] www.ft.com/content/85cbb2f8-abdd-11e6-9cb3-bb8207902122

Owens, J (2018) [accessed 30 April 2018] The Age of Post-Authenticity and the Ironic Truths of Meme Culture, *Medium*, 11 April [Online] https://medium.com/s/story/post-authenticity-and-the-real-truths-of-meme-culture-f98b24d645a0

Perry, E (2018) [accessed 20 April 2018] Facebook Is Fighting Fake News with Third-Party Fact-Checkers, *Social Media Week*, 4 April [Online] https://socialmediaweek.org/blog/2018/04/facebook-is-fighting-fake-news-with-third-party-fact-checkers/

Philp, C (2018) [accessed 14 July 2018] Russian Spies Charged by Justice Department over Meddling in US Election, *The Times*, 14 July [Online] https://www.thetimes.co.uk/edition/world/russian-spies-charged-by-justice-department-over-meddling-in-us-election-jmwmb0shs

Rand Corporation (2018) [accessed 20 April 2018] Truth Decay: Fighting for Facts and Analysis [Online] www.rand.org/research/projects/truth-decay.html

Rankin, J (2018) [accessed 22 May 2018] Complaints That Zuckerberg 'Avoided Questions' at European Parliament, *The Guardian*, 22 May [Online] https://www.theguardian.com/technology/2018/may/22/no-repeat-of-data-scandal-vows-mark-zuckerberg-in-brussels-facebook

Reagan, R (1987) [accessed 2 April 2018] Address to the Nation on the Iran Arms and Contra Aid Controversy, *Reagan Library Archives*, 4 March [Online] www.reaganlibrary.gov/sites/default/files/archives/speeches/1987/030487h.htm

Reporters Without Borders (2017) [accessed 5 April 2018] Predators of Press Freedom Use Fake News As Censorship Tool, *Reporters Without Borders*, 17 March [Online] https://rsf.org/en/news/predators-press-freedom-use-fake-news-censorship-tool

Rifkind, H (2017) [accessed 4 April 2018] Is Vladimir Putin Meddling in British Politics? *The Times*, 9 November [Online] www.thetimes.co.uk/article/the-fight-against-fake-news-p007rjshk

Roberts, D (2010) [accessed 20 April 2018] Post-Truth Politics, *Grist*, 1 April [Online] https://grist.org/article/2010-03-30-post-truth-politics/

Satariano, A (2018) [accessed 30 April 2018] Facebook Faces Tough Questions in Britain That It Avoided in the U.S., *The New York Times*, 26 April [Online] https://mobile.nytimes.com/2018/04/26/business/facebook-british-parliament.html

Serhan, Y (2017) [accessed 4 April 2018] Macron, Standing Alongside Putin, Says Russian Media Spread 'Falsehoods', *The Atlantic*, 30 May [Online] www.theatlantic.com/news/archive/2017/05/macron-rt-supnik-are-agents-of-influence/528480/

Shaban, H (2017) [accessed 5 April 2018] Facebook, Google and Twitter Testified on Capitol Hill. Here's What They Said, *The Washington Post*, 31 October [Online] www.washingtonpost.com/news/the-switch/wp/2017/10/31/facebook-google-and-twitter-are-set-to-testify-on-capitol-hill-heres-what-to-expect/?utm_term=.2620524b7502

Shearer, E (2017) [accessed 3 April 2018] News Use Across Social Media Platforms 2017, *Pew Research*, 7 September [Online] www.journalism.org/2017/09/07/news-use-across-social-media-platforms-2017/

Soares, I (2017) [accessed 4 April 2018] The Fake News Machine: Inside a Town Gearing Up for 2020, *CNN* [Online] http://money.cnn.com/interactive/media/the-macedonia-story/

Solon, O (2017) [accessed 20 April 2018] Divisive Russian-Backed Facebook Ads Released to Public, *The Guardian*, 1 November [Online] https://www.theguardian.com/technology/2017/nov/01/facebook-ads-russia-us-election-fake-news-released-public

Swift, A (2016) [accessed 31 March 2018] Americans' Trust in Mass Media Sinks to New Low, *Gallup News*, 14 September [Online] http://news.gallup.com/poll/195542/americans-trust-mass-media-sinks-new-low.aspx

Tarnoff, B and Weigel, M (2018) [accessed 3 May 2018] Why Silicon Valley Can't Fix Itself, *The Guardian*, 3 May [Online] https://www.theguardian.com/news/2018/may/03/why-silicon-valley-cant-fix-itself-tech-humanism

Tesich, S (1992) [accessed 2 April 2018] A Government of Lies, *The Nation*, 6 January [Online] https://drive.google.com/file/d/0BynDrdYrCLNtdmt0SFZFeGMtZUFsT1NmTGVTQmc1dEpmUC1z/view

Tett, G (2017) [accessed 5 April 2018] Want to Change the Media? Don't Get Mad – Get Even, *Financial Times*, 21 July [Online] www.ft.com/content/2ba2f132-6c18-11e7-bfeb-33fe0c5b7eaa

Thompson, N (2018) [accessed 25 May 2018] Exclusive: Facebook Opens Up About False News, *Wired*, 23 May [Online] https://www.wired.com/story/exclusive-facebook-opens-up-about-false-news/?mbid=nl_052418_daily_list_p

Thornhill, J (2016) [accessed 20 April 2018] Year in a Word: Post-truth, *Financial Times*, 22 February [Online] https://www.ft.com/content/47761ace-c394-11e6-9bca-2b93a6856354

Trump, D (2017) [accessed 3 April 2018] Fox News Is Much More Important in the United States Than CNN, But Outside of the U.S., CNN International Is Still a Major Source of (Fake) News, and They Represent Our Nation to the World Very Poorly. The Outside World Does Not See the Truth from Them! @realDonaldTrump, 25 November [Online] https://twitter.com/realdonaldtrump/status/934551607596986368?lang=en

Turner, J (2017) [accessed 4 April 2018] Labour Turns a Blind Eye to Its Vile Trolls, *The Times*, 15 July [Online] www.thetimes.co.uk/article/labour-turns-a-blind-eye-to-its-vile-trolls-phj39g32j

Wallace, G (2016) [accessed 3 April 2018] Voting Turnout at 20-Year Low in 2016, *CNN*, 30 November [Online] https://edition.cnn.com/2016/11/11/politics/popular-vote-turnout-2016/index.html

Waterson, J (2018) [accessed 3 July 2018] Google and Facebook Won: Old Guard of Advertising under Threat in Cannes, *The Guardian*, 22 June [Online] https://www.theguardian.com/media/2018/jun/22/google-facebook-won-old-guard-advertising-under-threat-cannes-lions

Whale, S (2017) [accessed 5 April 2018] Damian Collins: Voters Have a Right to Know About Russian Interference in UK Politics, *Politics Home*, 16 November [Online] www.politicshome.com/news/uk/sport/house/house-magazine/90669/damian-collins-voters-have-right-know-about-russian

White, J (2017) [accessed 4 April 2018] Facebook Says 126 Million Americans May Have Been Exposed to Russia-Linked US Election Posts, *The Independent*, 31 October [Online] www.independent.co.uk/news/world/americas/us-politics/facebook-russia-adverts-americans-exposed-trump-us-election-2016-millions-a8028526.html

World Advertising Research Center (WARC) (2018) [accessed 30 May 2018] CNN calls for new definition of brand safety, *WARC News*,

29 May [Online] https://www.warc.com/newsandopinion/news/cnn_
calls_for_new_definition_of_brand_safety/40536

World Economic Forum (2018) [accessed 31 March 2018] Fake News vs
Real Politics, *Davos 2018*, 24 January [Online] www.weforum.org/
events/world-economic-forum-annual-meeting-2018/sessions/fake-
news-versus-real-politics

Chapter 2

BBC News (2018) [accessed 5 May 2018] The UK's Data Watchdog Has
Ordered the Parent Company of Cambridge Analytica to Hand over
the Data of a US Citizen, *BBC News*, 5 May [Online] https://www.bbc.
co.uk/programmes/b0b0lzsd

BBC Technology (2018) [accessed 30 April 2018] Amazon Patents 'Voice-
Sniffing' Algorithms, *BBC News*, 11 April [Online] www.bbc.co.uk/
news/technology-43725708

Big Brother Watch (2013) [accessed 30 April 2018] New Research: Global
Attitudes to Privacy Online, *Big Brother Watch*, 24 June [Online]
https://bigbrotherwatch.org.uk/2013/06/new-research-global-attitudes-
to-privacy-online/

Bridge, M (2018a) [accessed 30 April 2018] Alexa the Robot
Saleswoman Will Follow You Around the House, *The Times*, 24 April
[Online] www.thetimes.co.uk/article/014db2ae-47c9-11e8-8db5-
58268675bbb1

Bridge, M (2018b) [accessed 7 May 2018] Facebook Puts Isis Supporters
in Touch, *The Times*, 7 May [Online] https://www.thetimes.co.uk/
article/1b13e762-516f-11e8-9795-08ef69e784e8

Bridge, M (2018c) [accessed 7 May 2018] Cambridge Analytica Must
Return Data to US Academic, *The Times*, 7 May [Online] https://www.
thetimes.co.uk/article/de8da302-517b-11e8-9795-08ef69e784e8

Brown, D (2016) [accessed 30 April 2018] New UN Resolution on the
Right to Privacy in the Digital Age: Crucial and Timely, *Internet Policy
Review*, 22 November [Online] https://policyreview.info/articles/news/
new-un-resolution-right-privacy-digital-age-crucial-and-timely/436

Cadwalladr, C (2018a) [accessed 05 May 2018] UK Regulator Orders
Cambridge Analytica to Release Data on US Voter, *The Guardian*,

5 May [Online] https://www.theguardian.com/uk-news/2018/may/05/
cambridge-analytica-uk-regulator-release-data-us-voter-david-carroll

Cadwalladr, C (2018b) [accessed 6 May 2018] Cambridge Analytica Has
Gone. But What Has It Left in Its Wake? *The Guardian*, 6 May [Online]
https://www.theguardian.com/uk-news/2018/may/06/cambridge-
analytica-gone-what-has-it-left-in-its-wake?CMP=share_btn_tw

Cadwalladr, C and Graham-Harrison, E (2018a) [accessed 25 May
2018] Facebook Accused of Conducting Mass Surveillance through
Its Apps, *The Guardian*, 25 May [Online] https://www.theguardian.
com/technology/2018/may/24/facebook-accused-of-conducting-mass-
surveillance-through-its-apps

Cadwalladr, C and Graham-Harrison, E (2018b) [accessed 24 May 2018]
Zuckerberg Set Up Fraudulent Scheme to 'Weaponise' Data, Court Case
Alleges, *The Guardian*, 24 May [Online] https://www.theguardian.com/
technology/2018/may/24/mark-zuckerberg-set-up-fraudulent-scheme-
weaponise-data-facebook-court-case-alleges

Chinese Govt State Council Notice (2015) [accessed 30 April 2018]
Planning Outline for the Construction of the Social Credit System
(2014–2020), *China Copyright and Media*, 14 June [Online]
https://chinacopyrightandmedia.wordpress.com/2014/06/14/planning-
outline-for-the-construction-of-a-social-credit-system-2014-2020/

Dwoskin, E (2018) [accessed 30 April 2018] Facebook's Rules for
Accessing User Data Lured More Than Just Cambridge Analytica,
The Washington Post, 19 March [Online] www.washingtonpost.com/
business/economy/facebooks-rules-for-accessing-user-data-lured-more-
than-just-cambridge-analytica/2018/03/19/31f6979c-658e-43d6-a71f-
afdd8bf1308b_story.html?utm_term=.a59357bbe0d3

Fortson, D (2018) [accessed 30 April 2018] Mark Zuckerberg in
Facebook 'Shadow Profiles' Row, *The Times*, 15 April [Online]
www.thetimes.co.uk/article/mark-zuckerberg-in-facebook-shadow-
profiles-row-mxzfhmh7z

Green, S (2015) [accessed 30 April 2018] Consumer Privacy in the Digital
Age, *Harvard Business Review*, 14 May [Online] https://hbr.org/
ideacast/2015/05/consumer-privacy-in-the-digital-age

Halpern, S (2017) [accessed 30 April 2018] How He Used Facebook
to Win, *NYBooks*, 8 June [Online] www.nybooks.com/
articles/2017/06/08/how-trump-used-facebook-to-win/

Hern, A (2018) [accessed 30 April 2018] Five Things We Learned from Mark Zuckerberg's Facebook Hearing, *The Guardian*, 11 April [Online] www.theguardian.com/technology/2018/apr/11/mark-zuckerbergs-facebook-hearing-five-things-we-learned

Hern, A and Sabbagh, D (2018) [accessed 29 May 2018] EU referendum won through fraud, whistleblower tells MPs, *The Guardian*, 27 May [Online] https://www.theguardian.com/uk-news/2018/mar/27/brexit-groups-had-common-plan-to-avoid-election-spending-laws-says-wylie

Hoffman, B (2018) [accessed 30 April 2018] Ad Industry's Irresponsibility Continues Unabated, *Twitter*, 25 April [Online] https://twitter.com/AdContrarian/status/989294834014863360

Hoyle, B (2018) [accessed 30 April 2018] Apple Boss Tim Cook on Data Privacy, Screen Time and Secrecy in Silicon Valley, *The Times*, 28 April [Online] www.thetimes.co.uk/article/apple-boss-tim-cook-on-data-privacy-screen-time-and-secrecy-in-silicon-valley-dpt3fzdxf

ICO (2017) [accessed 30 April 2018] ICO Survey Shows Most UK Citizens Don't Trust Organisations with Their Data, *ICO*, 6 November [Online] https://ico.org.uk/about-the-ico/news-and-events/news-and-blogs/2017/11/ico-survey-shows-most-uk-citizens-don-t-trust-organisations-with-their-data/

Ingram, D (2018) [accessed 30 April 2018] Exclusive: Facebook to Put 1.5 Billion Users Out of Reach of New EU Privacy Law, *Reuters*, 19 April [Online] www.reuters.com/article/us-facebook-privacy-eu-exclusive/exclusive-facebook-to-put-1-5-billion-users-out-of-reach-of-new-eu-privacy-law-idUSKBN1HQ00P

Kranish, M and Romm, T (2018) [accessed 5 May 2018] Cambridge Analytica, Data Consultant for Trump Campaign and Others, *The Washington Post*, 20 March [Online] https://www.washingtonpost.com/politics/cambridge-analytica-data-consultant-for-trump-campaign-and-others-suspends-ceo-amid-federal-probe-of-its-use-of-facebook-data/2018/03/20/3f1d8a4c-2c75-11e8-b0b0-f706877db618_story.html?noredirect=on&utm_term=.b5394bbab03e

Kunz, B (2018) [accessed 30 April 2018] Lessons from a Rebooted SXSW Interactive, *Thought Gadgets*, 14 March [Online] www.thoughtgadgets.com/?p=9568

Lemire, J (2018) [accessed 6 May 2018] Mueller Examining Cambridge Analytica, Trump Campaign Ties, *The Denver Post*, 22 March [Online] https://www.denverpost.com/2018/03/22/cambridge-analytica-donald-trump-robert-mueller

Lewis, P and Hilder, P (2018) [accessed 30 April 2018] Cambridge Analytica Misled MPs over Work for Leave.EU, Says Ex-Director, *The Guardian*, 23 March [Online] www.theguardian.com/news/2018/mar/23/cambridge-analytica-misled-mps-over-work-for-leave-eu-says-ex-director-brittany-kaiser

Ma, A (2018) [accessed 30 April 2018] China Has Started Ranking Citizens with a Creepy 'Social Credit' System – Here's What You Can Do Wrong and the Embarrassing, Demeaning Ways They Can Punish You, *Business Insider*, 8 April [Online] http://uk.businessinsider.com/china-social-credit-system-punishments-and-rewards-explained-2018-4?r=US&IR=T/#1-banning-you-from-flying-or-getting-the-train-1

Mac, R (2018) [accessed 04 May 2018] Facebook Placed an Employee Who Harvested User Data for Cambridge Analytica on Leave, 3 May [Online] https://www.buzzfeed.com/amphtml/ryanmac/facebook-joseph-chancellor-administrative-leave-cambrdige?utm_term=.lvWvMdxE7&__twitter_impression=true

McMillan, R and Knutson, R (2017) [accessed 30 April 2018] Yahoo Triples Estimate of Breached Accounts to 3 Billion, *The Wall Street Journal*, 3 October [Online] www.wsj.com/articles/yahoo-triples-estimate-of-breached-accounts-to-3-billion-1507062804?ns=prod/accounts-wsj

Morey, T and Forbath, T and Schoop, A (2015) [accessed 30 April 2018] Customer Data: Designing for Transparency and Trust, *Harvard Business Review*, May [Online] https://hbr.org/2015/05/customer-data-designing-for-transparency-and-trust?referral=00134

Oakes, O (2018a) [accessed 30 April 2018] Should Political Parties Be Allowed to Use Micro-Targeting? *Campaign*, 25 April [Online] www.campaignlive.co.uk/article/political-parties-allowed-use-micro-targeting/1463000?bulletin=campaign_agencies_bulletin&utm_medium=EMAIL&utm_campaign=eNews%20Bulletin&utm_source=20180425&utm_content=Campaign%20Agencies%20(25-04-2018)::www_campaignlive_co_uk_ar_11&email_hash=

Oakes, O (2018b) [accessed 30 April 2018] IPA Calls for Suspension of Micro-Targeted Political Ads, *Campaign*, 20 April [Online] www.campaignlive.co.uk/article/ipa-calls-suspension-micro-targeted-political-ads/1462598

O'Brien, C (2018) [accessed 5 April 2018] Elliot Schrage on Facebook Backlash: 'We Have Not Done as Good a Job as We Need to Do', *Venturebeat*, 22 January [Online] https://venturebeat.com/2018/01/22/elliot-schrage-on-facebook-backlash-we-have-not-done-as-good-a-job-as-we-need-to-do/

Osborne, H and Sabbagh, D (2018) [accessed 30 April 2018] Cambridge Analytica: Search of London HQ Delayed by Wait for Warrant, *The Guardian*, 22 March [Online] www.theguardian.com/uk-news/2018/mar/22/cambridge-analytica-warrant-high-court-adjourns-hearing-information-commissioner

Parakilas, S (2017) [accessed 5 April 2018] We Can't Trust Facebook to Regulate Itself, *The New York Time*s, 19 November [Online] www.nytimes.com/2017/11/19/opinion/facebook-regulation-incentive.html

Pendergast, T (2018) The Next Cold War Is Here, and It's All About Data, *Wire*d, 28 March [Online] www.wired.com/story/opinion-new-data-cold-war/ [accessed 30 April 2018]

Ritson, M (2018) [accessed 30 April 2018] Mark Ritson: This Is a Critical Point in Marketers' Relationship with Data Privacy, *Marketing Week*, 3 April [Online] www.marketingweek.com/2018/04/03/mark-ritson-marketers-data-privacy/

Sevak, T (2018) [accessed 30 April 2018] Targeting Personalised Ads to the Right Audience, *YouGov*, 26 March [Online] https://yougov.co.uk/news/2018/03/26/targeting-personalised-ads-right-audience/

Si, M (2018) [accessed 30 April 2018] Face Reading Gets AI Touch, *China Daily*, 9 April [Online] www.chinadaily.com.cn/a/201804/09/WS5acace25a3105cdcf6516e5b.html

Slaughter, A (2018) [accessed 30 April 2018] Our Struggle with Big Tech to Protect Trust and Truth, *Financial Times*, 6 February [Online] www.ft.com/content/ff7b7ec4-1aec-11e8-a748-5da7d696ccab

Sloane, G (2018a) [accessed 1 May 2018] Facebook, Very Busy, Working on a Dating Service and AR for Messenger, *AdAge*, 1 May [Online] http://adage.com/article/digital/f8-facebook-launches-dating-service-ar-messenger/313347/

Sloane, G (2018b) [accessed 30 April 2018] Facebook Says 'Most People' Likely Had Their Data Scraped from Its Platform, *AdAge*, 4 April [Online] http://adage.com/article/digital/facebook-close-data-holes-reveals-rampant-scraping/312991/

Sloane, G (2018c) [accessed 30 April 2018] Advertisers Signal to Facebook They Want More Data, Not Less, *AdAge*, 25 April [Online] http://adage.com/article/digital/advertisers-signal-facebook-data/313276/?utm_medium=Social&utm_source=Twitter&utm_campaign=SocialFlow

Solon, O (2018a) [accessed 3 May 2018] Cambridge Analytics Closing After Facebook Data Harvesting Scandal, *The Guardian*, 3 May [Online] https://www.theguardian.com/uk-news/2018/may/02/cambridge-analytica-closing-down-after-facebook-row-reports-say

Solon, O (2018b) [accessed 30 April 2018] How Europe's 'Breakthrough' Privacy Law Takes on Facebook and Google, *The Guardian*, 19 April [Online] www.theguardian.com/technology/2018/apr/19/gdpr-facebook-google-amazon-data-privacy-regulation

Sulleyman, A (2017) [accessed 30 April 2018] Google Home Mini Secretly Recorded Everything Its Owner Said, *The Independent*, 11 October [Online] www.independent.co.uk/life-style/gadgets-and-tech/news/google-home-mini-secretly-recording-everything-you-say-voice-assistant-my-activity-a7994261.html

Swift, J (2018) [accessed 30 April 2018] Voice: The Long and Short of It, *Contagious*, 18 April [Online] www.contagious.com/blogs/news-and-views/what-brands-should-speak-when-spoken-to?utm_source=Contagious+Newsletter&utm_campaign=1e5ca50d0c-EMAIL_CAMPAIGN_2018_04_03&utm_medium=email&utm_term=0_c637df1c24-1e5ca50d0c-368445117

Taplin, J (2018) [accessed 30 April 2018] 'Facebook Is a Profit Making Organisation That Is in the Surveillance Capitalism Business' Argues @ Jonathan Taplin, *BBC Newsnight Twitter*, 10 April [Online] https://twitter.com/BBCNewsnight/status/983829352969207810

The Times (2018) [accessed 30 April 2018] OpEd: Anti-Social Network, *The Times*, 12 April [Online] www.thetimes.co.uk/article/anti-social-network-htvdxqlsn

Tobitt, C (2018) [accessed 30 April 2018] Observer's Carole Cadwalladr: I Became a 'News Slave' in Pursuing Cambridge Analytica Data

Harvesting Scoop, *Press Gazette*, 22 March [Online] www.
pressgazette.co.uk/observers-carole-cadwalladr-i-became-a-news-slave-
in-pursuing-cambridge-analytica-data-harvesting-scoop/

Vizard, S (2018) [accessed 30 April 2018] The ICO Preps Campaign to
Educate Consumers on Data and GDPR, *Marketing Week*, 23February
[Online] www.marketingweek.com/2018/02/23/ico-preps-campaign-
educate-consumers-data-gdpr/

Waite, J (2017) [accessed 30 April 2018] Jeremy Waite – the Future of
AI in Marketing, *YouTube*, 25 June [Online] www.youtube.com/
watch?v=FfL5LvfYw-U

Watson, R (2016) *Digital vs Human: How we'll live, love and think in the
future*, Scribe Publications, London

Williams, A (2018) [accessed 30 April 2018] What's Really Stopping
Amazon and Google from Recording Us 24/7? *The Ambient*, 4 January
[Online] www.the-ambient.com/features/amazon-google-unauthorised-
data-capture-laws-186

Wong, J and Lewis, P (2018) [accessed 30 April 2018] Facebook Gave
Data About 57bn Friendships to Academic, *The Guardian*, 22 March
[Online] www.theguardian.com/news/2018/mar/22/facebook-gave-
data-about-57bn-friendships-to-academic-aleksandr-kogan

Yakob, F (2016) [accessed 30 April 2018] Personalized Advertising
Is an Oxymoron or: How We Forgot That Minority Report Was a
Dystopian Vision, *Context*, 10 October [Online] https://medium.com/
context/personalized-advertising-is-an-oxymoron-77c95f608fb5

Zuckerberg, M (2018) [accessed 30 April 2018] I Want to Share an
Update on the Cambridge Analytica Situation …, *Facebook*, 21 March
[Online] www.facebook.com/zuck/posts/10104712037900071

Chapter 3

Bain & Company (2018) [accessed 29 March 2018] Advanced Analytics,
Bain [Online] www.bain.com/consulting-services/advanced-analytics/
index.aspx

B&T (2017) [accessed 29 March 2018] Marc Pritchard: 'We Need the Next
Generation of Digital Ads, Because People Hate Ads', *B&T*, 14 September

[Online] www.bandt.com.au/media/marc-pritchard-need-next-generation-digital-ads-people-hate-ads

Braiker, B (2018) [accessed 02 July 2018] Cannes Gets Back to Business, *AdAge*, 22 June [Online] http://adage.com/article/special-report-cannes-lions/cannes-back-business/314015/

Bruell, A (2017) [accessed 29 March 2018] P&G Cuts More Than $100 Million in 'Largely Ineffective' Digital Ads, *The Wall Street Journal*, 27 July [Online] www.wsj.com/articles/p-g-cuts-more-than-100-million-in-largely-ineffective-digital-ads-1501191104

Bughin, J (2010) [accessed 29 March 2018] A New Way to Measure Word-of-Mouth Marketing, *McKinsey*, April [Online] www.mckinsey.com/business-functions/marketing-and-sales/our-insights/a-new-way-to-measure-word-of-mouth-marketing

Chahal, M (2016) [accessed 29 March 2018] Brand Strategy, Data and Customer Experience Are Marketers' New Priorities, *Marketing Week*, 9 May [Online] www.marketingweek.com/2016/05/09/importance-of-brand-strategy-data-and-customer-experience-have-grown-at-highest-rate-for-marketers/

Dash, C (2015) [accessed 29 March 2018] Three Beautiful 'Apartments' That Are Actually Stores (and We Want to Buy Everything in Them), *Vogue*, 26 October [Online] www.vogue.com/article/apartment-style-stores-sezane-the-line

Edelman (2017) [accessed 29 March 2018] 2017 Edelman Earned Brand Study, Beyond No Brand's Land, *Edelman*, 18 June [Online] www.slideshare.net/EdelmanInsights/2017-edelman-earned-brand

Finkelstein, H (2017) [accessed 29 March 2018] 5 Trends That Will Change the Way Your Customers Will Shop in 2017, *Forbes*, 16 January [Online] www.forbes.com/sites/harleyfinkelstein/2017/01/16/5-trends-that-will-change-the-way-you-shop-in-2017/#30fb7c31578a

Frean, A (2018) [accessed 29 March 2018] Still Winning Friends and Influencing People after 40 Years in Advertising, *The Times*, 13 January [Online] www.thetimes.co.uk/article/still-winning-friends-and-influencing-people-after-40-years-in-advertising-8d52vgrkg

Gallen, S (2017) [accessed 29 March 2018] Contagious Founder Paul Kemp on the Future of Advertising, *Forbes*, 10 December [Online] www.forbes.com/sites/berlinschoolofcreativeleadership/2017/12/10/

contagious-founder-paul-kemp-robertson-on-the-future-of-
advertising/#2a956f2978ea

Golding, D (2017) [accessed 29 March 2018] The Big Adland
Divide: Culture vs Collateral, *Campaign*, 20 February [Online]
www.campaignlive.co.uk/article/big-adland-divide-culture-vs-
collateral/1424173

Goodfellow, J (2016) [accessed 29 March 2018] Adidas' Dark Social
Experiment Is Darker Than Initially Thought, *The Drum*, 10 October
[Online] www.thedrum.com/news/2016/10/10/adidas-dark-social-
experiment-darker-initially-thought

Hammett, E (2018) [accessed 7 May 2018] Record Number of Ad
Complaints Sees Online Overtake TV, *Marketing Week*, 4 May
[Online] https://www.marketingweek.com/2018/05/04/ad-complaints-
online-tv/

Handley, L (2017a) [accessed 29 March 2018] People Wouldn't Care if
Three Quarters of Brands Disappeared, *CNBC*, 2 February [Online]
www.cnbc.com/2017/02/02/people-wouldnt-care-if-three-quarters-of-
brands-disappeared-survey.html

Handley, L (2017b) [accessed 29 March 2018] People Wouldn't Care
if Three Quarters of Brands Disappeared: Survey, *Yahoo Finance*,
2 February [Online] https://uk.finance.yahoo.com/news/people-
wouldn-t-care-three-070500342.html

Havas (2018) [accessed 29 March 2018] Meaningful Brands, *Havas
Media Group*, 2018 [Online] file:///Users/helen/Library/Containers/
com.apple.mail/Data/Library/Mail%20Downloads/7B026684-B1F3-
4D1B-A276-655446ABC3CC/Meaningful%20Brands®%20-%20
Havas%20Media%20Group.htm

Herring, L (2014) [accessed 29 March 2018] Making Stores Matter
in a Multichannel World, *McKinsey*, December [Online] www.
mckinsey.com/industries/retail/our-insights/making-stores-matter-in-a-
multichannel-world

Hirst, C (2018) [accessed 29 March 2018] The Year Ahead for
Advertising Agencies: Expect More Disruption and a Creative
Renaissance, *Campaign*, 9 January [Online] www.campaignlive.co.uk/
article/year-ahead-advertising-agencies-expect-disruption-creative-
renaissance/1453802

Hoffman, B (2017) Badmen: How Advertising Went from a Minor Annoyance to a Major Menace, Type A Group, United States

Ipsos MORI (2017) [accessed 29 March 2018] Veracity Index 2017 – All Professions Overview, Ipsos MORI, November [Online] www.ipsos.com/sites/default/files/ct/news/documents/2017-11/trust-in-professions-veracity-index-2017-slides.pdf

Jeffrey, P (2017) [accessed 29 March 2018] Cannes Lions / Outdoor, PR & Glass Winners, *Contagious*, 19 June [Online] www.contagious.com/blogs/news-and-views/cannes-lions-outdoor-pr-amp-glass-winners

Livingstone, R (2017) [accessed 29 March 2018] The Future of Online Advertising Is Big Data and Algorithms, *The Conversation*, 13 March [Online] http://theconversation.com/the-future-of-online-advertising-is-big-data-and-algorithms-69297

McMullan, C (2016) [accessed 29 March 2018] Adidas's Venture into the Underground Brings Branding to New Depth, *Digital Sport*, 29 November [Online] https://digitalsport.co/adidass-venture-into-the-underground-brings-branding-to-new-depths

Moore, M (2018) [accessed 02 July 2018] Unilever Dumps Celebrities Who Pay for Followers, *The Times*, 18 June [Online] https://www.thetimes.co.uk/article/eae8a1a4-7270-11e8-a4b0-c06c-25e9bae2

Neff, J (2016) [accessed 29 March 2018] P&G's Pritchard: Time to Cut the Crap – and the Pressure on Agencies, *AdAge*, 20 October [Online] http://adage.com/article/special-report-ana-annual-meeting-2016/p-g-s-pritchard-time-cut-crap-agency-pressure/306370/

Neff, J (2017) [accessed 29 March 2018] Two Seconds Is Not Enough for P&G: Pritchard Calls for 'Next Generation of Digital Ads', *AdAge*, 19 September [Online] http://adage.com/article/special-report-dmexco/p-g-s-pritchard-calls-generation-digital-ads/310442/

Nielsen (2015) [accessed 29 March 2018] Recommendations from Friends Remain Most Credible Form of Advertising Among Consumers, *Neilsen*, 28 September [Online] www.nielsen.com/eu/en/press-room/2015/recommendations-from-friends-remain-most-credible-form-of-advertising.html

Nudd, T (2017) [accessed 29 March 2018] 'Fearless Girl' Dominates the Clios, Winning the Grand Clio in 5 Catagories, *Adweek*, 28 September [Online] www.adweek.com/creativity/fearless-girl-dominates-the-clios-winning-the-grand-clio-in-5-categories/

Ogilvy, D (2014) *Ogilvy on Advertising: 'I hate rules'*, Prion Books, Chicago

Pritchard, M (2017) [accessed 30 April 2018] Proctor & Gamble Chief Issues Powerful Media Transparency Rallying Cry, *Campaign*, 30 January [Online] www.campaignlive.co.uk/article/procter-gamble-chief-issues-powerful-media-transparency-rallying-cry/1422599

R/GA (2017) [accessed 29 March 2018] Cannes Lions 2017: 'Change Your Methods, While You Are on Top', *Campaign India*, 21 June [Online] www.campaignindia.in/article/cannes-lions-2017-change-your-methods-while-youre-at-the-top/437503

Richards, K (2017) [accessed 29 March 2018] Fearless Girl Stole the World's Heart, But What Did It Do for the Client's Business? *Adweek*, 10 September [Online] www.adweek.com/brand-marketing/fearless-girl-stole-the-worlds-heart-but-what-did-it-do-for-the-clients-business/

Roberts, D (2014) *Sad Men: A memoir: It's advertising but know as you know it …*, Bantam Press, London

Roderick, L (2017) [accessed 29 March 2018] Why Bank Brands Are Taking a More Purposeful Marketing Approach, *Marketing Week*, 25 January [Online] www.marketingweek.com/2017/01/25/bank-brands-purposeful-approach/

Schumpeter (2018) [accessed 29 March 2018] Something Doesn't Ad Up About America's Advertising Market, *The Economist*, 18 January [Online] https://www.economist.com/news/business/21735029-stockmarket-investors-are-wrong-expect-enormous-surge-advertising-revenues-something

Sherwood, I-Hsien (2018) [accessed 3 June 2018] Fearless Girl Takes Top Honor at 2018 Effie Awards, *AdAge,* 31 May [Online] http://adage.com/article/agency-news/fearless-girl-takes-top-honor-2018-effie-awards/313709/?utm_visit=597492

Tencent (2017) [accessed 29 March 2018] Tencent's Cannes 'China Day' Marks China's Transformation from Follower to Leader, *PR Newswire*, 21 June [Online] www.prnewswire.com/news-releases/tencents-cannes-china-day-marks-chinas-transformation-from-follower-to-leader-629879443.html

The Fashion Law (2018) [accessed 29 March 2018] How Influencers Turned Word-of-Mouth Marketing into a $1 Billion Digital Goldmine, *The Fashion Law*, 16 January [Online] www.thefashionlaw.com/home/the-business-of-influencer-modern-day-word-of-mouth-marketing

The Network One (2016) [accessed 29 March 2018] Cannes Review 2016, The Network One [Online] https://thenetworkone.com

The Network One (2017) [accessed 29 May 2018] Cannes Review 2017, *The Network One* [Online] https://thenetworkone.com/wp-content/uploads/2017/01/thenetworkone-cannes-review-2017.pdf

The Network One (2018) [accessed 07 July 2018] Cannes Review 2018, *The Network One* [Online] https://thenetworkone.com

Trott, D (2013) *Predatory Thinking: A masterclass in out-thinking the competition*, Macmillan, London

Vallance, C (2017) [accessed 29 March 2018] Trust Me, I'm an Adman, *Campaign*, 6 November [Online] www.campaignlive.co.uk/article/trust-me-im-adman/1448758

Voight, J (2007) [accessed 29 March 2018] How to Define a Brand's Soul, *Adweek*, 18 June [Online] www.adweek.com/brand-marketing/how-define-brands-soul-89403/

Vranica, S (2016) [accessed 29 March 2018] Facebook Overestimated Key Video Metric for Two Years, *The Wall Street Journal*, 22 September [Online] www.wsj.com/articles/facebook-overestimated-key-video-metric-for-two-years-1474586951

Vranica, S (2017) [accessed 29 March 2018] 'Fearless Girl' Steals the Conversation, *The Wall Street Journal*, 19 June [Online] www.wsj.com/articles/fearless-girl-steals-the-conversation-1497864600

Weed, K (2017) [accessed 29 March 2018] Keith Weed: We Need Comparable Metrics in a Digital World, *Marketing Week*, 22 February [Online] www.marketingweek.com/2017/02/22/keith-weed-need-comparable-metrics-digital-world/

WFA (2016) [accessed 29 March 2018] WFA Issues Advice for Combatting Ad Fraud, *World Federation of Advertisers*, 6 June [Online] www.wfanet.org/news-centre/wfa-issues-first-advice-for-combatting-ad-fraud/

Whitler, K (2014) [accessed 29 March 2018] Why Word of Mouth Marketing Is the Most Important Social Media, *Forbes*, 17 July [Online] www.forbes.com/sites/kimberlywhitler/2014/07/17/why-word-of-mouth-marketing-is-the-most-important-social-media/#1c9df72d54a8

WOMMA & AMA (2013) [accessed 29 March 2018] 2 in 3 Marketers Say Word-of-Mouth Marketing More Effective Than Traditional Marketing, *Marketing Charts*, 25 November [Online] www.marketingcharts.com/digital/social-media-38330

Chapter 4

Barnes, R (2018) [accessed 28 March 2018] Is Purpose-Washing Damaging the Industry? *Campaign*, 12 February [Online] www.campaignlive.co.uk/article/purpose-washing-damaging-industry/1456451

Barton, D (2018) [accessed 23 April 2018] Reflections from Davos 2018, *McKinsey*, 30 January [Online] www.mckinsey.com/about-us/new-at-mckinsey-blog/reflections-from-davos-2018

Chouinard, Y (2006) *Let My People Go Surfing: The education of a reluctant businessman*, Penguin, London

Cushman, J (1998) [accessed 28 March 2018] Nike Pledges to End Child Labour and Apply US Rules Abroad, *The New York Times*, 13 May [Online] www.nytimes.com/1998/05/13/business/international-business-nike-pledges-to-end-child-labor-and-apply-us-rules-abroad.html

Economist (2009) [accessed 28 March 2018] Triple Bottom Line, *The Economist*, 17 November [Online] www.economist.com/node/14301663

Fournier, S (2009) [accessed 28 March 2018] Getting Brand Communities Right, *Harvard Business Review*, April [Online] https://hbr.org/2009/04/getting-brand-communities-right

Havea, M (2014) [accessed 28 March 2018] Bart Houlahan Thinks Business Can Change the World, *Dumbo Feather Magazine*, 3 September [Online] www.dumbofeather.com/conversations/bart-houlahan-thinks-business-can-change-the-world/

House of Vans (2017) [accessed 28 March 2018] Reflecting on Subcultures, *House of Vans and London College of Fashio*n [Online] http://houseofvanslondon.com/events/calendar/events/reflecting-on-sub-cultures

Jan, N (2017) [accessed 28 March 2018] Bring Back Bottle Deposits to Stop Plastic Pollution in Our Oceans, *38 Degrees blog*, 28 January [Online] https://home.38degrees.org.uk/2017/01/28/bring-back-bottle-deposits-stop-plastic-pollution-oceans/

Jones, G (2017) [accessed 28 March 2018] Brands and Activism: The Shift from Corporation to 'Community of Citizens', *The Drum*, 10 June [Online] www.thedrum.com/opinion/2017/06/10/brands-activism-the-shift-corporation-community-citizens

Keys, D (1985) *Earth at Omega: Passage to planetization*, Branden, Wellesley, MA

Lee, L (2009) [accessed 28 March 2018] The Power of Community in Marketing, *Forbes*, 6 April [Online] www.forbes.com/2009/04/06/lara-lee-community-branding-leadership-cmo-network-marketing.html#5767b3e23851

Lego (2018) [accessed 28 March 2018] Local Community Engagement [Online] www.lego.com/en-gb/aboutus/responsibility/caring-ethical-and-transparent/local-community-engagement

Lesko, S (2017) Oiselle, Bras, and Destiny, *Oiselle*, 22 May [Online] www.oiselle.com/blog/oiselle-bras-and-destiny [accessed 28 March 2018]

McKinsey (2017) [accessed 28 March 2018] Mapping the Benefits of a Circular Economy, *McKinsey Quarterly*, June [Online] www.mckinsey.com/business-functions/sustainability-and-resource-productivity/our-insights/mapping-the-benefits-of-a-circular-economy

Mycoskie, B (2012) *Start Something That Matters*, Random House, London

Parker, S (2017) [accessed 28 March 2018] Oiselle: When a Brand Really Means It, *The Union Metrics blog*, 27 May [Online] https://unionmetrics.com/blog/2017/05/oiselle-brand-really-means/

Sleaze Nation (1999) Jeunes revoltes en robe de coktail Molotov rassemblez vous, *Sleaze Nation Magazine*, November

Sormunen, K (2017) [accessed 28 March 2018] The Circular Economy Enters the World Stage, With Finland Leading The Way, *The Guardian*, 6 June [Online] www.theguardian.com/global-development-professionals-network/2017/jun/06/the-circular-economy-enters-the-world-stage-with-finland-leading-the-way

Strauss, K (2017) [accessed 28 March 2018] The 10 Companies with the Best CSR Reputations in 2017, *Forbes*, 13 September [Online] www.forbes.com/sites/karstenstrauss/2017/09/13/the-10-companies-with-the-best-csr-reputations-in-2017/#3354c572546b

Viner, K (2000) [accessed 28 March 2018] Hand-to-Brand-Combat, *The Guardian*, 23 September [Online] www.theguardian.com/books/2000/sep/23/society.politics

Chapter 5

Beauty Pie (2018) [accessed 29 March 2018] How It Works, *Beauty Pie* [Online] www.beautypie.com/uk/join-info

Bentahar, A (2017) [accessed 29 March 2018] Optimizing for Voice Search Is More Important Than Ever, *Forbes*, 27 November [Online] www.forbes.com/sites/forbesagencycouncil/2017/11/27/optimizing-for-voice-search-is-more-important-than-ever/#1795c7b64a7b

Botsman, R (2017) *Who Can You Trust? How technology brought us together – and why it could drive us apart*, Portfolio, London

Contagious (2017) [accessed 29 March 2018] The Most Contagious 2017 Report: Transparency and Trailblazers, *Contagious* [Online] http://resources.contagious.com/most-contagious-2017-report-0

Deloitte (2017) [accessed 29 May 2018] The Deloitte Millennial Survey, *Deloitte* [Online] https://www2.deloitte.com/content/dam/Deloitte/global/Documents/About-Deloitte/gx-deloitte-millennial-survey-2017-executive-summary.pdf

Deloitte (2018) [accessed 29 March 2018] Blockchain: Opportunities for Health Care, *Deloitte* [Online] www2.deloitte.com/us/en/pages/public-sector/articles/blockchain-opportunities-for-health-care.html

Ecoalf (2018) [accessed 29 March 2018] [Online] https://ecoalf.com/gb/

Economist (2018a) [accessed 29 March 2018] A Revolution in Health Care Is Coming: Welcome to Doctor You, *The Economist*, 1 February [Online] www.economist.com/news/leaders/21736138-welcome-doctor-you-revolution-health-care-coming

Economist (2018b) [accessed 29 March 2018] Surgical Intervention: Apple and Amazon's Moves In Health Signal A Coming Transformation, *The Economist*, 3 February [Online] www.economist.com/news/business/21736193-worlds-biggest-tech-firms-see-opportunity-health-care-which-could-mean-empowered

Euromonitor (2017) [accessed 29 March 2018] Megatrend Analysis: Putting the Consumer at the Heart of Business, *Ethical Living* [Online] http://go.euromonitor.com/white-paper-2017-megatrend-analysis.html

Fashion Revolution (2018) [accessed 29 March 2018] Why Transparency Matters, *Fashion Revolution* [Online] www.fashionrevolution.org/about/transparency/

Feed the Truth (2018) [accessed 29 March 2018] Our Mission: Truth, Transparency and Integrity [Online] www.feedthetruth.org/#truth-transparency-integrity

Hannam, K (2016) [accessed 29 March 2018] This emerging Tech Company Has Put Asia's Tuna on the Blockchain, *Forbes*,

30 September [Online] www.forbes.com/sites/keshiahannam/
2016/09/30/this-emerging-tech-company-has-put-asias-tuna-on-the-
blockchain/#437f660a2649

Happycius Blog (2017) [accessed 29 March 2018] Blockchain-Based
Applications: The Traceability Revolution That Will Disrupt the F&B
Sector, *The Happycius Blog* [Online] www.happycius.blog/blockchain-
based-applications-the-traceability-revolution-t/

Herzberg, B (2014) [accessed 29 March 2018] The Next Frontier for Open
Data: An Open Private Sector, *The World Bank*, 24 March [Online] http://
blogs.worldbank.org/voices/next-frontier-open-data-open-private-sector

Hsu, T (2018) [accessed 29 March 2018] Dr Alexa, I've Been Sneezing
and My Throat Is Sore, *NY Times*, 30 January [Online] www.nytimes.
com/2018/01/30/business/amazon-health-care-plan-reaction.html

Jardine, A (2017) [accessed 29 March 2018] Best of 2017 Integrated/
Interactive – No 7: This Supermarket Is Using Snapchat Stories to
Show How Fresh Its Fish Is, *AdAge*, 8 May [Online] http://creativity-
online.com/work/u-fresh-stories/51722

JWT (2017) [accessed 29 March 2018] The Future 100: 2018, *JWT*,
December [Online] www.jwtintelligence.com/trend-reports/the-
future-100-2018/

Leap (2018) [accessed 29 March 2018] Free, Not Farmed, *Leap* [Online]
www.leapwildsalmon.co.uk

Maloney, N (2017) [accessed 29 March 2018] How Marcia Kilgore is
Changing the Business of Beauty, One Brand at a Time, *Vanity Fair*,
6 December [Online] www.vanityfair.com/style/2017/12/how-marcia-
kilgore-is-changing-the-business-of-beauty-one-brand-at-a-time

McKinsey (2011) [accessed 29 March 2018] Transparency – the Most
Powerful Driver Of Health Care Improvement? *McKinsey* [Online]
www.mckinsey.com/~/media/mckinsey/dotcom/client_service/
Healthcare%20Systems%20and%20Services/Health%20International/
Issue%2011%20new%20PDFs/HI11_64%20Transparency_noprint.ashx

Mindshare (2017) [accessed 29 March 2018] Speak Easy 2017 [Online]
www.mindshareworld.com/uk/about/speak-easy

Mintel (2017) [accessed 29 March 2018] Mintel Announces Five Global
Food and Drink Trends for 2018, *Montel*, 26 October [Online] www.
mintel.com/press-centre/food-and-drink/mintel-announces-five-global-
food-and-drink-trends-for-2018

Nielsen (2014) [accessed 29 March 2018] Is Sharing the New Buying? *Nielsen*, 28 May [Online] www.nielsen.com/us/en/insights/news/2014/is-sharing-the-new-buying.html

NME blog (2017) [accessed 29 March 2018] Did Radiohead's 'In Rainbows' Honesty Box Actually Damage the Music Industry? *NME*, 9 October [Online] www.nme.com/blogs/nme-blogs/did-radioheads-in-rainbows-honesty-box-actually-damage-the-music-industry-765394

Ovum (2017) [accessed 29 March 2018] Virtual Digital Assistants to Overtake World Population by 2021, *Ovum*, 17 May [Online] https://ovum.informa.com/resources/product-content/virtual-digital-assistants-to-overtake-world-population-by-2021

Provenance (2015) [accessed 29 March 2018] Blockchain: The Solution for Transparency in Product Supply Chains, *Provenance*, 21 November [Online] www.provenance.org/whitepaper

Provenance (2017) [last accessed 29 May 2018] Unlocking the financial incentives that reward sustainability in supply chains, *Provenance*, 12 December [Online] https://www.provenance.org/news/us/unlocking-financial-incentives-reward-sustainability-supply-chains

Saner, E (2018) [accessed 29 March 2018] Free for All: The Psychology of Pay-What-You-Want Cafes, *The Guardian*, 4 February [Online] www.theguardian.com/lifeandstyle/shortcuts/2018/feb/04/psychology-of-pay-what-you-want-cafes

Schurmann, J (2015) [accessed 29 March 2018] Pricing across Borders: How Smart Manufacturers Maximize Value, *Boston Consulting Group*, 24 June [Online] www.bcg.com/en-gb/publications/2015/marketing-pricing-across-borders-how-smart-manufacturers-maximize-value.aspx

Tapscott, D (2018) [accessed 29 March 2018] The Blockchain Research Institution Manifesto, *Don Tapscott* [Online] http://dontapscott.com/2017/12/blockchain-research-institute-manifesto-realizing-new-promise-digital-economy/

Tufekci, Z (2017) [accessed 9 May 2018] We're Building a Dystopia Just to Make People Click on Ads, *TED Talks*, 17 September [Online] https://www.ted.com/talks/zeynep_tufekci_we_re_building_a_dystopia_just_to_make_people_click_on_ads

Tufekci, Z (2018) [accessed 9 May 2018] Google Assistant Making Calls – Tweet, 9 May [Online] https://twitter.com/zeynep/status/994233568359575552

Van Buskirk, E (2007) [accessed 29 March 2018] Thom Yorke Discusses 'In Rainbows' Strategy with David Byrne, *Wired*, 19 December [Online] www.wired.com/2007/12/thom-yorke-disc/

WARC (2018) [accessed 29 March 2018] Marketers Need a Better Understanding of Health Tech, *WARC*, 8 February [Online] www.warc.com/newsandopinion/news/marketers_need_a_better_understanding_of_health_tech/40002

Whole Foods (2018) [accessed 29 March 2018] Wholefoods Market Reveals Top Food Trends for 2018, *Whole Foods*, 2018 [Online] https://media.wholefoodsmarket.com/news/whole-foods-market-reveals-top-food-trends-for-2018

Wynne, A (2017) [accessed 29 March 2018] Maison Standards Innovates with 'Pay What You Want' Model, *WWD*, 23 June [Online] http://wwd.com/fashion-news/fashion-scoops/maison-standards-innovates-pay-what-you-want-model-10927623/

Chapter 6

Baer, D (2014) [accessed 28 March 2018] The Making of Tesla: Invention, Betrayal, and the Birth of the Roadster, *Business Insider*, 11 November [Online] http://uk.businessinsider.com/tesla-the-origin-story-2014-10

Charny, D (2011) *Power of Making: The case for making and skills*, V&A Publishing, London

Goodwin, T (2018) *Digital Darwinism: Survival of the fittest in the age of business disruption*, Kogan Page Inspire, London

Just an allusion (2014) [accessed 28 March 2018] There's a New Sheriff in Town and Auto Experts Know It, *Tesla Forums*, 21 November [Online] file:///Users/helen/Library/Containers/com.apple.mail/Data/Library/Mail%20Downloads/7B5B5EEE-3810-4243-B1EC-AEE64A57C266/There's%20A%20New%20Sheriff%20In%20Town%20And%20Auto%20Experts%20Know%20It%20_%20Tesla.htm

Levitt, T (1983) [accessed 28 March 2018] The Globalization of Markets, *Harvard Business Review*, May [Online] https://hbr.org/1983/05/the-globalization-of-markets

Mackie, G (2017) [accessed 28 March 2018] BrewDog Pledges to Give Staff and Charities 20% Of Profits, *The Scotsman*, 29 August [Online] www.scotsman.com/business/companies/brewdog-pledges-to-give-staff-and-charities-20-of-profits-1-4545162

Moulds, J (2017) [accessed 28 March 2018] Even the Big Brewers Are Fans, So Why Is Craft Beer's Glass Half-Full? *The Times*, 25 September [Online] www.thetimes.co.uk/article/carlsburg-london-fields-trumans-even-the-big-brewers-are-fans-so-why-is-craft-beer-s-glass-half-full-6pjzb8kp6

Northover, D (2014) [accessed 28 March 2018] Brands Need to Wake Up to Maker Culture, *The Guardian*, 12 March [Online] www.theguardian.com/media-network/media-network-blog/2014/mar/12/brands-maker-culture-do-it-yourself-technology

Rose, L (2017) [accessed 28 March 2018] Something's Changing Documentary, *Lucy Rose* [Online] https://www.lucyrosemusic.com

Schwaner-Albright, O (2015) [accessed 28 March 2018] Five-Star Dining on Leftover Scraps? *The Wall St Journal*, 22 June [Online] www.wsj.com/articles/zero-waste-restaurants-five-star-dining-on-leftover-scraps-1434386371

The Disappearing Dining Club (2018) [accessed 28 March 2018] About DDC [Online] www.disappearingdiningclub.co.uk/dinner-parties/unusual-private-spaces#

Chapter 7

Anholt, S (nd) [accessed 29 March 2018] What Is a Nation Brand? *Superbrands* [Online] www.superbrands.com/turkeysb/trcopy/files/Anholt_3939.pdf

Anholt, S (2010) [accessed 29 March 2018] Why 'Nation Branding' Doesn't Exist, *The Economic Times*, 14 April [Online] https://economictimes.indiatimes.com/magazines/brand-equity/why-nation-branding-doesnt-exist/articleshow/5799304.cms

Anholt-GfK (2017) [accessed 29 March 2018] Anholt-GfK Nation Brands Index, *Anholt-GfK* [Online] http://nation-brands.gfk.com

Bartlett, J (2018) *The People vs Tech: How the internet is killing democracy (and how we save it)*, Ebury Press, London

Born, M (2003) [accessed 29 March 2018] Advertisers Urged to Stay Away from Stars and Stripes, *The Telegraph*, 4 April [Online] www.telegraph.co.uk/news/uknews/1426553/Advertisers-urged-to-shy-away-from-Stars-and-Stripes.html

Braun, T (2004) *The Philosophy of Branding: Great philosophers think brands*, Kogan Page, London

Campbell, T (2017) [accessed 29 March 2018] Cool Britannia Symbolised Hope – But All It Delivered Was a Culture of Inequality, *The Guardian*, 5 July [Online] www.theguardian.com/inequality/commentisfree/2017/jul/05/cool-britannia-inequality-tony-blair-arts-industry

Collins, P (2017) [accessed 29 March 2018] Issue 11: Renewal Britannia, *Demos*, 20/6 [Online] https://quarterly.demos.co.uk/article/issue-11/foreword-by-philip-collins/

Dinnie, K (2015) *Nation Branding: Concepts/Issues/Practice*, Routledge, London

Gibson, O (2012) [accessed 29 March 2018] Danny Boyle's Olympics Opening Ceremony: Madcap, Surreal and Moving, *The Guardian*, 27 July [Online] www.theguardian.com/sport/2012/jul/27/olympic-opening-ceremony

Gov.uk (2011) [accessed 29 March 2018] Prime Minister Launches Drive to Promote Britain, *Gov.uk*, 21 September [Online] www.gov.uk/government/news/prime-minister-launches-drive-to-promote-britain

Gray, A (2017) [accessed 23 April 2018] France Becomes the World No 1 for Soft Power, *World Economic Forum*, 27 June [Online] https://www.weforum.org/agenda/2017/07/france-new-world-leader-in-soft-power/

Gwynn, S (2016) [accessed 29 March 2018] National Stereotypes Still Score for Euro 2016 Brands, *Campaign*, 19 May [Online] www.campaignlive.co.uk/article/national-stereotypes-score-euro-2016-brands/1395247

Harris, J (2017) [accessed 29 March 2018] Cool Britannia: Where Did It All Go Wrong? *New Statesman*, 1 May [Online] www.newstatesman.com/1997/2017/05/cool-britannia-where-did-it-all-go-wrong

Kamp, D (1997) [accessed 29 March 2018] London Swings! Again! *Vanity Fair*, 7 February [Online] www.vanityfair.com/magazine/1997/03/london199703

Kelly, J (2017) [accessed 29 March 2018] These Are the Most Dynamic Cities in the world – and They're Not the Ones You'd Expect,

World Economic Forum, 16 January [Online] www.weforum.org/
agenda/2017/01/these-are-the-most-dynamic-cities-in-the-world-and-
they-re-not-the-ones-you-d-expect/

Kerr, P (2013) *Diplomacy in a Globalising World: Theories and practices*,
Oxford University Press, New York

Monocle (2017) [accessed 29 March 2018] Soft Power Survey 2017,
Monocle, December [Online] https://monocle.com/film/affairs/soft-
power-survey-2017-18/

NED (2017) [accessed 29 March 2018] Sharp Power: Rising
Authoritarian Influence: New Forum Report, *National Endowment for
Democracy*, 5 December [Online] www.ned.org/sharp-power-rising-
authoritarian-influence-forum-report/

Sachs, M (2014) [accessed 29 March 2018] Storytelling at the Cannes
Lions, *Forbes*, 16/6 [Online] www.forbes.com/sites/maryleesachs/
2014/06/16/storytelling-at-the-cannes-lions/#5e84af2d2596

Sinek, S (2011) *Start with Why: How great leaders inspire everyone to
take action*, Penguin, London

The Partners (2017) [accessed 29 March 2018] To Be Or Not to Be:
Decoding the Great British Identity Crisis: Building Great British
Brands Post-Brexit, *The Partners' Perspectives* [Online] https://static1.
squarespace.com/static/55a3c285e4b0bd1e115082d8/t/590b02f029687
f2f54ee9512/1493893924865/To+Be+or+Not+To+Be+-+The+Partners

Tyers, A (2016) [accessed 29 March 2018] BBC Imagine on 2012
London Olympics: Danny Boyle, Being British and Not Mentioning
the War, *The Telegraph*, 17 July [Online] www.telegraph.co.uk/
olympics/2016/07/17/bbc-imagine-on-2012-london-olympics-danny-
boyle-being-british-no/

VisitBritain (2017) [accessed 29 March 2018] Britain's Image
Overseas, *VisitBritain* [Online] www.visitbritain.org/britain's-image-
overseas

Wang, J (2013) *Shaping China's Global Imagination: Branding nations*,
Palgrave Macmillan, New York

WEF (2015) [accessed 29 March 2018] Which Countries Come Top for
'Soft Power'? *World Economic Forum*, 17 July [Online]
www.weforum.org/agenda/2015/07/which-countries-come-top-for-
soft-power/

Chapter 8

Added Value (2017) [accessed 30 March 2018] Cultural Value –
Mastering the New Marketing Currency, *Added Value*, 3 August
[Online] http://added-value.com/2017/08/03/cultural-value-mastering-
the-new-marketing-currency/

Baudrillard, J (1994) *Simulacra and Simulation*, University of Michigan
Press, Ann Arbor

Cohn & Wolfe (2014) [accessed 30 March 2018] Authentic Brand 2014:
Key Findings Report [Online] www.cohnwolfe.com/en/
authenticbrands/keyfindings [accessed 30 March 2018]

Enrail, K (1999) The Burning Man 1999: Are your festival memories
lacking in colour? *Sleaze Nation Magazine*, November

Gaufman, Y (2017) [accessed 23 April 2018] How to Reinvent a Brand in
an Authentic Way, *Campaign*, 24 May [Online] https://
www.campaignlive.co.uk/article/reinvent-brand-authentic/1434472

Hilfiger, T (2016) *American Dreamer: My life in fashion and business*,
Random House Publishing Group, New York

Indvik, L (2017) [accessed 30 March 2018] Tommy Hilfiger's On-Again,
Off-Again Relationship with Hip-Hop is Back in Full Swing, *Billboard*,
2 August [Online] www.billboard.com/articles/news/magazine-
feature/7677920/tommy-hilfiger-hip-hop-relationship

Kemp, N (2017) [accessed 30 March 2018] Xenia Tchoumi: How
to Influence the Influencers, *Campaign*, 15 September [Online]
www.campaignlive.co.uk/article/xenia-tchoumi-influence-
influencers/1443270

Kuchler, H (2017) [accessed 30 March 2018] Burning Man Keeps Silicon
Valley Fired Up, *Financial Times*, 30 August [Online] www.ft.com/
content/539c2324-8d0c-11e7-a352-e46f43c5825d

PARK Social Soccer Co (2018) [accessed 23 April 2018] *Passion is
Universal* [Online] https://www.parkssc.com/aboutpassaball/

Petridis, A (2014) [accessed 30 March 2018] Youth Subcultures: What
Are They Now? *The Guardian*, 20 March [Online] www.theguardian.
com/culture/2014/mar/20/youth-subcultures-where-have-they-gone

Pinsker, J (2017) [accessed 30 March 2018] How on Earth Does an Ad
Like Pepsi's Get Approved? *The Atlantic*, 8 April [Online]
www.theatlantic.com/business/archive/2017/04/pepsi-kendall-jenner-
ad-how/522423/

Rahman, A (2017) [accessed 30 March 2018] Late-Night TV Savages Kendall Jenner Pepsi Ad: It's a Protest for Attractive Lives Matter, *The Hollywood Reporter*, 4 May [Online] www.hollywoodreporter.com/news/pepsi-kendall-jenner-ad-slammed-by-late-night-hosts-stephen-colbert-seth-meyers-trevor-noah-991

Robinson, B (1998) *Withnail and I*, Bloomsbury, London

Rooney, J (2013) [accessed 30 March 2018] The Ten Most Culturally Vibrant Brands, *Forbes*, 20 March [Online] www.forbes.com/sites/jenniferrooney/2013/03/20/the-10-most-culturally-vibrant-brands/#6b47ab846029

Schultz, H (1998) *Pour Your Heart Into It: How Starbucks built a company one cup at a time*, Hyperion, New York

Schwartz, B (2005) *The Paradox of Choice: Why more is less*, Harper Perennial, New York

Sisodia, R (2014) *Conscious Capitalism, with a new preface by the authors: Liberating the heroic spirit of business*, Harvard Business Review Press, Boston, MA

Variety (2017) [accessed 30 March 2018] Late-Night Hosts Skewer Kendall Jenner's Pepsi Ad, *NBC News*, 6 April [Online] www.nbcnews.com/pop-culture/tv/late-night-hosts-skewer-kendall-jenner-s-pepsi-ad-n743561

Watercutter, A (2017) [accessed 30 March 2018] Pepsi's Kendall Jenner Ad Was so Awful It Did the Impossible: It United the Internet, *Wired*, 4 May [Online] www.wired.com/2017/04/pepsi-ad-internet-response/

West, G (2017) [accessed 30 March 2018] Kendall Jenner Breaks Silence over Controversial Pepsi Ad, *The Drum*, 3 September [Online] www.thedrum.com/news/2017/09/03/kendall-jenner-breaks-silence-over-controversial-pepsi-ad

Chapter 9

Beer, J (2015) [accessed 28 March 2018] How the Truth Campaign Plans to End Youth Smoking Once and for All, *Fast Company*, 13 August [Online] www.fastcompany.com/3049629/how-the-truth-campaign-plans-to-end-youth-smoking-once-and-for-all

Belam, M (2017) [accessed 23 April 2018] Fact-checking Isn't Enough. To Fight Far Right, the Media Must Spread the Truth, *The Guardian*,

7 February [Online] www.theguardian.com/commentisfree/2017/
feb/07/fact-checking-far-right-media-truth-donald-trump-terrorist

Boseley, S (2017) [accessed 28 March 2018] Threats, Bullying, Lawsuits:
Tobacco Industry's Dirty War for the African market, *The Guardian*,
12 July [Online] www.theguardian.com/world/2017/jul/12/big-
tobacco-dirty-war-africa-market

Centers for Disease Control and Prevention (2017a) [accessed 28 March
2018] Tobacco Use in Top-Grossing Movies, *CDC.gov*, 7 July [Online]
www.cdc.gov/mmwr/volumes/66/wr/mm6626a1.htm

Centers for Disease Control and Prevention (2017b) [accessed 28 March
2018] Data & Statistics, *CDC.gov*, 5 September [Online] www.cdc.
gov/tobacco/data_statistics/index.htm

Coffee, P (2014) [accessed 28 March 2018] 72andSunny Goes
Revolutionary in Anti-Smoking PSA, *Adweek*, 11 August [Online]
www.adweek.com/agencyspy/72andsunny-goes-revolutionary-in-anti-
smoking-psa/71199

Elliott, S (1998) [accessed 28 March 2018] CP+B Coordinates Florida's
Anti-Smoking Campaign by and for Teenagers, *The New York Times*, 14
April [Online] www.nytimes.com/1998/04/14/business/media-business-
advertising-crispin-porter-bogusky-coordinates-florida-s-anti.html

Frank, T (1997) *The Conquest of Cool: Business culture, counterculture,
and the rise of hip consumerism*, University of Chicago Press, Chicago

Hicks, B (2004) *Love All the People: Letters, lyrics, routines*, Constable &
Robinson, London

Hicks, J (2001) [accessed 28 March 2018] The Strategy Behind
Florida's 'Truth' Campaign, *Tobacco Freedom.org* [Online]
www.tobaccofreedom.org/msa/articles/truth_review.html

Hoyle, B (2017) [accessed 28 March 2018] Smoking on Screen Has
Health Experts Fuming, *The Times*, 13 July [Online] www.thetimes.
co.uk/article/smoking-on-screen-has-health-experts-fuming-nxsc8stvz

Knight, V (2017) [accessed 28 March 2018] Tobacco Use Jumps 80%
in Top-Grossing Movies, *CNN*, 10 July [Online] https://edition.cnn.
com/2017/07/10/health/tobacco-movies-teen-smoking-study/index.html

Lasn, K (1999) *Culture Jam: The uncooling of America*, Eagle Brook,
New York

Morrison, M (2014) [accessed 28 March 2018] Legacy names 72 and
Sunny to handle Creative on Anti-Tobacco Crusade, *AdAge*, 25

February [Online] http://adage.com/article/agency-news/72andsunny-picks-legacy-creative-account/291866/

Surgeon General (2014) [accessed 28 March 2018] Preventing Tobacco Use Among Youth and Young Adults Fact Sheet, *US Surgeon General* [Online] www.surgeongeneral.gov/library/reports/preventing-youth-tobacco-use/factsheet.html

Teinowitz, I (2000) [accessed 28 March 2018] Philip Morris USA Slams 'Truth' Ads from Foundation, *AdAge*, 14 February [Online] http://adage.com/article/news/philip-morris-usa-slams-truth-ads-foundation/31620/

Vander Weyer, M (2002) [accessed 28 March 2018] Nike Can Make a Nicer World, *The Telegraph*, 4 May [Online] www.telegraph.co.uk/culture/4727780/Nike-can-make-a-nicer-world.html

Wipperfurth, A (2005) *Brand Hijack: Marketing without marketing*, Portfolio, London

Zyman, S (2002) *The End of Advertising as We Know It*, John Wiley & Sons, Hoboken, NJ

Chapter 10

Kim, E (2014) [accessed 7 May 2018] Alibaba CEO Jack Ma: we earned the trust of people today, *Business Insider*, 19 September [Online] http://www.businessinsider.com/alibaba-jack-ma-says-he-earned-the-trust-2014-9?IR=T

Leader section (2001) [accessed 7 May 2018] The case for brands, *The Economist*, 6 September [Online] https://www.economist.com/node/771049

INDEX

TOM
GOODWIN

DIGITAL
DARWINISM

SURVIVAL OF
THE FITTEST
IN THE AGE OF
BUSINESS
DISRUPTION

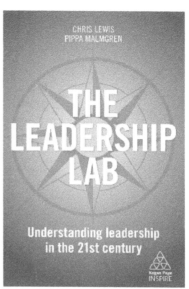

CHRIS LEWIS
PIPPA MALMGREN

THE
LEADERSHIP
LAB

Understanding leadership
in the 21st century

HUMANITY
WORKS

MERGING TECHNOLOGIES
AND PEOPLE FOR
THE WORKFORCE
OF THE FUTURE

ALEXANDRA LEVIT

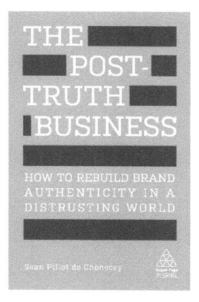

THE
POST-
TRUTH
BUSINESS

HOW TO REBUILD BRAND
AUTHENTICITY IN A
DISTRUSTING WORLD

Sean Pillot de Chenecey

Cutting-edge thinking from

Kogan Page Inspire

www.koganpage.com/inspire

CPSIA information can be obtained
at www.ICGtesting.com
Printed in the USA
BVHW09s0501141018
530109BV00011B/17/P